Practical Linux Infrastructure

Syed Ali

Apress®

Practical Linux Infrastructure

ISBN-13 (pbk): 978-1-4842-0512-9

ISBN-13 (electronic): 978-1-4842-0511-2

Trademarked names, logos, and images may appear in this book. Rather than use a trademark symbol with every occurrence of a trademarked name, logo, or image we use the names, logos, and images only in an editorial fashion and to the benefit of the trademark owner, with no intention of infringement of the trademark.

The use in this publication of trade names, trademarks, service marks, and similar terms, even if they are not identified as such, is not to be taken as an expression of opinion as to whether or not they are subject to proprietary rights.

Managing Director: Welmoed Spahr
Lead Editor: Louise Corrigan
Technical Reviewer: Jose Diego Castro
Editorial Board: Steve Anglin, Mark Beckner, Ewan Buckingham, Gary Cornell, Louise Corrigan, Jim DeWolf, Jonathan Gennick, Robert Hutchinson, Michelle Lowman, James Markham, Matthew Moodie, Jeff Olson, Jeffrey Pepper, Douglas Pundick, Ben Renow-Clarke, Dominic Shakeshaft, Gwenan Spearing, Matt Wade, Steve Weiss
Coordinating Editor: Christine Ricketts
Copy Editor: Catherine Ohala
Compositor: SPi Global
Indexer: SPi Global
Artist: SPi Global
Cover Designer: Anna Ishchenko

Distributed to the book trade worldwide by Springer Science+Business Media New York, 233 Spring Street, 6th Floor, New York, NY 10013. Phone 1-800-SPRINGER, fax (201) 348-4505, e-mail orders-ny@springer-sbm.com, or visit www.springeronline.com. Apress Media, LLC is a California LLC and the sole member (owner) is Springer Science + Business Media Finance Inc (SSBM Finance Inc). SSBM Finance Inc is a Delaware corporation.

For information on translations, please e-mail rights@apress.com, or visit www.apress.com.

Apress and friends of ED books may be purchased in bulk for academic, corporate, or promotional use. eBook versions and licenses are also available for most titles. For more information, reference our Special Bulk Sales–eBook Licensing web page at www.apress.com/bulk-sales.

Any source code or other supplementary material referenced by the author in this text is available to readers at www.apress.com. For detailed information about how to locate your book's source code, go to www.apress.com/source-code/.

Dedicated to the free software and open source community

Contents at a Glance

Contents

About the Author

Syed Ali is a senior site reliability engineering manager who has extensive experience with virtualization and cloud computing. His experience as an entrepreneur in infrastructure cloud computing offers him deep insight into how businesses can leverage the power of the cloud to their advantage. Syed is a firm believer in free software and open source software. When he is not working on technology, Syed likes to spend time enjoying the outdoors. He can be reached at alicsyed@gmail.com.

About the Technical Reviewer

Jose Dieguez Castro is a senior system administrator employed currently as a freelance consultant. He has worked on a wide range of projects—from small to large infrastructures, from private to public sectors. When is asked about his specialty, he replies, "Get the job done." Jose thinks of himself as a developer as well, who cares too much about software libre. Photography, sports, music, and reading are his ways to free his mind from work. He can be reached at jose@jdcastro.eu.

Acknowledgments

Without GNU/Linux and the countless free and open source software that make up the Internet, the world would be a different place. Having been a benefactor of the free software and open source movement, I have attempted to give back to the community by writing a book that takes the best of free and open source software and uses it advantageously.

Writing a book takes a lot of time away from family. I thank my wife, Mariam, and my children, Mehdi and Zayn, who were very patient with me and tolerated my obsession with getting this book completed on time. I know I was not able to spend all the time with them that they deserved, and I owe them a big thank you for giving me the space needed to finish this book. I hope this book serves as an inspiration for both of you to eventually write your own book.

I thank my mother, Parvin, and my brother, Sameer, for being a pillar of support for me.

My colleagues Matt Heck and Adam Faris provided feedback for parts of this book, and I thank them for their help. Their input provided valuable insight.

The Apress staff was very helpful in getting this book to completion. I want to thank everyone who took part in its success, especially the folks I dealt with directly: Louise Corrigan, Christine Ricketts, Catherine Ohala, and Jose Diego Castro.

Introduction

GNU/Linux (`https://www.gnu.org/gnu/linux-and-gnu.html`) is a fundamental building block of the Internet. Many of the most visited Internet sites run some flavor of GNU/Linux. Along with GNU/Linux is other free and open source software that is used to build infrastructures for organizations. This book serves as a guide to engineers who want to use free and open source software to build their infrastructure.

There are a lot of very interesting and relevant topics that need to be visited when building an infrastructure. The topics I picked are based on my personal experience and on what I think is most relevant to engineers now and in the future. I dedicated entire chapters to topics that I believe deserve deeper discussion, such as Apache HTTP Server and kernel-based virtual machine (KVM). For other services that are commonly being used in the software-as-a-service model, such as e-mail, I chose to share that chapter with other topics.

Although cloud computing is gaining in popularity, there are questions about infrastructure management that need to be answered, such as monitoring, logging, configuration management, and name service in the cloud. In addition, if you want to be cloud agnostic, then you have to build services in the cloud that do not lock you in to a particular cloud provider. For instance, instead of using Google SQL, you may chose to use MariaDB installed on a virtual instance in Google Compute Engine. This strategy might make it easier for you to migrate to another cloud provider in the future, if needed.

The software I explain in this book is among the more popular in their respective fields. Apache HTTP Server and MySQL are often used for Internet-facing applications. Nagios and Cacti are leading monitoring and trend analysis software. KVM is the most popular open source free virtualization software. OpenVPN and iptables are very useful for edge protection and remote connectivity. Internet companies for source code management use Git extensively. Puppet is used to manage systems and also for application deployment. BIND is the reference architecture implementation for domain name system (DNS) and rsyslog is the default installation for managing logs on Linux.

Google Cloud Platform is the only platform I cover in this book that is not free, but this is because I am not aware of any public cloud provider that is free. You can get demo accounts with public cloud providers for a limited time, and some of them offer a very limited—and free—basic tier, but none of them allow you to build an entire infrastructure and run it for free.

There are hundreds of Linux distributions (`http://distrowatch.com/`). For the purpose of this book, I have referenced CentOS 6.x/RedHat 6.x. Location of configuration files might be different if you use another Linux distribution.

Readers of this book include those who want to build a GNU/Linux–based infrastructure. You could be a junior, mid-level, or senior system administrator, site reliability engineer, DevOps or developer, and you can still benefit from this book. The knowledge you acquire from these pages hopefully helps you design a fault-tolerant, resilient GNU/Linux–based infrastructure you can be proud of, and one that is able to enhance your business value though the use of free open source software.

CHAPTER 1

Managing Large-Scale Infrastructure

This chapter is about the issues that come up in infrastructure management at a large scale. Mission-critical decisions such as infrastructure architecture, and decisions on matters such as licensing and support, are all part of infrastructure design. When managing a small infrastructure, many of these issues do not have the same criticality as they do in a large enterprise. A scalable architecture is an important foundation for a successful, large infrastructure.

Infrastructure management can be divided into two components: application deployment and infrastructure architecture. First we review application deployment and then look at different infrastructure architecture models. We also review the components that make up a scalable infrastructure.

Application Deployment

From design to production, a scalable infrastructure enables developers to code, test, and deploy applications quickly. The traditional deployment model has not been effective at speeding up the design-to-production pipeline. Figure 1-1 shows the traditional deployment model where a major hurdle to reaching production is testing. After developers have written code, they pass it to a quality assurance (or QA) team that tests the code manually and sends it back to the development team for fixing. After the fixes are complete, the code is tested again. When the tests pass, the code is sent to staging. Staging is a replica of production. After the code passes through staging, the operations team deploys the code to production using a change management process. This entire process for a single line of change in code might take two to four weeks.

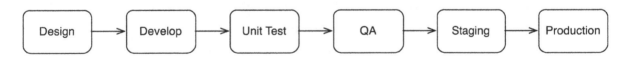

Figure 1-1. *Traditional design-to-production model*

Realizing that this model is not a very effective one, a newer model came into existence—that of continuous integration and continuous delivery (CI/CD). With this model, as soon as unit testing is complete and code is checked into the source code repository, the CI/CD pipeline kicks in. The pipeline consists of an automated build system, using tools such as Jenkins (http://jenkins-ci.org). The build system takes the code and builds it, outputting a compiled binary. The binary can then be taken and installed into production in an automated manner (Figure 1-2).

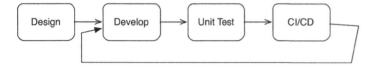

Figure 1-2. *Continuous integration and continuous delivery*

The CI/CD pipeline automates as many tests as possible to gain confidence in the code. In addition, it performs a complete build of the software system and ensures the code that has been checked in does not cause anything to break. Any failure has to be investigated by a developer. There are numerous software products that can help implement a CI/CD pipeline, including the following:

- Jenkins (http://jenkins-ci.org)

- CruiseControl (http://cruisecontrol.sourceforge.net)

- Buildbot (http://buildbot.net)

Software Development Automation

Software development automation is the process of automating as many components of software development as possible. The goal of software development automation is to minimize the time between when a developer checks in code to the time a product is in the hands of an end user or is being used in production. Without software development automation there is a significant delay in getting software products to end users. There are various components of software development automation, a few of them are listed in the following sections, along with the tools that can help accomplish the automation needed.

Build Automation

Build automation is the process of automating the immediate tasks that need to happen after a developer checks in code. This process includes actually building the code. The build is triggered on a check-in by the developer. Some of the features of build automation are as follows:

- Frequent builds to catch problems with code sooner than later

- Incremental build management, an attempt to build modules and then integrate them

- Build acceleration, so that a large code base does not slow down the build

- Build status reporting and failure detection

Some of the tools that can help with build automation are the following:

- Gradle (http://www.gradle.org)

- Apache Ant (http://ant.apache.org)

- Apache Maven (http://maven.apache.org)

- Gnu Make (http://www.gnu.org/software/make/)

Software Configuration Management

Software configuration management (SCM) is an integral component of software development automation. A few questions that need to be answered in software configuration management are

- Which source code management system do we use?

- How do we do code branches?

- What kind of revisions in software will we support?

Anything that has to do with managing the actual code itself is considered part of SCM. The following is a list of some of the tools that can help with the source code control part of SCM:

- Git (`http://git-scm.com`)

- SVN (`https://subversion.apache.org`)

- Mercurial (`http://mercurial.selenic.com`)

SCM is more of a process than a selection of tools, and includes questions about how to manage branches, versions, merging, and code freeze, and should be answered with policy rather than a product.

Continuous Integration

There can be many different components of a large software project. After a developer checks in code, it has to be integrated with the rest of the code base. It is not feasible for one developer to work on integrating his or her components with all other components. Continuous integration (CI) ensures all different components of code are eventually merged into one mainline that can then be built and a complete product released. The components of an effective CI are as follows:

- The CI process should start automatically with a successful build of code.

- Developers should commit code frequently to catch issues early.

- The CI build should be self-testing.

- The CI build should be fast.

An example of a CI process is that of a web services application divided into a PHP front end and a Java back end with MariaDB as a database. Any change on the PHP front-end code should trigger a full CI pipeline build that also builds Java and does a full test that includes database calls.

Continuous Delivery

So far, we have automated builds using build automation, we have integrated our code with other components using CI, and we have now arrived at the final step of continuous delivery (CD). CD is the process of getting code out to production as soon as a successful CI is complete. This is one of the most crucial steps in software development; a botched CD can cause an outage in your environment. The output of CI can be packaged binary. Software that can help with CD includes the following:

- Gnu AutoConf (`https://www.gnu.org/software/autoconf/`)

- Go (`http://www.go.cd`)

- Chef (`https://www.getchef.com/chef/`)

- SaltStack (`http://www.saltstack.com`)

3

The output of a CI pipeline can be a `war` file in case of Java or a `tar.gz` file or a package that is based on your production distribution. The CD process has to take this output and get in on a running production server. This should be done within the scope of release management.

Change Management

Change control plays a very important role in effective infrastructure management. Change management is the process of reviewing, approving, and executing changes relating to infrastructure components. To operate at a large scale, there has to be an effective change management process. The process should not be that of rubber-stamping changes without reviewing them. It also should not be so burdensome that engineers become wary of changes as a result of the burden required in getting changes pushed out.

Changes can be classified into the following categories:

- Low risk

- Medium risk

- High risk

A low-risk change is one that does not affect an infrastructure's uptime. An example is adding a few comments to code in a production environment and deploying them to production. It is possible the software engineer will forget to add the appropriate blocks of code that denote a comment, but this causes, at most, build failure, not the failure of the application. Hence, this type of change can be classified as low risk.

A medium-risk change can be classified as something that might potentially affect production. An example is adding a new virtual machine to a load balancer group. A misconfiguration on the load balancer might knock out the entire cluster; however, these chances are low because the change is not modifying the existing servers behind the load balancer.

An example of a high-risk change is upgrading an entire application to a new version of the code base, with significant changes in it. This certainly affects production because it involves code changes, and it involves the entire application cluster.

An organization should have published policies on what types of changes fall into the low-, medium-, and high-risk categories. No one should be allowed to make changes to production without following the change process in place.

Regardless of the type of change, medium to large organizations have a change control board that reviews changes, either daily or a few times a week. The board approves changes that are then executed by engineers. Changes may not be allowed during certain times of the year. If you are working for an online retailer, then no changes may be allowed to the infrastructure during the holiday season in an effort to minimize anything that affects sales. In the United States, a "freeze" might go into effect starting November 1 and lasting until January 5, because during this time a lot of online retail shopping happens for the holiday season.

A question may arise regarding how change control integrates into CI/CD or into the model where code is pushed to production in an automated manner as soon as it is ready. There are times when the CI/CD model should be placed on hold, such as during the freeze period for online retailers. During other times, software itself can integrate with a change control system so that all changes are documented, even if they are pushed out automatically. In addition, large-scale changes such as upgrading the entire code base should perhaps be reviewed and supervised by a team of engineers, instead of allowing it to be fully automated.

Release Management

Release management is the process of planning, designing, and building the framework needed to bring a product or software into production. When it comes to infrastructure management, release management plays the role of ensuring that infrastructure components are deployed into production in an efficient manner. Relating to software, release management ensures that new code is delivered to the end users or on end systems that will be using the code. Some of the items that should be tracked as part of release management are as follows:

- Feature requests
- Software packaging tools
- Delivery methodology
- Issues and risks with the release

Waterfall Methodology

When managing projects, an infrastructure, or software deployment, the traditional approach is called *waterfall methodology*, and it consists of the steps shown in Figure 1-3. First, requirements for the project are gathered. After that, a design is created based on the initial requirements. After the design is complete, implementation starts, followed by testing or verification of the implementation. Last, the software or infrastructure goes in maintenance mode.

This methodology has its limitations, because it assumes that all requirements are known upfront—something that may not be necessarily true. In addition, when a phase is over—such as the requirements phase—and the next phase starts, there is no room to revisit the earlier phase in case something was missed. If the requirements are revisited, then implementation stops until requirements gathering is complete. As such, it takes a lot time to implement the waterfall methodology.

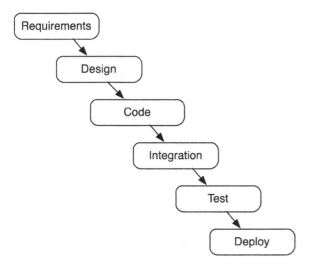

Figure 1-3. *Waterfall methodology*

For both software and infrastructure design, the waterfall model has fallen out of favor because of its limitations; Agile has become more popular.

Agile Methodology

Agile is an umbrella framework for numerous project management methods based on the Agile manifesto. The Agile manifesto is as follows:

> *"We are uncovering better ways of developing software by doing it and helping others do it. Through this work we have come to value:*
>
> - *Individuals and interactions over processes and tools*
>
> - *Working software over comprehensive documentation*
>
> - *Customer collaboration over contract negotiation*
>
> - *Responding to change over following a plan*
>
> *That is, while there is value in the items on the right, we value the items on the left more."*
>
> (http://en.wikipedia.org/wiki/Agile_software_development)

Agile has gained popularity over the waterfall methodology because the chances of having a successful project increase dramatically when Agile is followed correctly. One of the reasons of increased chances of success is that, with Agile, it is not assumed that all requirements are known upfront, and at the beginning of each sprint, the requirements can be reviewed again. Agile includes numerous methods:

- Kanban (http://en.wikipedia.org/wiki/Kanban_(development))

- Scrum (http://en.wikipedia.org/wiki/Scrum_(software_development))

- Lean (http://en.wikipedia.org/wiki/Lean_software_development)

There are many more Agile methods. You can read about them at http://en.wikipedia.org/wiki/Agile_software_development.

Agile methodology for infrastructure engineering is increasing in adoption due to the need of developers to do both development and operational tasks.

Scrum

Let's take a look at the Scrum methodology, which is part of the Agile framework. Scrum is a framework for learning about the products and the process used to build them. Figure 1-4 shows Scrum in action.

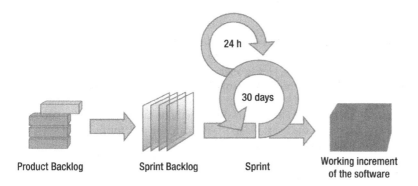

Product Backlog   Sprint Backlog   Sprint   Working increment of the software

Figure 1-4. *Scrum at work*

Scrum provides roles, meetings, and artifacts. There are three roles defined in Scrum: product owner, Scrum development team, and Scrum master.

The product owner focuses on "what" over the "how." He interfaces with customers and figures out a product road map. He prioritizes the product backlog, which contains a list of software features wanted by customers. He is the single point of contact for interfacing with the team.

The development team is cross-functional and consists of developers, testers, and the Scrum master. The team is comprised ideally of four to nine people.

The Scrum master has no management authority over the team. He or she is a facilitator, protects the team from distractions and interruptions, and removes hurdles the team encounters. He or she also promotes good engineering practices, and acts as a checks and balances person. You can read more about what a Scrum master does at http://scrummasterchecklist.org.

Scrum consists of two important artifacts: the product backlog and the sprint backlog. The backlog is a ranked list of everything that needs to be done. If it's not in the backlog, then it not something the team should be working on. Items in the backlog are written in user story format, or in use case scenarios. A user story is a documented requirement from an end user written from the users perspective. For example, "I want a website that allows me to sell clothing online" could be a user story that translates into a more defined backlog.

The sprint backlog is what the team is currently committed to doing, and as such it has an end date. Sprints are usually not longer than two weeks. Sprints consist of a working, tested, shippable product. A sprint is a short iteration.

There is the "what" and the "how" in the sprint backlog. The "what" is the product backlog item for this sprint. The "how" is the not-yet-started, in-progress, and completed tasks in the sprint.

There are four meetings defined by Scrum (Figure 1-5):

1. Sprint planning meeting

2. Daily Scrum

3. Sprint review meeting

4. Sprint retrospective meeting

There could be one more meeting, called the backlog-grooming meeting. Let's assume the sprint is a two-week sprint. At the beginning of the two weeks, a sprint planning meeting is held. During the meeting, items that are high priority are taken from the backlog and discussed. The outcome of the meeting is a ranked list of tasks for that particular sprint.

Every day there is a 15-minute daily Scrum meeting. During the meeting, three things are discussed: what you did yesterday, what you plan on doing today, and what the blockers are.

Sprint review meeting is at the end of each sprint, before the sprint retrospective meeting. In the review meeting items that were completed from the backlog are shown, and any items that could not be completed are discussed and placed in the product backlog.

The sprint ends with a sprint retrospective meeting during which the team discusses what went well in the given sprint and could have been done better.

During the sprint backlog-grooming meeting, the product backlog is reviewed. Large items are broken down into smaller items that can be done in two weeks. Also, the items in the backlog may be ranked. Figure 1-5 provides an overview of the meetings.

Scrum is one framework within Agile, and your team should review the other methods mentioned earlier, such as Lean, Kanban, and others, and pick one based on what suits the team the most. You can also pick the best processes of each of these methods and combine them into a new method that works for you.

Following Agile can speed up infrastructure project delivery and help your enterprise operate at a large scale.

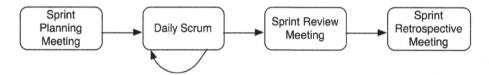

Figure 1-5. *Scrum meetings*

Even for small teams, following Agile can help in delivering infrastructure sooner rather than later to both internal and external customers.

Resources to learn more about Agile can be found at

- `http://agilemethodology.org`
- `http://scrummethodology.com`
- `http://agilemanifesto.org`

Web Architecture

So far in this chapter we have looked at software development and project management methods for scalable infrastructure design. The next section of this chapter focuses on a scalable web architecture. There are numerous designs that can be used for web architectures. I start off explaining the most basic one—single tier—and move on to more complex designs.

Single-Tier Architecture

In a single-tier architecture, there is one server that hosts the application and is being accessed remotely. This is the most basic design in infrastructure engineering for web services. The single server might host a web server and a database server, if needed. There are no failover capabilities and it is difficult to grow this architecture horizontally. Figure 1-6 shows this type of design. It is not recommended to use this design unless you have a non-mission critical, very low-volume use application that you want to use for testing and development.

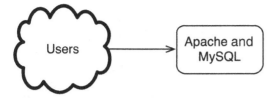

Figure 1-6. *Single-tier architecture*

Two-Tier Architecture

Adding to the single-tier architecture is the two-tier architecture. With this design we split the database from the web server. This type of design adds a bit of fault tolerance, because if the database goes down, the web server can still serve static content that is not dependent on the database. Or, if the web server goes down, the database can still be accessed by setting up another web server. Figure 1-7 shows how to set this up. This design has some of the same flaws as the single-tier architecture; it is not a very scalable design because it we cannot grow horizontally or vertically.

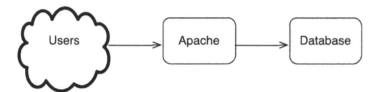

Figure 1-7. *Two-tier architecture*

Three-Tier Architecture

With the three-tier architectural model, we start to introduce a load balancer in front of the web servers (Figure 1-8). This strategy makes our design a bit more scalable. As our load increases, we can add more web servers and scale. We can also set up autoscaling so that the web servers increase in number automatically as needed, and decrease in number as needed, as well. One caveat of this design is that we can potentially overload the database as more web servers are added.

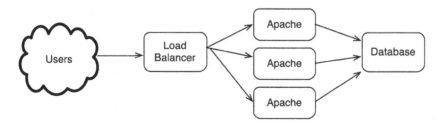

Figure 1-8. *Three-tier architecture*

Four-Tier Architecture

We can add one more tier between the web server and the database to make our design more scalable. This layer is a database caching technology such as Memcache (http://memcached.org). We can start to scale, not just the web server layer, but also the database layer to handle load and be more fault tolerant. We add more database servers and split the workload among them. This can be done via a Cassandra (http://cassandra.apache.org) multinode implementation, for instance. This design is now more complex, but it is also more fault tolerant and able to scale as needed (Figure 1-9).

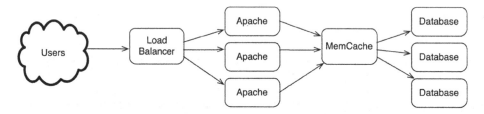

Figure 1-9. *Four tier architecture*

Five-Tier Architecture

When serving web content, we can have dynamic and static web content. For instance, if you look at Figure 1-10, the web-serving layer is split into Apache and a Java application server running Jetty or JBoss. Apache serves any static content and the application server serves any content that is dynamic, or generated on the fly. An example of this type might be the FAQ section of a support web site. Because FAQ page contents are fairly static, the list might be served a lot quicker from Apache. However, the ticketing system that allows interacting with customers might be served from the application layer of Jetty.

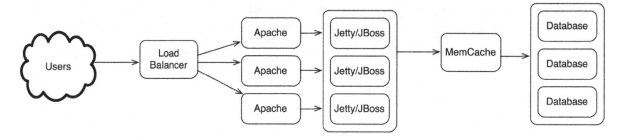

Figure 1-10. *Five-tier architecture*

Six-Tier Architecture

We can get even more fancy than the five-tier architecture and add a content delivery network (CDN) from which users can download content. Let's say that customers download Android images from your web site. Instead of streaming hundreds of megabytes of data from your web site, push that content to a CDN and let the CDN serve the downloads. The rest of the web site can still run in your infrastructure (Figure 1-11). This is useful for web sites that serve videos or any other type of data that require a large download.

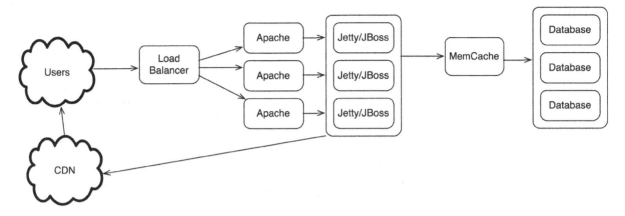

Figure 1-11. *Six-tier architecture*

Global Architecture

In today's global world, your users can be anywhere. Consolidating data centers and pushing content through one or more central data centers that host your content may not be sufficient. One way to improve efficiency is to build point-of-presence sites globally. These are small caching-only sites that reside close to your users and can push content to users with low latency. Figure 1-12 presents an example of such a design, with two core data centers—one in Chicago and the other in Austin. The other sites, such as in Taiwan or Geneva, are caching-only sites that contact the two primary data centers, download data used more frequently by the users in that particular region, and store it. You need an application such as Apache Traffic Server (`http://trafficserver.apache.org`) running in your point-of-presence sites to support such a design. If building such an infrastructure is cost prohibitive, then consider using a CDN, such as those offered by Akamai, Amazon, Rackspace, and other providers, to achieve the same results.

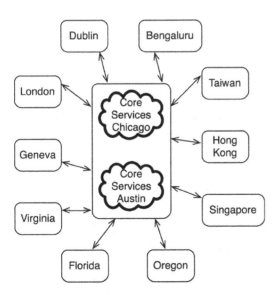

Figure 1-12. *Global scalable architecture*

Autoscaling

Autoscaling is the process of increasing or decreasing infrastructure resources to meet varying traffic demands. Let's take the example of Netflix. Their infrastructure might see a large spike in incoming streaming requests on Saturday morning, when a lot of children are home and want to watch cartoons. On the other hand, they may have much lower use on a Monday morning, when most people are at work and children are in school. To handle this variance in traffic, autoscaling might come in handy. During peak hours, the load balancer can check uptime or some other metric from the real web servers and, based on a threshold, spin up new instances of web servers (Figure 1-13). When traffic slows down, the virtual instances can be deleted (Figure 1-14). This strategy allows for the cost to Netflix to vary based on need, and they do not have to spin up and keep the high-watermark instances up and running all the time.

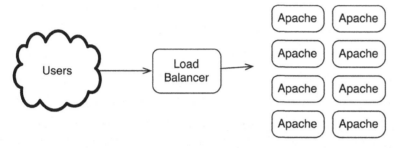

Figure 1-13. *Peak usage*

Auto scaling is offered in Amazon Web Services and in other clouds, such as Google Cloud. For private clouds, you have to create your own autoscaling mechanism unless your private cloud vendor provides it.

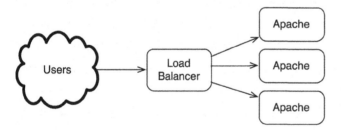

Figure 1-14. *Autoscaling during normal traffic patterns*

Rolling Deployments

When a new version of code is available in production for deployment, the traditional approach for upgrading existing code in production was to schedule some downtime during which the service is not available. This was often called a *maintenance window*, and is still used by some organizations. During the maintenance window, all users are drained from a service, and access to the service is disabled. Code is upgraded and tested, and then traffic is allowed back into the production cluster. A disadvantage of this method is that, if your web site is revenue generating, you will lose revenue during the maintenance window. Especially in today's global setting, where your external-facing web site may be accessed from anywhere in the world, keeping your site up 100% of the time is becoming more crucial.

An alternative approach to this is rolling deployments. Rolling deployments entails upgrading a small portion of your infrastructure, testing it, and then upgrading more servers. There are two ways of doing this: one method is to deploy code on new servers, or virtual machines, that will be added to the pool behind a load balancer. If things appear to work OK on the new servers, then you keep adding more new servers with the new code base. After you reach 100% of new code base servers, you can then start to turn off the old code base servers. Another approach is to replace an existing server in the pool with a newer version of code (Figure 1-15). Of the eight servers for a given application, all eight are running v1.0 of the code, but we have to upgrade the code to v2.0.

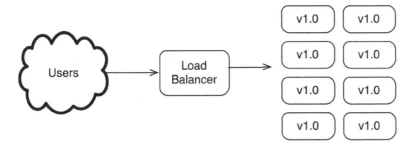

Figure 1-15. *Server running 100% of v1.0 code*

In Figure 1-16, we replace a single server with v2.0 of the code. We can do this in two ways: either upgrading code directly onto the server or shutting the server down and creating a new server with v2.0 of the code. We then monitor this new server that receives one-eighth of the traffic if the load balancer is using a round-robin load-balancing methodology.

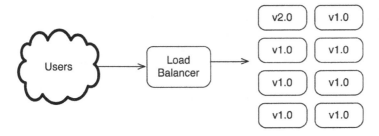

Figure 1-16. *One-eighth of servers running the new version 2.0 of code*

If the newer version of the code is functioning well, we then proceed to change 50% of the servers with the new code (Figure 1-17). As before, we can simply deploy new virtual machines and replace the older ones, or we can upgrade the code on them without actually installing new virtual machines.

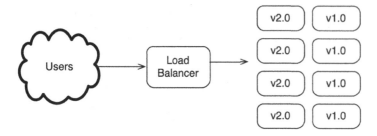

Figure 1-17. *Fifty percent of servers running version 2.0 of code*

Last, if things are looking good, we proceed to deploy the new code on 100% of the virtual machines, thereby completing our upgrade without affecting end users (Figure 1-18).

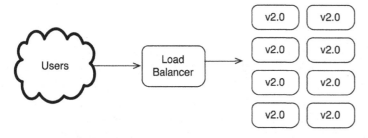

Figure 1-18. *One hundred percent of servers running new code version 2.0*

An important part of rolling upgrades is constant monitoring and ensuring the new code does not cause any issues. In the case when new code is not compatible with the existing version, and both cannot exist at the same time, another option is to create a new set of virtual machines or servers behind a load balancer, and add that load balancer to the global traffic manager. Or, you can use round-robin domain name system (DNS) and have the IP address of both load balancers with the same A record.

Licensing

When deciding on software solutions for an enterprise, the various licenses for which software is available should be reviewed and taken into account before deciding on a specific product. For an enterprise to operate securely at scale, there has to be a top-down strategy for which licenses are acceptable in the company. Similarly, there should be a strategy for contributing to open source projects with specific licenses.

One of the big issues to be addressed is whether commercial software is given preference over open source software, or vice versa. In the Linux world, open source software is very much prevalent, especially because Linux itself is open source. Linux is licensed under GPL v2.

There are a number of open source licenses under which free software is available. Some of them include the following:

- Apache License 2.0

- GNU General Public License (GPL)

- Common Development and Distribution Licenses

- BSD {2,3} License

You can view a more complete list at http://opensource.org/licenses/alphabetical.

An example of how the choice of using software with a particular open source license can affect an organization is the GNU Affero General Public License (AGPL). AGPL requires that if you modify the open source software, you must make it available to all network users of the software. The problem with this is that, if your company has any proprietary software, and you use AGPL-licensed open source software, then your proprietary software can be at risk of being forced into the open source world. Public web sites are particularly affected by this clause. Some of the more popular open source software using AGPL are:

- MongoDB (http://www.mongodb.org)

- Launchpad (https://launchpad.net/)

- PHP-Fusion (https://www.php-fusion.co.uk/home.php)

- SugarCRM (http://www.sugarcrm.com)

Similarly, when contributing to open source projects, issues about licensing of the code being contributed should be addressed. Many open source projects have a Contributor License Agreement under which you are allowed to contribute. There can be an individual contributor agreement, if you are contributing as an individual, and a corporate contributor agreement. Generally speaking, you give up the copyright to your code when you contribute to an open source project.

Support

After addressing the licensing issue there is the question of support to consider. Operating at scale means having a defined strategy on what, if any, support is available for the software being used in the company. With the proliferation of open source software, support of the software has become an even more important issue.

If you are using software that has no support, and your production environment depends on it, then you could potentially have a risk that is not mitigated. As part of your corporate strategy, if you are using a Linux operating system, then perhaps a distribution with support makes more sense for mission-critical systems, and one without support for non-mission critical systems.

Another possibility is to hire subject matter experts on the open source software being used, thereby reducing risk. In case of a problem with the software, the subject matter experts can be relied on for help. Some large Internet-based companies hire Linux kernel developers and use their own custom distribution, thereby ensuring an enhanced level of support.

You could, of course, rely on the open source community itself for software that has no commercial support. Quite often, user groups, Internet Relay Chat (IRC) channels, and mailing lists are good sources of getting support on issues. Unfortunately, none of them are guaranteed, and when a business is losing money because of a software bug, you want to know there is someone in the wings who can fix it.

Various Linux distributions have different support models. Some have no commercial support at all, whereas others do have commercial support. Fedora does not have commercial support, but RedHat does.

Support Model for Customers

Support can be divided into two major types: one is internal facing and the other is external facing. External-facing support is for an organization's customers. Internal-facing support is among different teams in the company. Tracking support requests is important and should be done through a ticketing system. A few open source ticketing systems include

- osTicket (http://osticket.com)

- Request Tracker (http://www.bestpractical.com/rt/)

- OTRS (http://www.otrs.com/software/open-source/)

The same solution can work at times for internal and external customers, with different views. You can also have homegrown systems or purchase commercial products. Regardless of your choice, to scale, you must keep track of issues and use extensive reporting so that problem spots can be figured out and resolved sooner rather than later.

Network Operations Center

Another important component of operating at scale is having 24/7 support for your products or services. This can be accomplished through various ways, including the following:

- *Follow the sun's rotation*: Have staff working in the world where there is sunlight—for example, starting off with teams in San Francisco, who then hand off to India, who then hand off to, say, Ireland.

- *Have a single global location with 24/7/365 coverage*: This means having a night shift as well in the single location.

- *Overlap shifts*: Have one shift that overlaps in part with another. An example is to start off in San Francisco, then move calls to Ireland. This entails long days for employees in San Francisco and Ireland.

Self-Service Support

In today's connected world, having one type of support option, such as phone or e-mail is not sufficient. Customers, both internal and external, expect support through varies means:

- Online user and support forums

- Social media such as Twitter and Facebook

- Online knowledge portal

- Web and phone based

- Remote screen sharing based

To operate at scale, enterprises have to adopt one or more of the previously mentioned methods. As the user base of a given application grows, different users turn to different methods of seeking help. The more you are able to empower your end users to solve their problem, the easier it will be on your organization to support them.

Bug Reporting

Tracking bugs and ensuring they are resolved helps in operating efficiently. This, in turn, enables large-scale operations. A few open source bug tracking tools include the following:

- Bugzilla (http://www.bugzilla.org/)

- Mantis (http://www.mantisbt.org/)

- Trac (http://trac.edgewall.org/)

Even for infrastructure-related issues, these bug tracking tools can be used in addition to ticketing tools to keep track of infrastructure issues. Or, you can use these bug reporting tools in lieu of ticketing tools, although you may lose some needed functionality that is specific to ticketing software and is not part of bug reporting software.

Inventory Management

Data center inventory management (DCIM) is a component of inventory management. Inventory management is generally used by finance to keep track of assets, and DCIM is useful for this; however, it adds an extra layer on top of infrastructure management. DCIM tools prove to be very helpful in the following scenarios:

- Capacity planning

  - Power requirements

  - Space planning

- System provisioning

- Contract negotiations

- Hardware life cycle management

  - Older hardware procurement

  - New hardware procurement

When dealing with hardware vendors, it is helpful to be able to go to them with numbers on mean time between failures to negotiate with the vendor on better pricing or product improvements.

Capacity planning in relation to power and space can be made a lot easier if an enterprise knows how many servers are present and how much power they consume.

What kind of data should be present in a DCIM system? The more the merrier is the right policy in this case. At a minimum, the following items should be present:

- Server make, model, year purchased, cost, and a link to the purchase order

- Storage, processors, memory, and any peripherals

- Operating system flavor and version, and applications running on the system

- Technical contact for the server administrator, and escalation contacts

- Ethernet address, power supplies, and remote console information

A lot more information can be stored in a DCIM, and it should also integrate with your server provisioning system, such as Kickstart. To provision a system, a script can pull down the media access control address from the DCIM and create a PXE config file. Then, using the console information, you can reboot the system for operating system installation.

Hardware

The choice of hardware plays a very important role in the scaling of the infrastructure of an organization. Processors, memory, and storage technologies can make or break an application as well as a budget. In the following sections I try to make sense of the different choices available and how to pick solutions that suit your needs the most.

Processors

Between the two major vendors in the industry for server processors, Intel and AMD, there exist a wide variety of processor families. When purchasing hardware at scale, you have to be careful which processor family you buy into, and at what time of the processor cycle you are buying as well. If you look at the Intel microarchitecture (https://en.wikipedia.org/wiki/Intel_Tick-Tock), every 12 to 18 months there is either a new microarchitecture or a die shrink of the processor technology. You can capitalize on this and purchase hardware at different times of the cycle to optimize cost versus performance.

In addition to cost, power consumption plays a key role in picking a processor architecture. A low-power processor that performs just as fast as a high-power processor might be more suitable for large-scale deployment to reduce the cost of running a data center. Low-power ARM-based (http://www.arm.com) processors are also gaining a market share.

As of this writing, the current Intel microarchitecture is Haswell, and the upcoming one by the end of 2014 is called Broadwell. Haswell is a new architecture compared with the previous one, called Ivy Bridge. Broadwell is a die shrink of Haswell. Die shrink allows for cost reduction.

When purchasing a server, take into consideration its microarchitecture and the stage of the microarchitecture. This affects your application performance and your financial costs. You cannot afford to ignore this factor when operating at scale.

Memory

Another aspect of operating at a large scale is to pick the right type of memory at the right price. Prices of memory vary a lot throughout the year. The right type of memory is dependent on the chipset of the motherboard on your server, and the requirements of the application. Yes, faster is better in this case, but cost is an important consideration and so is power consumption.

There are different types of memory, such as

- DDR4 (1600 MHz–3200 MHz)

- DDR3 PC3-6400, -8500, -10600, and -12800

- DDR2 PC2-4200, -5300, -6400, and 8000

- DDR PC1600, PC2100, PC2700, and PC3200

- SDRAM PC100, 125 MHz, and PC133

As of this writing, DDR4 is the latest memory type; it is not backward compatible with DDR3. DDR4 has high module density compared with DDR3 and lower voltage requirements.

If the cost of DDR4 is a concern, then consider using DDR3. The speed of DDR3 is shown in Table 1-1.

Table 1-1. *Memory Speeds*

Friendly name	Industry name	Peak transfer rate (MB/sec)	Data transfers/sec (in millions)
DDR3-800	PC3-6400	6400	800
DDR3-1066	PC3-8500	8533	1066
DDR3-1333	PC3-10600	10,667	1333
DDR3-1600	PC3-12800	12,800	1600

Testing application requirements with the memory type can help in getting the most optimized type of memory. If you are purchasing 10,000 servers in a year, the savings based on the appropriate memory can be in hundreds of thousands of dollars, if not millions of dollars.

Additional references are available at

- `http://www.crucial.com/usa/en/support-memory-speeds-compatability`

- `http://en.wikipedia.org/wiki/DDR4_SDRAM`

Storage

Picking the right storage technology can help keep your applications humming and your costs down. There are numerous types of disk technologies for enterprises, and numerous disk configurations as well. Some of the common types of disk technologies are

- ATA, parallel and serial (`http://en.wikipedia.org/wiki/Serial_ATA`)

- SAS (`http://en.wikipedia.org/wiki/Serial_attached_SCSI`)

- SSD (`http://en.wikipedia.org/wiki/Solid-state_drive`)

- SCSI (`http://en.wikipedia.org/wiki/SCSI`)

I am going to explain solid state drives (SSD) in detail, because it is the latest storage technology as of this writing. SSD consist of a circuit board, NAND flash, Serial Advanced Technology Attachment (SATA) controller, and SATA connector. Flash is non-volatile electronic storage. A hard disk drive (HDD) consists of a platter, spindle, actuator arm, SATA connector, and actuator.

The advantages of SSDs over HDDs are the following:

- Faster

- More durable

- Less power consumption

- Lighter

- Cost-efficient

- Cooler

- Quieter

Challenges with Flash based SSD:

- *Data retention*: Flash cells lose their charge over time. Weaker cells lose charge faster. Ask your vendor how often they refresh data to account for the loss of charge.

- *Endurance*: Flash cells get worn out over time as you erase and rewrite data on them. The more you write to a cell, the weaker it becomes.

- *Faster failure*: Multilevel cells can begin to fail faster than single-level cells.

- *Variation in performance*: Reading and writing are asymmetric in size and duration; hence, you can get a significant variance in performance.

Flash products consist of:

- Flash array
- Flash appliance
- PCIe card

Table 1-2 shows a brief comparison among the different flash solutions available. IOPS stands for input-output operations per second.

Table 1-2. *Comparing Flash solutions*

Friendly name	Performance	Cost ($/GB)	Scalability
Flash array	400,000 IOPS; latency, <1 msec	5–10	100TBs usable
Flash appliance	500,000 IOPS; latency, 100 msec	20–40	5–20TB usable
PCIe flash card	500,000 IOPS; latency, <1 msec, potentially 100 msec	10	2TB

When picking a flash vendor, ask the following questions:

- How does your system write to flash?
- How do you account for bit disturbance and losses in the flash cells over time?
- How do you minimize the wearing out of flash cells caused by writes?
- How do you minimize write amplification?
- How do you read from an SSD that is busy writing?
- How do you ensure you have the right data before they are served?
- What type of flash are you using?
- What is the expected life of the flash you are using?
- What do you do to ensure no data loss?

For an additional reference, see `http://ocz.com/consumer/ssd-guide/ssd-vs-hdd`.

System Profiles

Operating at a large scale requires all systems to operate at the most optimized settings. A large-scale infrastructure has virtual hosts, virtual machines, and a wide variety of systems.

Performance-related issues are a high percentage of trouble spots in an infrastructure. In a preemptive measure to reduce the number of issues arising from a system that is not properly tuned, configure `tuned`. `tuned` is a daemon in CentOS/RedHat that can modify system settings dynamically in conjunction with `ktune`. Listing 1-1 shows how to interact with `tuned`.

Listing 1-1. Tuned Profiles

First, view all the different profiles available. These profiles apply specific kernel-level tuning parameters for network, disk, power, and memory to match performance to the requirements of the profile.

```
# tuned-adm list
Available profiles:
- sap
- virtual-guest
- spindown-disk
- default
- server-powersave
- latency-performance
- enterprise-storage
- laptop-ac-powersave
- throughput-performance
- laptop-battery-powersave
- desktop-powersave
- virtual-host
```

Next, view which profile is active. In our case, a virtual host profile is active. This is probably a hypervisor, and hence this profile is active.

```
# tuned-adm active
Current active profile: virtual-host
Service tuned: enabled, running
Service ktune: enabled, running
```

To select another profile, simply type in the profile name after the profile keyword.

```
# tuned-adm profile throughput performance
Reverting to saved sysctl settings:                    [  OK  ]
Calling '/etc/ktune.d/tunedadm.sh stop':               [  OK  ]
Reverting to cfq elevator: dm-0 dm-1 dm-2 dm-3 dm-4 dm-5 dm[  OK  ]dm-8 sda
Stopping tuned:                                        [  OK  ]
Switching to profile 'throughput-performance'
Applying deadline elevator: dm-0 dm-1 dm-2 dm-3 dm-4 dm-5 d[  OK  ] dm-8 sda
Applying ktune sysctl settings:
/etc/ktune.d/tunedadm.conf:                            [  OK  ]
Calling '/etc/ktune.d/tunedadm.sh start':              [  OK  ]
Applying sysctl settings from /etc/sysctl.d/libvirtd
Applying sysctl settings from /etc/sysctl.conf
Starting tuned:                                        [  OK  ]
```

If you want to view all the different settings that have been changed for a given profile, you can do so by looking at the /etc/tune-profiles/ directory, which lists each profile and the settings that are changed based on the profile.

Tuning TCP/IP

In addition to using system profiles, you should look at TCP parameters on your systems and determine whether there is a need to tune them. As part of provisioning systems, pretuned systems help maintain a large-scale network with fewer issues.

Linux maintains a buffer for TCP/IP packets. The buffer size is adjusted dynamically; however, you can set some limits on it. There are two different parameters that can be adjusted. One is a receive window and the other is a send window. The receive window is the amount of data a recipient is willing to accept. The send window is the amount of data the sender can receive at a given time. Listing 1-2 shows how to view and adjust these TCP parameters.

Listing 1-2. Tunning TCP

Inspect the TCP socket buffer status on the system using netstat. If we see packets that are pruned or collapsed, we will have to adjust the TCP send and receive window to prevent the pruning. In this example, we can see 70 packets were pruned and 9325 packets were collapsed.

```
# netstat -s | grep socket
    3118 resets received for embryonic SYN_RECV sockets
    70 packets pruned from receive queue because of socket buffer overrun
    75756 TCP sockets finished time wait in fast timer
    23 delayed acks further delayed because of locked socket
    9325 packets collapsed in receive queue due to low socket buffer
```

Review the existing size of the rmem and wmem parameters. rmem is the receive window and wmem is the send window. The first number is the smallest the buffer gets, the middle number is the default size with which a socket is opened, and the last number is the largest the buffer gets.

```
#  cat /proc/sys/net/ipv4/tcp_rmem
4096    87380    4194304

# cat /proc/sys/net/ipv4/tcp_wmem
4096    16384    4194304
```

Let's increase the size and reset the counters for netstat. For servers with 1GB or 10GB network cards, the maximum size of the buffers is 16MB. To reset the counters, you have to reboot the system. To preserve these settings across reboot, enter them in /etc/sysctl.conf.

```
# echo "4096 87380 16777216" > /proc/sys/net/ipv4/tcp_wmem
# echo "4096 87380 16777216" > /proc/sys/net/ipv4/tcp_rmem

#  cat /proc/sys/net/ipv4/tcp_rmem
4096    87380    16777216

# cat /proc/sys/net/ipv4/tcp_wmem
4096    87380    16777216
```

Increasing these values to a large number can result in high latency and jitter (packet delay variation), also known as *buffer bloat* (https://en.wikipedia.org/wiki/Bufferbloat). The overall throughput of a network can be reduced because of buffer bloat. Applications such as VoIP are very sensitive to jitter. An application that can be used to check for buffer bloat is ICSI Netalyzr (http://netalyzr.icsi.berkeley.edu/).

CPU Scheduling

CPU scheduling is the process of scheduling jobs on the processor. The kernel's job is to ensure the CPU is as busy as possible. There are two scheduling categories:

- Real time
  - SCHED_FIFO
  - SCHED_RR

- Normal

  - SCHED_OTHER
  - SCHED_BATCH
  - SCHED_IDLE

Real-time threads are scheduled first using one of the real-time CPU schedulers. The normal scheduler is used for all threads that do not need real-time processing.

In large-scale computing, you might have a need to adjust the CPU scheduling policy. You can check if an adjustment is needed by keeping a tab on the nonvoluntary_ctxt_switches parameter, as shown in Listing 1-3. Here we are checking the context switching of the init process that has a process ID (PID) of 1. You can replace the PID with any other running PID on the system to get information about the context switching of that PID.

Listing 1-3. R eviewing CPU Scheduling

```
# grep voluntary /proc/1/status
voluntary_ctxt_switches:        136420
nonvoluntary_ctxt_switches:     59
```

If the nonvoluntary context switches are high, then you might want to consider changing the scheduler. For data throughput relating to network bandwidth and disk input/output, use the SCHED_OTHER scheduler.

If latency is a concern, then use SCHED_FIO. Latency is defined as event response time. It is different than throughput, because the goal of throughput is to send as much data as possible, but latency is sending as fast as possible.

Normal policies result in better throughput than real-time policies because they do not preempt processes, as the real-time scheduler might do to ensure real-time processing.

The command chrt (http://linux.die.net/man/1/chrt) can be used to manipulate the scheduling policy for a process. Listing 1-4 shows how to manipulate the CPU scheduling for a process.

Listing 1-4. Modifying CPU scheduling

View the existing priority of PID 1 (init).

```
# chrt -p 1
pid 1's current scheduling policy: SCHED_OTHER
pid 1's current scheduling priority: 0
```

Each scheduling policy has limits. We can use the -m option to view them. Larger numbers mean greater priority.

```
# chrt -m
SCHED_OTHER min/max priority     : 0/0
SCHED_FIFO min/max priority      : 1/99
SCHED_RR min/max priority        : 1/99
SCHED_BATCH min/max priority     : 0/0
SCHED_IDLE min/max priority      : 0/0
```

Switch the scheduler to SCHED_FIFO from SCHED_OTHER, using a priority of 50.

```
# chrt -f -p 50 1
```

View the scheduler being used after making the switch to SCHED_FIFO.

```
# chrt -p 1
pid 1's current scheduling policy: SCHED_FIFO
pid 1's current scheduling priority: 50
```

Change the scheduler back to SCHED_OTHER.

```
# chrt -o -p 0 1
```

Confirm the change to SCHED_OTHER has occurred.

```
# chrt -p 1
pid 1's current scheduling policy: SCHED_OTHER
pid 1's current scheduling priority: 0
```

Conclusion

In this chapter we looked at a number of issues that arise in large-scale computing. The issues can be divided into the following categories

- Application development
- Project management
- Multitier web architecture
- Housekeeping issues around licensing, support, and inventory
- Large-scale hardware selection

All these issues are important considerations when you manage large-infrastructure environments. With careful consideration, and decision making based on data, you can build and support a practical Linux infrastructure that lasts a long time.

■ ■ ■

## CHAPTER 2

Hosted Cloud Solutions Using Google Cloud Platform

This chapter is about how to integrate a private or public cloud solution into your enterprise environment. The cloud infrastructure has become very prevalent and has helped startup companies as well as enterprises reduce cost and deploy applications quickly compared with traditional brick-and-mortar infrastructures. In particular, this chapter covers the Google Cloud Platform (GCP), which includes a range of public cloud solutions for your enterprise.

To Cloud or Not to Cloud

Should you invest in a public or a private cloud? Are clouds a trend that will phase out with time? Cloud computing has been gaining in popularity and, for the time being, it does not look as if there is a way of stopping its growth. What exactly is cloud computing? definition According to NIST, "Cloud computing is a model for enabling ubiquitous, convenient, on-demand network access to a shared pool of configurable computing resources (e.g., networks, servers, storage, applications, and services) that can be rapidly provisioned and released with minimal management effort or service provider interaction." (http://csrc.nist.gov/publications/nistpubs/800-145/SP800-145.pdf). The question of whether to invest in cloud computing should be considered carefully by your enterprise.

Infrastructure as a service, platform as a service (PaaS), and software as a service (SaaS) can all benefit from the implementation of a cloud computing environment. Instead of focusing on infrastructure issues, development engineers can focus on writing code and pushing it out to production as soon as possible. With continuous integration, continuous delivery, and continuous deployment taking over the software engineer's world, a cloud computing solution can make all three seamless. Continuous integration is the process of merging development code with the mainline or trunk of code. Continuous delivery is the sustained promotion of code to different environments, such as staging, quality assurance (QA), and production. Continuous deployment is installing code in production as soon as it is ready.

The cost of a cloud solution can be an impediment depending on the size of the enterprise. However, the capital investment up front for an in-house solution is often worth the long-term gains, especially in developer productivity. Even if an in-house solution does not make sense, it does not mean that a public cloud solution is out of the question.

Types of Clouds

There are at least two kinds of cloud solutions—three, if you include hybrids. A private cloud is an in-house cloud solution, using software such as OpenStack (http://www.openstack.org/), VMware's vCloud (http://www.vmware.com/cloud-computing/private-cloud). The second type of cloud, a public cloud, is hosted in a provider's data center instead of your own and is a pay-per-use model. Public cloud solutions are numerous, with the most popular ones offered by Amazon, Oracle, Google, Microsoft, and Rackspace. Hybrid cloud solutions involve an in-house cloud solution and use of a public cloud. OpenShift from RedHat is another on-premise and hosted PaaS solution, and hence can be classified as a hybrid (https://www.openshift.com/products/enterprise).

Private Cloud

Selecting a private cloud entails building a cloud infrastructure in your own data center. This option can be expensive, depending on how much investment is required and the size of your organization. OpenStack, for instance, is a distributed, in-house cloud solution that requires an extensive investment not only in hardware, but also in engineering skills to manage the solution. The following is a brief list of topics to keep in mind when deciding to opt for an in-house private cloud.

- Vendor choice

- Hardware requirements

- Availability of engineers who can manage the cloud

- Integration with your existing environment

- Ongoing licensing costs, in some cases

- The ease/difficulty of managing the cloud

- Life cycle management of the cloud

- Total cost of ownership of the private cloud

The exercise of hosting your own cloud can be simplified if you have a robust infrastructure with the tools needed to deploy new hardware quickly. There are numerous private cloud software solutions; I listed two earlier—OpenStack, which is free, and VMware, for which you must pay. Although OpenStack is free, this does not mean the cost of implementing it is less than that of VMware. Keep in mind that you should always look at the total cost of ownership when considering your options. A private cloud architecture is shown in Figure 2-1.

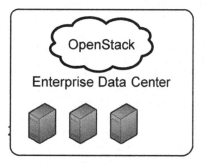

Figure 2-1. *Private cloud solution*

Public Cloud

A public cloud solution can end up being more expensive than a private cloud or less, depending on the size of an enterprise. Some cloud providers such as Amazon and Google provide a cost calculator. Using this calculator you can determine the approximate monthly cost of hosting your infrastructure on the provider's premises. Amazon's calculator can be found at https://calculator.s3.amazonaws.com/index.html and Google's calculator is located at https://cloud.google.com/products/calculator/. Microsoft has its own cloud platform called *Azure,* and Salesforce.com is a market leader in the SaaS cloud solution provider space. Figure 2-2 gives an example of a public cloud.

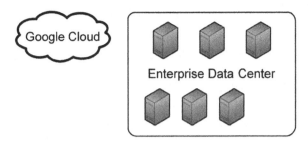

Figure 2-2. *Public cloud solution*

Hybrid Cloud

Hybrid cloud solutions include an in-house cloud solution and an external public cloud, as shown in Figure 2-3. This type of solution can be used for multiple purposes. For instance, one use could be disaster recovery. If the in-house cloud fails, the public cloud takes over serving data. Another alternative is to use the in-house cloud for development and staging, and the public cloud for production release. Hybrid clouds can also help save money, because you may end up hosting only a production infrastructure in the pay-per-use public cloud and use a smaller scale, less expensive in-house cloud for nonproduction environments such as development, QA, and staging. As mentioned, OpenShift from RedHat is a hybrid cloud solution; it has an on-premise and hosted infrastructure. The advantage of using an integrated solution such as OpenShift is that you only need to develop once, for a single platform, and you can deploy both on-premise and in a public cloud using the same deployment engine.

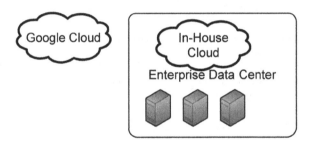

Figure 2-3. *Hybrid cloud solution*

Components of a Cloud

Cloud platforms—private, public, or hybrid—have some common components, including the following:

- Compute: virtual machines or instances that are available to install applications on and use for computing

- App Engine: application containers to upload code into the cloud; runs in the cloud without you having to manage any virtual machine or instances

- Storage: object base storage or nonrelational database storage

- Databases: MySQL or something similar

- Application programming interface (API): used to access cloud components, such as compute, app, and storage

- Metering: a way of tracking usage and either increasing or decreasing usage based on certain metrics; also used for billing

- Networking: used for communication between the cloud based virtual machines, and from external sources into the cloud

An enterprise does not necessarily have to use all the components of a cloud. One or more components may be in the cloud, but others are outside the cloud. Similarly, one or more components may be in the public cloud but other components reside in the private cloud.

Migrating to the Cloud

Moving applications to the cloud can be a daunting task. Assuming that an enterprise does not have a cloud solution but has decided to adopt one, how does it go about migrating existing infrastructure applications to the cloud? In this section I explain a few things you should keep in mind to have a successful migration.

First, you should conduct a cost analysis. Using any of the cloud calculators I mentioned earlier, calculate the cost of using a cloud such as Google Cloud. Then, compare the cost with that of using an in-house cloud such as OpenStack. To calculate the cost of OpenStack you have to include items such as hardware, both server and network, engineers, and support costs. A word of caution about online cloud cost calculators is that your answers may vary between the costs they predict and the actual cost you end up paying. Factor in a margin of error with the online calculators.

The next step is to figure out which applications are good candidates to run in the cloud. Not all applications run well in the cloud; some may be better running in-house. There could be regulations in certain industries that prohibit using external cloud providers. For instance, if you are in the health care industry, then privacy concerns may restrict you from uploading data to an external cloud.

Another concern with privacy may be in regard to the laws of a country. For instance, Germany has very strict individual privacy laws that may prohibit German companies from uploading German customer data to an international cloud providers network.

Next, it is crucial to develop a project plan that outlines which applications are moving and when. One possible way of migrating existing applications is to use the existing code base and push it in the cloud. This is perhaps not the most ideal way, because legacy applications not designed to run in the cloud may not work well in the cloud. For instance, if your application needs a database such as MySQL, MySQL may not be available in the cloud and you may have to use another database. Another thing to keep in mind is that some applications are very sensitive to disk input/output speed requirements and, because a majority of the cloud is based on virtualization, it will be slower than having direct disk access. Therefore these types of applications may not work well in the cloud. There are some cloud providers that lease physical servers instead of virtual environments, but at this point it's hard to see an advantage in using hosted physical servers.

As an application developer you also have to decide which cloud components are needed by an application. For enterprise applications that are within a corporate infrastructure, there are a host of other infrastructure services, such as monitoring, backup, and network operations center (NOC), that provide support services. These are not available in the same format in the cloud.

For instance, Google Cloud's SQL backup policy, which can be found at `https://developers.google.com/cloud-sql/docs/backup-recovery`, states that last seven backups of an instance are stored without any charge. If your organization has a need to back up data longer than that, then how can it be done and the cost of doing so must be considered.

For monitoring applications, some cloud providers provide a framework that can be used programmatically, and alerts can be sent on certain trigger activations. Google Cloud provides an API (`https://developers.google.com/cloud-monitoring/`) that lets you read monitoring metrics such as CPU, disk usage, and more, and sends alerts based on those metrics. An enterprise has to decide whether it makes sense to use this API or to leverage its existing monitoring infrastructure and extend it into the cloud.

Overall, the process of migrating to the cloud cannot be a sudden cutover. After the issues just presented have been sorted out, one strategy is to migrate partial data into the cloud and serve, say, 5% of traffic from the cloud. If this works, then you can increase traffic to the cloud slowly until it reaches 100%. Avoid situations in which immediate cutovers to the cloud are done; you don't want your customers experience an outage. The speed and reliability of Internet connectivity should also factor into your cloud migration strategy. Developing regions may not have the same access to the Internet as more developed countries. Terms of service, availability of the cloud, and privacy of data are also important factors to consider before and during migration. Figure 2-4 shows a flowchart for a cloud migration strategy.

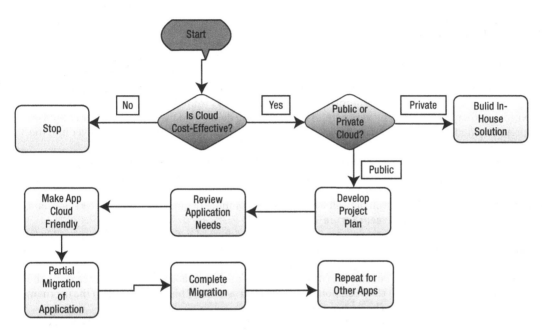

Figure 2-4. *Flowchart of cloud migration strategy*

DevOps

Who manages the cloud applications is an important discussion to have before preparing the cloud migration strategy. In a traditional enterprise, there are developers and operations engineers. Developers write code; operations engineers then push the code to production and manage the production environment. However, in the case of an enterprise using a public cloud, the public cloud infrastructure is managed by the provider, so what role will operations play?

The simplistic version is that ops will not play any role. Developers will push code to the public code as needed, and any alerts from the application are sent to the developers, who are on call 24/7 and who will resolve the issue. This approach has the advantage of having the shortest turnaround time for bug fixes and new features from developers into production. However, this approach also has the highest risk, because there is an assumption that, before code is deployed into the cloud, developers have tested it and are following the proper procedures for deploying code.

Another approach is to stay with the traditional model and have developers write code and hand it over to the operations staff, who then push it to the cloud. In general, this is how things have worked in traditional enterprises. With the proper checks and balances incorporated into this process, it is perhaps a safer way of deploying code. However, the advantage of leveraging rapid code deployment in the cloud can be lost if you adhere to this approach without any modifications.

A third option that is perhaps more popular is a hybrid approach. With this type of approach, developers write code; however, they cannot push it to the cloud without operational overview. For instance, change management has to be incorporated into the process, which requires operational oversight. In addition, most enterprises maintain an NOC that has to be involved to coordinate and provide 24/7 first-level support for incidents arising from code deployments or other actions. In general, security review comes under the purview of the operations umbrella and, as such, new-application migration to the cloud should be overseen by the corporate security team.

As you can see, the strategy most suitable for an enterprise depends on a lot of factors. There is no one-size-fits-all when it comes to managing the cloud.

Security in the Cloud

Security is always a concern for an enterprise and it becomes more of a concern when applications are deployed in a public cloud, because the usual controls of an enterprise such as firewalls and intrusion prevention/detection software may not be readily available in the public cloud. Connecting a virtual public cloud infrastructure to an enterprise network with a VPN makes your enterprise vulnerable to attacks from the public cloud if it is compromised. Needless to say, you have to be very careful when pushing data out to the public cloud. In the case of a private, on-premise cloud, the same controls that apply to other noncloud entities can be ported over into the cloud, with some modifications.

So how do you handle security in a public cloud such as Google Cloud Platform (GCP)? One advantage of GCP is that, in your project, your resources are isolated from other projects, even if they belong to the same organization. This provides some level of security. In addition, if your instances do not use public Internet Protocol (IP) addresses, they are not reachable from the Internet. The built-in firewall within Google Compute Engine (GCE) is secure as well, and by default blocks all incoming connections except Secure Shell (SSH).

Intrusion detection and intrusion prevention are topics that are not addressed in GCE, so you are responsible for setting up your own if you so desire.

When using SaaS, such as `Salesforce.com`, or other hosted solutions, the location from which your data in the cloud is accessed is also a security concern. For example if your employees access SaaS from an Internet café and the café computers are infected with a virus, the virus can potentially log all keystrokes. This would result in the username and password of your employees' SaaS access being compromised.

In the Google App Engine (GAE) world, the security of your application is dependent primarily on the application and your faith in Google's infrastructure. You have little to no control over the infrastructure; therefore, a majority of what you do from a security perspective is based on your application.

Google Cloud Platform

Google Cloud Platform (GCP) provides the building blocks needed to run your applications on Google's hosted servers. The services that GCP offers can be divided into compute, storage, big data, and development tools. For the purpose of this chapter, big data is included in the discussion of storage. To get started with GCP, head over to `https://cloud.google.com/products/` and take a look at the different offerings in relation to compute, storage, big data, and development. You need a Google account to sign up for GCP. After you sign in at `https://console.developers.google.com`, you can start to create GCP resources. The following is a list of products that GCP offers as of the writing of this chapter:

- Compute
  - Google App Engine (GAE)
  - Google Compute Engine (GCE)

- Storage
    - Google Cloud Storage (GCS)
    - Google Cloud DataStore (GCD)
    - Cloud SQL (GSQL)
    - BigQuery
- Development tools
    - Google Cloud SDK
    - Cloud Playground
    - Google Plugin for Eclipse
    - Push to Deploy
    - Android Studio

Accessing GCP is done through the web interface at `https://cloud.google.com`. There is also a software development kit (SDK) that can be used to manage GCP; however, some level of web user interface is required, at least initially, to set up your project. You can view extensive documentation on this above topics at `https://developers.google.com/cloud/`.

Projects

Projects in GCP are a way of grouping resources. For instance, if there are ten applications, each might get its own project. The name of a project is entirely up to you. Each project has a project name and a project ID. The project name can be changed later, but the project ID cannot be changed. A project also has a project number that is assigned automatically and cannot be changed.

For instance, if your company is `Example.com`, then the project might be named Example-Web-Front-End, with a project ID of example-web-fe. The project ID also is the subdomain in the `.appspot.com` URL for GAE. All projects have permissions and billing. Without enabling billing, you cannot create any resources in the project. Providing a credit card number enables billing, as does providing a bank account number. Premier accounts do not need a credit card account; instead, they are billed on a monthly basis. Enterprises generally sign up with a premier account when they know for sure that they want to deploy in GCP.

One possible way of handling projects is to create three projects per application: one for development, another for QA or staging, and the third for production. Developers can be given access to the developer project, QA engineers to the QA project, and operations staff to the production project.

Permissions

The permissions in Google Cloud Platform are all based on Google accounts, which are used to log in to GCP, and are applied in projects. There are three kinds of permissions in a project. "Is owner" allows full access, which includes billing and administrative control. "Can edit" allows full access to the applications, but not to billing and administrative control. "Can view" allows view permission without the ability to modify any setting.

Permissions are crucial to a project, and having unnecessary permissions can result in a security breach, so be extra careful when providing permissions. An example is that most projects should have different permissions for cloud management engineers versus developers versus the NOC. However, if all three categories of people are given the same level of access, then one group may override the settings put in place by another group, causing virtual instances of the project not to be accessible. You can read more about permissions at `https://cloud.google.com/developers/articles/best-practices-for-configuring-permissions-on-gcp`.

Google Compute Engine

GCE provides virtual machines, also known as instances that can be used to deploy code. They consist of disks, images, instances, networks, load balancers, and more. GAE is an alternative to GCE for certain types of applications. With GAE, you do not have a lot of the flexibility present in GCE. For instance, in GCE you can control networks, firewalls, load balancers, and virtual machine configuration—none of which is feasible in GAE. If you need this level of control over your application, then use GCE and not GAE. You can get more information about GCE at https://developers.google.com/compute/.

Virtual Machines

To create a virtual machine in GCE, you can use the Google Cloud SDK or the web interface. There are different configurations available for virtual machines. A full list can be found at https://cloud.google.com/products/compute-engine/. Pricing varies based on instance type. Listing 2-1 is an example of creating a virtual machine using the default settings.

Listing 2-1. Create a Virtual Machine

```
##########
#Install the Google Cloud SDK
$ curl https://sdk.cloud.google.com | bash


##########
#Log in to GCP; this will open a web browser that will ask you to give permission for GCP
$ gcloud auth login


##########
#Add an instance to project webexample
$ gcutil --project=webexample addinstance www1-example-com
Select a zone:
1: asia-east1-a
2: asia-east1-b
3: asia-east1-c
4: europe-west1-a
5: europe-west1-b
6: us-central1-a
7: us-central1-b
8: us-central1-f
>>> 6
Select a machine type:
1: n1-standard-1        1 vCPU, 3.75 GB RAM
2: n1-standard-16       16 vCPUs, 60 GB RAM
3: n1-standard-2        2 vCPUs, 7.5 GB RAM
4: n1-standard-4        4 vCPUs, 15 GB RAM
5: n1-standard-8        8 vCPUs, 30 GB RAM
6: n1-highcpu-16        16 vCPUs, 14.4 GB RAM
7: n1-highcpu-2         2 vCPUs, 1.8 GB RAM
8: n1-highcpu-4         4 vCPUs, 3.6 GB RAM
9: n1-highcpu-8         8 vCPUs, 7.2 GB RAM
10: n1-highmem-16       16 vCPUs, 104 GB RAM
11: n1-highmem-2        2 vCPUs, 13 GB RAM
```

```
12: n1-highmem-4        4 vCPUs, 26 GB RAM
13: n1-highmem-8        8 vCPUs, 52 GB RAM
14: f1-micro            1 vCPU (shared physical core) and 0.6 GB RAM
15: g1-small            1 vCPU (shared physical core) and 1.7 GB RAM
>>> 3
Select an image:
1: projects/centos-cloud/global/images/centos-6-v20140718
2: projects/debian-cloud/global/images/backports-debian-7-wheezy-v20140807
3: projects/debian-cloud/global/images/debian-7-wheezy-v20140807
4: projects/rhel-cloud/global/images/rhel-6-v20140718
5: projects/suse-cloud/global/images/sles-11-sp3-v20140712
>>> 1
INFO: Waiting for insert of instance www1-example-com. Sleeping for 3s.
[SNIP]


Table of resources:

+------------------+-------------+----------------+---------------+---------+
| name             | network-ip  | external-ip    | zone          | status  |
+------------------+-------------+----------------+---------------+---------+
| www1-example-com | 10.240.93.2 | 146.148.37.192 | us-central1-a | RUNNING |
+------------------+-------------+----------------+---------------+---------+


Table of operations:

+--------------------------------+----------+------------------------------+---------------+
| name                           | status   | insert-time                  | operation-type|
+--------------------------------+----------+------------------------------+---------------+
| operation-140790998[SNIP]-4641f474 |   DONE   | 2014-08-12T23:06:27.376-07:00 |    insert     |
+--------------------------------+----------+------------------------------+---------------+


##########
#SSH to the instance created earlier
$ gcutil --project webexample ssh www1-example-com
```

The type of instance you create depends on the computing requirements of the application. Be careful when picking the type of instance, because if you overestimate you will end up paying for capacity that is not being used. If you underestimate, you can always add more instances. For example, instance type n1-standard-4 consists of four virtual cores, 15GB of memory, and costs $0.280 in the United States. If you pick n1-standard-16 instead, then the cost is $1.120/hour for 16 cores and 64GB of memory.

You can figure out whether you are logged in a GCE virtual instance by searching for "Google" in the output of the dmidecode command:

```
$ sudo dmidecode -s bios-vendor | grep Google
Google
```

By default, instances are assigned ephemeral IP addresses. All instances have a network IP that is addressable only within the network. You can also assign a public IP address to an instance. The public IP address can be static or ephemeral. By default, the following ports are allowed to an instance:

- Incoming Secure Shell (SSH) from anywhere

- Incoming Remote Desktop Protocol (RDP) on port 3389

- Any port and any protocol for intrainstance traffic in the same network in a given project

Instances can have numerous operations performed on them, some of which are listed here:

```
##########
#list instances in a project
$ gcloud compute instances list
NAME        ZONE          MACHINE_TYPE  INTERNAL_IP    EXTERNAL_IP     STATUS
vm1         us-central1-b n1-standard-2 10.240.64.102  23.251.145.124  RUNNING
vm2         us-central1-b n1-standard-1 10.240.73.218  23.236.61.138   RUNNING

#if an instance is "stuck" you can power cycle it
$ gcloud compute  instances reset vm2 --zone us-central1-b
Updated [https://www.googleapis.com/compute/v1/projects/webexample/zones/us-central1-b/instances/vm2]


##########
#SSH to an instance without using gcutil
#key file is normally ~/.ssh/google_compute_engine
#replace USER@IP_ADDRESS with your username in GCE and IP_ADDRESS with the instance public IP
address. You cannot SSH to instances that do not have a public IP address.
$ ssh -i KEY_FILE -o UserKnownHostsFile=/dev/null -o CheckHostIP=no -o StrictHostKeyChecking=no
USER@IP_ADDRESS


##########
#delete an instance
$ gcloud compute  instances delete vm1 --zone us-central1-b
The following instances will be deleted. Attached disks configured to
be autodeleted will be deleted unless they are attached to any other
instances. Deleting a disk is irreversible and any data on the disk
will be lost.
 - [vm1] in [us-central1-b]

Do you want to continue (Y/n?  Y
Deleted [https://www.googleapis.com/compute/v1/projects/webexample/zones/us-central1-b/instances/vm1].
```

■ **Note** When creating a virtual machine, check firewall rules first so that you do not allow incoming traffic inadvertently to an instance that is not supposed to receive traffic from the Internet.

Networks

A virtual machine resides on a network. By default, in GCE there is a network called *default*. This network is 10.240.0.0/16. Each network has firewall rules associated with it. Networks can belong to one project only and cannot be shared between projects. By default, all incoming traffic is blocked. Firewall rules regulate incoming traffic to the instances only, not outgoing. If you want to block outgoing traffic from a virtual machine, then you have to use iptables.

Google also blocks all outgoing traffic from GCE to the Internet on port 25. If you wish to use "deliver mail" outside of GCE, then you have to sign up for an account with SendGrid (http://sendgrid.com/), which is the only supported mail relay as of the writing of this chapter. You can read more about how to setup outbound email at https://cloud.google.com/compute/docs/sending-mail. Outgoing ports 465 and 587 are also blocked, except to known Google IP addresses, because all three ports (25, 465, and 587) are used for SMTP service. You can get a list of known Google IP addresses by querying the Sender Policy Framework (SPF) record for Google, as shown at https://support.google.com/a/answer/60764.

■ **Note**   A project in GCE can contain multiple networks; however, each instance or virtual machine can be attached to a single network only. GCE currently does not support IPv6, only IPv4, so all networks have to be IPv4.

For an enterprise that is creating instances in GCE, if the instances are going to stay isolated from the corporate network, then using the default network within GCE might be convenient. On the other hand, if the enterprise wants to setup a VPN between the GCE instances and its corporate network, then it may be suitable for the enterprise also to manage the networks within GCE. For instance, if an enterprise has its corporate network in the range 192.168.0.0/16 and would prefer to extend that network into GCE instead of using the default 10.240.0.0/16, it can set up a VPN that connects the two networks. Figure 2-5 shows GCE and Corporate connected with VPN and having different network numbers.

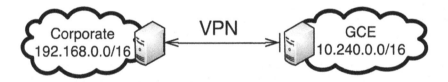

Figure 2-5. *VPN between public cloud and corporate network*

To connect your corporate network to GCE via VPN, on the GCE side you have to use an instance with VPN software installed, such as OpenVPN. On the corporate end, you can use OpenVPN as well or a dedicated VPN appliance.

■ **Note**   GCE networks support point-to-point IPv4 traffic only. They do not support multicast or broadcast.

You can find out more information about networks and firewalls at https://developers.google.com/compute/docs/networking.

Regions and Zones

GCE instances can be deployed in various regions and zones. Resources such as disk, instance, and IP address are zone specific. For example, an instance in us-central1-a cannot use a disk from us-central-1b. Regions are collections of zones. For instance us-central1 is a region that consists of zones a,b, and f. Two sample zones that are available in GCE as of this writing are depicted in Figure 2-6.

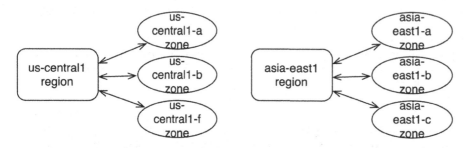

Figure 2-6. *Sample GCE regions and zones*

You can view all the zones available using the command shown here:

```
$ gcloud compute zones list
https://www.googleapis.com/compute/v1/projects/webexample/zones/asia-east1-a
https://www.googleapis.com/compute/v1/projects/webexample/zones/asia-east1-c
https://www.googleapis.com/compute/v1/projects/webexample/zones/asia-east1-b
https://www.googleapis.com/compute/v1/projects/webexample/zones/europe-west1-a
https://www.googleapis.com/compute/v1/projects/webexample/zones/europe-west1-b
https://www.googleapis.com/compute/v1/projects/webexample/zones/us-central1-a
https://www.googleapis.com/compute/v1/projects/webexample/zones/us-central1-f
https://www.googleapis.com/compute/v1/projects/webexample/zones/us-central1-b
```

To come up with an enterprise strategy for which zones to deploy in, the recommendation from Google is to spread instances between at least two zones. If one zone has an issue, your application will be up if it has another copy running in another zone. If the enterprise is a U.S.-only enterprise, then select regions that are based in the United States. On the other hand, if the enterprise is a global, then select regions where the enterprise does business.

■ **Tip**   For fault tolerance, when creating instances, create at least two of each in different zones.

Support for processors also varies across zones. For instance, as of this writing Intel Sandy Bridge is not available in us-central1-f. When you view the processor information of a virtual machine, you will see the type of processor that has been provided. An example is shown here for a dual-core virtual machine:

```
$ egrep 'vendor_id|model name'  /proc/cpuinfo
vendor_id        : GenuineIntel
model name       : Intel(R) Xeon(R) CPU @ 2.60GHz
vendor_id        : GenuineIntel
model name       : Intel(R) Xeon(R) CPU @ 2.60GHz
```

You can read more about regions and zones at https://developers.google.com/compute/docs/zones.

Quotas

Because GCE is a shared environment, Google implements quotas to ensure that no single customer is able to use all the resources and affect another customer. There are two kinds of quotas: one is projectwide quota and the other is regionwide quota. Quotas are on resources such as static IP address, images, networks, and firewall rules. Project quota limitations are listed in Table 2-1.

Table 2-1. *GCE Quotas*

Resource	Limit
Firewalls	100
Forwarding rules	50
Health checks	50
Images	100
Networks	5
Routes	100
Snapshots	1000
Target pools	50

To view a list of networks being used in your project, use the following command:

```
$ gcloud compute networks list
NAME            IPV4_RANGE        GATEWAY_IPV4
default         10.240.0.0/16     10.240.0.1
corp-net        192.168.0.0/16    192.168.0.1
```

■ **Caution**   Not being mindful of quotas on projects can result in production outages, especially for autoscaling resources.

For an enterprise, it is crucial to get the right amount of resources—both for projects and for regions. If the project is using autoscaling and growing instances on demand, hitting a quota limitation may affect production. You can request Google to increase the quota by using the web interface. It may take them a few days to do so, so plan ahead. The form to request a quota increase is at https://docs.google.com/forms/d/1vb2MkAr9JcHrp6myQ3oTxCyBv2c7Iy c5wqIKqE3K4IE/viewform. Monitor your usage and the quota limit closely, and make the request at least a few days in advance. You can view a list of quotas limitations at https://developers.google.com/compute/docs/resource-quotas.

Firewalls

By default, all networks in GCE are protected by a firewall that blocks incoming traffic. You can connect from an external network only to those GCE instances that have a public IP address. If an instance does not have an external IP and you attempt to SSH to it, you will get an error such as the one shown here:

```
ERROR: (gcloud.compute.ssh) Instance [vm1] in zone [us-central1-b] does not have an external IP
address, so you cannot SSH into it. To add an external IP address to the instance, use [gcloud
compute instances add-access-config].
```

You can access instances within a GCE network that do not have an external IP from other instances within GCE, because GCE uses the internal address of that host. For instance, if you are on web-server2 and you ping web-server1, GCE will use the internal address of web-server1:

```
[web-server2 ~]$ ping web-server1 -c 1
PING web-server1.c.webexample.internal (10.240.107.200) 56(84) bytes of data.
64 bytes from web-server1.c.webexaple.internal (10.240.107.200): icmp_seq=1 ttl=64 time=0.642 ms

--- web-server1.c.webexample.internal ping statistics ---
1 packets transmitted, 1 received, 0% packet loss, time 0ms
rtt min/avg/max/mdev = 0.642/0.642/0.642/0.000 ms
```

If you have one or more web servers behind a GCE load balancer, you do not have to assign an external IP address to the web server instances for them to accept incoming traffic. When you create the load balancer, GCE assigns the load balancer a public IP address, which is where all incoming traffic arrives. The load balancer then forwards the traffic to the web servers. On the other hand, if the instance is not behind a GCE load balancer, then it has to have a public IP address for it to accept incoming connections from the Internet.

For enterprises, assigning public IP addresses to instances is not recommended for security reasons, unless needed. You can create a gateway host, SSH to which is allowed from the corporate network. From the gateway host you can then SSH to all other instances within GCE.

Iptables is not configured by default on GCE instances; however, it can be used in addition to the network firewall that GCE provides for added security, as shown in Listing 2-2.

Listing 2-2. GCE Firewall

```
##########\
#list the firewall rules associated with all networks in a given project of GCE
#we have just one network called 'default'
$ gcloud compute firewall-rules list
NAME                      NETWORK    SRC_RANGES    RULES                              SRC_TAGS TARGET_TAGS
default-allow-internal  default    10.0.0.0/8    tcp:1-65535,udp:1-65535,icmp
default-https           default    0.0.0.0/0     tcp:443
default-ssh             default    0.0.0.0/0     tcp:22
http                    default    0.0.0.0/0     tcp:80

##########
#view detailed information about the http rule
$ gcloud compute firewall-rules describe http
allowed:
- IPProtocol: tcp
  ports:
  - '80'
creationTimestamp: '2013-12-18T18:25:30.514-08:00'
id: '170364142249969095876'
kind: compute#firewall
name: http
network: https://www.googleapis.com/compute/v1/projects/webexample/global/networks/default
selfLink: https://www.googleapis.com/compute/v1/projects/webexample/global/firewalls/http
sourceRanges:
- 0.0.0.0/0
```

```
##########
#create a new firewall rule that allows incoming TCP traffic on port 7000
#call the firewall rule 'my-app'
$ gcloud compute firewall-rules create my-app --allow tcp:7000 --source-ranges 0.0.0.0/0
Created [https://www.googleapis.com/compute/v1/projects/webexample/global/firewalls/my-app].
NAME    NETWORK SRC_RANGES RULES    SRC_TAGS TARGET_TAGS
my-app default 0.0.0.0/0  tcp:7000


##########
#verify that the new rule, which we called 'my-app,' is visible when a firewall rule listing is done
$ gcloud compute firewall-rules list | grep -i my-app
my-app default 0.0.0.0/0 tcp:7000


##########
#check the details of the new rule called 'my-app'
$ gcloud compute firewall-rules describe my-app
allowed:
- IPProtocol: tcp
  ports:
  - '7000'
creationTimestamp: '2014-08-17T10:00:56.611-07:00'
id: '9293032300921518370'
kind: compute#firewall
name: my-app
network: https://www.googleapis.com/compute/v1/projects/webexample/global/networks/default
selfLink: https://www.googleapis.com/compute/v1/projects/webexample/global/firewalls/my-app
sourceRanges:
- 0.0.0.0/0


##########
#update the new rule to allow TCP port 8001 instead of port 7000
$ gcloud compute firewall-rules update my-app --allow tcp:8001
Updated [https://www.googleapis.com/compute/v1/projects/webexample/global/firewalls/my-app].


##########
#verify that the update went through
$ gcloud compute firewall-rules describe my-app
allowed:
- IPProtocol: tcp
  ports:
  - '8001'
creationTimestamp: '2014-08-17T10:00:56.611-07:00'
id: '9293032300921518370'
kind: compute#firewall
name: my-app
network: https://www.googleapis.com/compute/v1/projects/webexample/global/networks/default
selfLink: https://www.googleapis.com/compute/v1/projects/webexample/global/firewalls/my-app
sourceRanges:
- 0.0.0.0/0
```

Images

Images are bootable operating system resources that include a boot loader and a system partition. There are public as well are private images. Public images are available for anyone who uses GCE. Private images are project specific. You can create your own image, upload it in a project, and deploy instances from that instance.

Some images have an additional cost associated with them whereas others are free. For instance, the centos-6-v20140718 web image is a free public image. On the other hand, the rhel-6-v20140718 image incurs additional charges because RedHat is a licensed operating system. Listing 2-3 shows some basic image operations, including creating an image.

Listing 2-3. Image Operations

```
##########
#list images available
$ gcloud compute images list
NAME                                 PROJECT            DEPRECATED STATUS
centos-6-v20140718                   centos-cloud                  READY
coreos-alpha-402-2-0-v20140807       coreos-cloud                  READY
coreos-beta-367-1-0-v20140715        coreos-cloud                  READY
coreos-stable-367-1-0-v20140724      coreos-cloud                  READY
backports-debian-7-wheezy-v20140807  debian-cloud                  READY
debian-7-wheezy-v20140807            debian-cloud                  READY
opensuse-13-1-v20140711              opensuse-cloud                READY
rhel-6-v20140718                     rhel-cloud                    READY
sles-11-sp3-v20140712                suse-cloud                    READY
##########
#Create an instance based on the latest centos-6 image, call the instance centos-vm1
$ gcloud compute instances create centos-vm1 --image centos-6 --zone us-central1-a
Created [https://www.googleapis.com/compute/v1/projects/webexample/zones/us-central1-a/instances/
centos-vm1].
NAME       ZONE         MACHINE_TYPE  INTERNAL_IP  EXTERNAL_IP   STATUS
centos-vm1 us-central1-a n1-standard-1 10.240.35.23 23.251.150.5 RUNNING

##########
#ensure that the instance is running
$ gcloud compute instances list centos-vm1
NAME       ZONE         MACHINE_TYPE  INTERNAL_IP  EXTERNAL_IP   STATUS
centos-vm1 us-central1-a n1-standard-1 10.240.35.23 23.251.150.5 RUNNING

##########
#attempt to SSH to the instance we created just now
$ gcutil ssh centos-vm1
INFO: Zone for centos-vm1 detected as us-central1-a.
INFO: Running command line: ssh -o UserKnownHostsFile=/dev/null -o CheckHostIP=no -o
StrictHostKeyChecking=no -i /Users/syedali/.ssh/google_compute_engine -A -p 22 23.251.150.5 --
[centos-vm1 ~]$ hostname
centos-vm1
[centos-vm1 ~]$ exit
Logout
Connection to 23.251.150.5 closed.
```

You can also create your own image and use that to deploy instances, as seen in Listing 2-4.

Listing 2-4. Creating a Custom Image

```
##########
#create an instance called web-server, using the centos-6 image, in zone us-central1-b
#we specify the scope of storage-rw and compute-rw to allow access to Google Cloud Storage
#you can learn more about scopes using the command 'gcloud compute instances create --help'
$ gcloud compute instances create web-server --scopes storage-rw compute-rw --image centos-6 --zone
us-central1-b
Created [https://www.googleapis.com/compute/v1/projects/webexample/zones/us-central1-b/instances/
web-server].
NAME        ZONE           MACHINE_TYPE   INTERNAL_IP    EXTERNAL_IP   STATUS
web-server us-central1-b n1-standard-1 10.240.111.65 108.59.82.59 RUNNING


##########
#SSH to the instance we created earlier
#install httpd
$ gcloud compute ssh web-server --zone us-central1-b
[web-server ~]$ sudo yum install httpd -y
Loaded plugins: downloadonly, fastestmirror, security
Determining fastest mirrors
 * base: mirror.us.oneandone.net
 * extras: mirror.wiredtree.com
 * updates: centos.corenetworks.net
.....[SNIP].....
Installed:
  httpd.x86_64 0:2.2.15-31.el6.centos
.....[SNIP].....
Complete!
[web-server ~]$ exit
logout
Connection to 108.59.82.59 closed.


##########
#delete the instance while keeping the boot disk, because we don't need the instance anymore
#you can also keep the instance for future modifications if you want
$ gcloud compute instances delete web-server --keep-disks boot --zone us-central1-b
The following instances will be deleted. Attached disks configured to
be auto-deleted will be deleted unless they are attached to any other
instances. Deleting a disk is irreversible and any data on the disk
will be lost.
 - [web-server] in [us-central1-b]

Do you want to continue (Y/n)?  y

Updated [https://www.googleapis.com/compute/v1/projects/webexample/zones/us-central1-b/instances/
web-server].
Deleted [https://www.googleapis.com/compute/v1/projects/webexample/zones/us-central1-b/instances/
web-server].
```

```
##########
#now create a new image called web-server-image using the boot disk of the previous instance on
which we installed httpd
#the --source-disk provides the name of web-server, because that was the name of the disk from the
earlier instance
$ gcloud compute images create web-server-image --source-disk web-server --source-disk-zone us-central1-b
Created [https://www.googleapis.com/compute/v1/projects/webexample/global/images/web-server-image].
NAME              PROJECT            DEPRECATED STATUS
web-server-image  webexample                    READY


##########
#list the images and make sure you see the web-server-image
$ gcloud compute images list
NAME                        PROJECT            DEPRECATED STATUS
web-server-image            webexample         READY
centos-6-v20140718          centos-cloud       READY
.....[SNIP].....
rhel-6-v20140718            rhel-cloud         READY
sles-11-sp3-v20140712       suse-cloud         READY


##########
#attempt to create a new instance called web-server2 using the web-server-image we created earlier
$ gcloud compute instances create web-server2  --image web-server-image --zone us-central1-b
Created [https://www.googleapis.com/compute/v1/projects/webexample/zones/us-central1-b/instances/
web-server2].
NAME         ZONE           MACHINE_TYPE   INTERNAL_IP    EXTERNAL_IP    STATUS
web-server2  us-central1-b  n1-standard-1  10.240.84.183  108.59.82.59   RUNNING


##########
#once the instance is up, SSH to it and verify that httpd is present on it
$ gcloud compute ssh web-server2 --zone us-central1-b
[web-server2 ~]$ hostname
web-server2
[web-server2 ~]$ rpm -qa | grep -i httpd
httpd-tools-2.2.15-31.el6.centos.x86_64
httpd-2.2.15-31.el6.centos.x86_64
[web-server2 ~]$ exit
logout
    Connection to 108.59.82.59 closed.
```

Network Load Balancing

Load balancing in GCE is straightforward. It does not support multiple load-balancing algorithms as of this writing. The algorithm supported is protocol based; in other words, it is based on address, port, and protocol type. By default, GCE picks real servers based on a hash of the source IP and port, and the destination IP and port. Incoming connections are spread across the real servers, not by packet, but by connection. For instance, if there are three real servers and a connection is to a given real server, until the connection is closed, all packets for that connection will go to the same server.

■ **Note**   Google does not support different load-balancing algorithms, such as least connection, dynamic round robin, weighted round robin, predictive, and observed.

To set up load balancing, first create a target pool. The pool should consist one or more real servers to which traffic will be sent. A pool can contain instances in different zones as long as they are in the same region.

After creating a pool, create a forwarding rule that forwards traffic to the previously created target pool. The type of traffic that is forwarded can be TCP or UDP and you can specify a range of ports.

Last, open the ports being forwarded on the firewall that are going to the real servers so that traffic can flow to them.

If encryption is being done, then it has to be set up at the instance level; the load balancer does not do any decryption for you. You cannot terminate a secure sockets layer at the load balancer and expect it to communicate unencrypted with the real servers. The general steps are summarized here and are shown in Listing 2-5:

1. Create web server instances.

2. Install httpd, and start httpd on servers.

3. Tag the web servers with a tag such as www.

4. Create a firewall rule to allow HTTP traffic to target tag www.

5. Verify that you can access the web servers remotely on port 80.

6. Create a health check on port 80 for the load balancer.

7. Define a target pool and add the two instances to the pool.

8. Create a load balancer forwarding rule to forward http port 80 traffic to the previously created target pool.

9. Ensure the forwarding rule works.

Listing 2-5. Load-Balanced Web Server Deployment

```
###############
#view a list of instances in our project
#it looks like we have only one instance called web-server2
$ gcloud compute instances list
NAME           ZONE          MACHINE_TYPE  INTERNAL_IP    EXTERNAL_IP    STATUS
web-server2    us-central1-b n1-standard-1 10.240.84.183  108.59.82.59   RUNNING

###############
#because we want to test load balancing, we are going to create another web server
#the second web server will be called web-server1, because the earlier one is called web-server2
#this web server is going to be in another zone, in the same region, for fault tolerance in case one
zone goes down
$ gcloud compute instances create web-server1  --image web-server-image --zone us-central1-a
Created [https://www.googleapis.com/compute/v1/projects/webexample/zones/us-central1-a/instances/
web-server1].
NAME           ZONE          MACHINE_TYPE  INTERNAL_IP    EXTERNAL_IP     STATUS
web-server1    us-central1-a n1-standard-1 10.240.107.200 199.223.235.248 RUNNING
```

```
###############
#ensure that both the instances are running
$ gcloud compute instances list --regex '^web.*'
NAME         ZONE          MACHINE_TYPE   INTERNAL_IP      EXTERNAL_IP       STATUS
web-server1  us-central1-a n1-standard-1  10.240.107.200   199.223.235.248   RUNNING
web-server2  us-central1-b n1-standard-1  10.240.84.183    108.59.82.59      RUNNING

###############
#create a file on each of the web servers
[root@web-server1 html]# cat > index.html
web-server1
#repeat the above step on web-server2, using hostname web-server2 in index.html

###############
#we need to start Apache on each of the web servers
$ gcloud compute ssh web-server1 --zone us-central1-a
[web-server1 ~]$ sudo /etc/init.d/httpd start
Starting httpd:                                    [  OK  ]
[web-server1 ~]$ exit
logout
Connection to 199.223.235.248 closed.

$ gcloud compute ssh web-server2 --zone us-central1-b
[web-server2 ~]$ sudo /etc/init.d/httpd start
Starting httpd:                                    [  OK  ]
[web-server2 ~]$ logout
Connection to 108.59.82.59 closed.

###############
#now that we have two web servers, we are going to tag them both with www
#tags are one way of grouping instances; it makes it easy to apply firewall rules
$ gcloud compute instances add-tags web-server1 --tags www --zone us-central1-a
Updated [https://www.googleapis.com/compute/v1/projects/webexample/zones/us-central1-a/instances/
web-server1].
$ gcloud compute instances add-tags web-server2 --tags www --zone us-central1-b
Updated [https://www.googleapis.com/compute/v1/projects/webexample/zones/us-central1-b/instances/
web-server2].

###############
#because we tagged both web servers, we can now create a firewall rule allowing incoming port 80
traffic to
#all instances that have been tagged with www
$ gcloud compute firewall-rules create www --target-tags www --allow tcp:80
Created [https://www.googleapis.com/compute/v1/projects/webexample/global/firewalls/www].
NAME NETWORK SRC_RANGES RULES  SRC_TAGS TARGET_TAGS
www   default 0.0.0.0/0  tcp:80          www
```

```
###############
# check to make sure that Apache is running and is accessible on both web servers
$ curl -I 199.223.235.248
HTTP/1.1 200 OK
Date: Sat, 16 Aug 2014 04:02:01 GMT
Server: Apache/2.2.15 (CentOS)
Last-Modified: Sat, 16 Aug 2014 03:47:01 GMT
ETag: "44de-c-500b6fd85c69c"
Accept-Ranges: bytes
Content-Length: 12
Connection: close
Content-Type: text/html; charset=UTF-8

$ curl -I 108.59.82.59
HTTP/1.1 200 OK
Date: Sat, 16 Aug 2014 04:02:21 GMT
Server: Apache/2.2.15 (CentOS)
Last-Modified: Sat, 16 Aug 2014 03:48:14 GMT
ETag: "44e5-c-500b701e8f71b"
Accept-Ranges: bytes
Content-Length: 12
Connection: close
Content-Type: text/html; charset=UTF-8

###############
#create a health check called www-check on port 80
$ gcloud compute http-health-checks create www-check
Created [https://www.googleapis.com/compute/v1/projects/webexample/global/healthChecks/www-check].
NAME       HOST PORT REQUEST_PATH
www-check        80   /

###############
#once we create the health check we can check to make sure it is working
$ gcloud compute http-health-checks describe www-check
checkIntervalSec: 5
creationTimestamp: '2014-08-15T16:56:33.068-07:00'
healthyThreshold: 2
id: '9586071737643618960'
kind: compute#httpHealthCheck
name: www-check
port: 80
requestPath: /
selfLink: https://www.googleapis.com/compute/v1/projects/webexample/global/httpHealthChecks/www-check
timeoutSec: 5
unhealthyThreshold: 2

###############
#create a target pool called www-pool in the us-central1 region using health check www-check
$ gcloud compute target-pools create www-pool --region us-central1 --health-check www-check
Created [https://www.googleapis.com/compute/v1/projects/webexample/regions/us-central1/targetPools/www-pool].
NAME       REGION       SESSION_AFFINITY BACKUP HEALTH_CHECKS
www-pool us-central1 NONE                         www-check
```

```
###############
#add instances to the pool www-pool
$ gcloud compute target-pools add-instances www-pool --instances web-server1 --zone us-central1-a
Updated [https://www.googleapis.com/compute/v1/projects/webexample/regions/us-central1/targetPools/
www-pool].
$ gcloud compute target-pools add-instances www-pool --instances web-server2 --zone us-central1-b
Updated [https://www.googleapis.com/compute/v1/projects/webexample/regions/us-central1/targetPools/
www-pool].


###############
#create a forwarding rule in the load balancer
$ gcloud compute forwarding-rules create www-rule --region us-central1 --port-range 80 --target-pool www-pool
Created [https://www.googleapis.com/compute/v1/projects/webexample/regions/us-central1/
forwardingRules/www-rule].
NAME       REGION       IP_ADDRESS       IP_PROTOCOL   TARGET
www-rule   us-central1  173.255.119.47   TCP           us-central1/targetPools/www-pool


###############
#check the forwarding rule
$ gcloud compute forwarding-rules describe www-rule  --region us-central1
IPAddress: 173.255.119.47
IPProtocol: TCP
creationTimestamp: '2014-08-15T17:26:05.071-07:00'
id: '11261796502728168445'
kind: compute#forwardingRule
name: www-rule
portRange: 80-80
region: https://www.googleapis.com/compute/v1/projects/webexample/regions/us-central1
selfLink: https://www.googleapis.com/compute/v1/projects/webexample/regions/us-central1/
forwardingRules/www-rule
target: https://www.googleapis.com/compute/v1/projects/webexample/regions/us-central1/targetPools/
www-pool


###############
#we can use curl to check the web server
#the reason we see web-server1 and web-server2 is that the load balancer is sending the requests to
each of the
#web servers
$ while true; do curl -m1 173.255.119.47; done
web-server1
web-server2
web-server1
web-server2
web-server2
web-server2
```

You can read more about network load balancing in the GCE world at https://developers.google.com/compute/docs/load-balancing/network/.

Maintenance

Google performs scheduled maintenance on the GCE infrastructure periodically. Maintenance can be transparent, which is within a zone, or it can affect an entire zone. In case of transparent maintenance, instances are moved between hypervisors, and as such you may not notice it. The movement of the instance may result in minor performance degradation. For complete zone maintenance, instances are not moved onto another zone and therefore are shut down. If your application is running in only a single zone, then it will be down during the maintenance window, which can be two weeks.

By default, Google live-migrates instances during a scheduled maintenance window. You can set an instance to terminate and restart during the maintenance instead of using live migration. If this option is set, then Google sends a signal to the instance to shut down. After that, Google terminates the instance and then performs the scheduled maintenance. After maintenance is complete, the instance is powered back on. You can view the operations performed on instances in a zone that includes maintenance operations by using the operations list command as shown here:

```
$ gcloud compute operations list --zones us-central1-b
NAME                            TYPE     TARGET                       HTTP_STATUS  STATUS
operation-..[SNIP]..-9e593195   delete   us-central1-b/instances/vm1  400          DONE
operation-..[SNIP]..327480ef    delete   us-central1-b/instances/vm2  200          DONE
operation-..[SNIP]..-33aa0766   reset    us-central1-b/instances/vm3  200          DONE
systemevent-..[SNIP]..tances.migrateOnHostMaintenance ..[SNIP]..vm4   200          DONE
```

You can also configure GCE to restart an instance automatically if it crashes. This can be done through the web console or the API.

As an enterprise strategy, using transparent maintenance has an advantage, because you do not have to worry about an instance being shut down during maintenance. In addition, if you enable the autorestart feature of an instance, in case the instance crashes, it comes back online automatically. You can read more about Google's maintenance policy at https://developers.google.com/compute/docs/robustsystems.

Google Cloud Storage

So far we have looked at GCE, or Google Compute Engine, which is an instance-based environment for building a cloud infrastructure. In addition to the compute environment, Google also provides a robust storage environment. The components included in cloud storage are Google Cloud Storage (GCS), Google Cloud DataStore (GCD), Cloud SQL (GSQL), and BigQuery.

Google Cloud Storage (https://cloud.google.com/products/cloud-storage/) is an object store service. Access is available through an API and also the GCS web interface. There are two types of storage solutions in GCS: standard storage or durable reduced availability (DRA). DRA is suitable for backups and batch jobs, because some unavailability should be acceptable for DRA applications. DRA costs less than standard storage. The price difference between the two can be viewed at https://developers.google.com/storage/pricing#storage-pricing.

Google Cloud SQL (https://developers.google.com/cloud-sql/) is a relational database, similar to MySQL. It is instance based and offers automatic backups and replication as well.

Google Cloud Datastore (https://developers.google.com/datastore/) is a managed, schema-less database for storing nonrelational data. It is a NoSQL database that is highly scalable and reliable. For cases when GSQL will not do, GCD might be a better option.

Google BigQuery (https://developers.google.com/bigquery/) is a data analytical environment, not a data store. You can bulk upload data from GCS or stream it in. There is a browser interface, command line, and API access.

The choice of a storage solution depends entirely on the application. If a data center inventory management system is being developed and the data are suitable for a relational database, GSQL might be a good solution. On the other hand, if a social networking application is being developed, GCD might be a better solution because of the volatility of the data.

Google App Engine

Google App Engine (`https://developers.google.com/appengine/`) is a PaaS environment that lets you upload applications to the cloud and run them on Google's infrastructure. Unlike GCE, there are no compute instances to maintain; you simply upload your application and Google runs the application.

GAE supports Java, Python, PHP, and Go. To develop applications for GAE, you can download the SDK (`https://developers.google.com/appengine/downloads`) and then start writing code, which, once uploaded into GAE using the SDK, can be run. GAE integrates well with other Google Cloud solutions, such as GCE and GCS.

For an enterprise to invest in GAE, it is crucial to understand which applications are likely candidates. Security is a huge concern with GAE, because a poorly written application can cause a data leak on the Internet. Authentication, authorization, and encryption are key components of a successful GAE deployment strategy. An in-depth discussion of GAE is out of scope for this chapter, because there is no infrastructure to run or manage.

Deployment Tools

There are numerous tools available to interact with GCP. Cloud Playground (`https://code.google.com/p/cloud-playground/`) is a quick way to try different Google cloud services without downloading the SDK. Google Plugin for Eclipse (`https://developers.google.com/eclipse/`) lets you interact with GCP from within Eclipse. It is a very useful tool for developers who want to upload code to GCP from within an integrated development environment.

Push to Deploy (`https://developers.google.com/cloud/devtools/repo/push-to-deploy`) is a way to deploy code into GCP by pushing to a Git repository. This method is part of a "release pipeline" that saves the effort of uploading to GCP using the SDK.

Android Studio (`https://developer.android.com/sdk/installing/studio.html`), which is an Android development environment, also supports a back end for GCP. This makes it easy to test and deploy to a GCP back end for Android applications (`https://developers.google.com/cloud/devtools/android_studio_templates/`).

Google Cloud SDK

The SDK is an essential tool for managing GCE. As mentioned earlier, the way to install the SDK is by using `curl`:

```
curl https://sdk.cloud.google.com | bash
```

When an update is available for the SDK, you will see a message similar to that shown here anytime you attempt to use the SDK:

```
There are available updates for some Cloud SDK components.  To
install them, please run:
 $ gcloud components update
```

To update the SDK, run the following command:

```
$ gcloud components update
```

```
The following components will be updated:
-------------------------------------------------------------------------------
| App Engine Launcher Application for Mac            |      1.9.7 |   7.3 MB |
| App Engine SDK for Java                            |      1.9.7 | 153.1 MB |
| App Engine SDK for Java (Platform Specific)        |      1.9.6 |   < 1 MB |
| BigQuery Command Line Tool                         |     2.0.18 |   < 1 MB |
[SNIP]
Do you want to continue (Y/n)?  Y
```

```
Creating update staging area...

Uninstalling: App Engine Launcher Application for Mac ... Done
Uninstalling: App Engine SDK for Java ... Done
Uninstalling: App Engine SDK for Java (Platform Specific) ... Done
Uninstalling: BigQuery Command Line Tool ... Done
Uninstalling: BigQuery Command Line Tool (Platform Specific) ... Done
..... [SNIP].....
Creating backup and activating new installation...
Done!
```

gcutil is a command that is part of the SDK and can be used to interact with GCP. You can view some very useful tips on gcutil at https://developers.google.com/compute/docs/gcutil/tips. ccutil is considered legacy, and the replacement for it is gcloud. Information about using gcloud can be found at https://developers.google.com/compute/docs/gcloud-compute/.

GCP Support

Google provides bronze, silver, gold, and platinum support levels. Each level costs more than the previous one. Bronze-level support is free and provides support through the online help center. For an enterprise that needs 24/7 support, gold and platinum are the choices available. The platinum level provides a dedicated technical account management team. More details can be found at https://cloud.google.com/support/. Google also maintains a healthy FAQ at https://developers.google.com/compute/docs/faq.

For their storage products, the service-level agreement (SLA) in monthly uptime percentage is greater than or equal to 99.9%. This translates to a little more than 43 minutes of downtime per month. There are some GCP products that are not included in the service-level agreement because they may be in preview mode or may be experimental. Be sure to read up on which feature is experimental at https://developers.google.com/storage/sla. Keep in mind that there is always a risk of any cloud provider going down, as is evident from historical cases when Amazon Web Services was unavailable and caused an outage for Instagram, Vine, Airbnb, and IFTTT.

For an enterprise, one way of handling GCP support is through the NOC. The NOC should be the first to get alerted in the case of a problem with an application. It can then coordinate or triage the teams needed to resolve the application issue. This should be done via run books. For instance if a web front end fails, perhaps the NOC can try out some well-documented steps to look at certain errors and restart certain services, such as the web server. If those steps fail, then the NOC can engage the on-call operations engineer, who can do more troubleshooting. Failing that, the developer can be engaged to look into the issue. Google telephone support can also be engaged through their support portal for platinum- and gold-level support.

For some applications, operations staff may not necessarily be paged, and the developers many be engaged directly by the NOC. This occurs for cases when the operations staff does not support an application. Figure 2-7 shows a flowchart for GCP support.

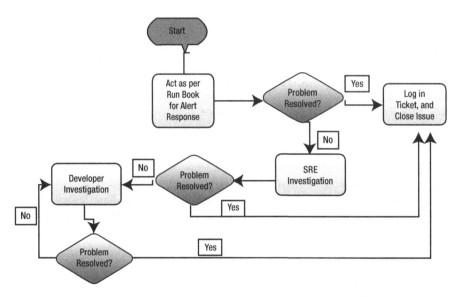

Figure 2-7. *GCP support flowchart*

Change Management

Changes in production in enterprises are generally controlled through change management. Whether it's done by using a change control board or through another method, change management is all the more crucial in the cloud. Because it is relatively easy to create and delete compute instances in production projects, and for developers to have administrative access to projects, an enterprise may struggle with unintended downtime as a result of having a lax change management policy.

All changes in production relating to instances, firewall rules, load balances, and GCS solutions should go through an approved and vetted change management process. For instance, if uploading production applications in GAE is with the help of Git, no developer should be allowed to check applications into the production Git repository without a change requisition. This repository is not the same one where source code is stored, but this is the one that Google uploads automatically into GAE.

Rollback is also very crucial. There is no undelete button for GCE instances or for storage buckets that are in GCS. As such, changes to production projects should be analyzed carefully. An example of a simple mistake that can create vulnerability through a production project is that of firewall rules. If the destination of a firewall rule is to a tag such as www, allowing inbound port 80 TCP traffic, then accidentally change the destination from a tag, to all instances will allow inbound traffic to all instances on port 80 that have a public IP. This might result in a security incident.

Google deprecates certain public images over time. If an instance is using a certain soon-to-be-deprecated image, then you will have to migrate to another image that is supported. Certain kernel versions, for instance, may be deprecated, and using them is not supported.

Conclusion

As of the this writing , cloud computing does not appear to be a trend, but a viable way of running applications. There are numerous decisions to be made with respect to cloud computing, and I hope the information in this chapter helps you make those critical decisions. Whether it's an in on-premise cloud, a hosted cloud, or a combination of both, investing in a cloud can help an enterprise reduce time to deployment for production applications.

Furthermore, many corporations have enjoyed enormous savings, by investing in cloud computing and moving away from traditional brick-and-mortar infrastructure services. Computing as a service makes it easy for application developers to focus on writing the application, rather than focusing on the infrastructure that runs it.

Although GCP is relatively new compared with, say, Amazon Web Services or Rackspace, GCP is gaining rapidly in popularity and offers a viable solution for an enterprise to run its applications.

CHAPTER 3

Virtualization with KVM

This chapter covers designing and implementing enterprise-class virtualization solutions. I focus on Kernel-Based Virtual Machine (KVM) because it is Linux based. The topics in this chapter include how to understand virtualization, select hardware, and configure networks; storage; file system choices; optimization; security concerns; and a reference architecture to put it all together.

What Is Virtualization?

Virtualization of the operating system is creating a virtual machine (VM) within another machine. The host is called the *hypervisor* and the guest is called a *virtual machine*. As seen in Figure 3-1, five VMs are running on a single physical box. Assuming the host, or hypervisor, is running RedHat or CentOS, and the VMs are also running the same, you end up with six copies of the operating system.

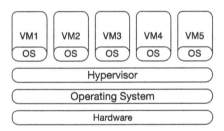

Figure 3-1. *Virtualization in a nutshell*

With KVM, you first install the base operating system, then the KVM packages, and after that you can start creating VMs.

Some advantages of using virtualization for an enterprise are as follows:

- Reduced capital expenditure because you buy fewer servers

- Faster provisioning because you can scale on demand

- Reduced energy costs because of fewer servers

- Disaster recovery made easier using high availability

- Easier to support legacy applications

- One step closer to moving to the cloud

- Reduced support requirements because of smaller data center footprint

Virtualization is not a panacea, by any means. Some cons of using virtualization are as follows:

- The abstraction layer of virtualization adds a performance penalty.

- Overprovisioning is easy to do on a virtualization platform, resulting in degraded system performance during peak hours.

- Slow adoption of software-defined networks has resulted in difficult-to-manage virtual networks, and congested virtual networks.

- Rewriting of applications to be more virtual/cloud friendly can result in additional up-front costs of adoption.

- Loss of a hypervisor can result in the loss of numerous VMs on the hypervisor.

- Virtualization administration requires additional training and processes in the operations world.

Virtualization Solutions

Some of the different enterprise-class virtualization solutions available are the following:

- LXC

  `https://linuxcontainers.org/`

- OpenVZ

  `http://openvz.org/Main_Page`

- QEMU/KVM

  `http://www.linux-kvm.org/page/Main_Page`

- VMware

  `http://www.vmware.com/`

- XenServer

  `http://www.xenserver.org/`

- Microsoft's Hyper-V, Windows based

  `http://www.microsoft.com/en-us/server-cloud/solutions/virtualization.aspx`

- Bhyve, FreeBSD based

  `http://bhyve.org/`

This chapter covers KVM. The choice for which platform to pick can be complex. One possible option is to compare two or more solutions in your environment using virtualization benchmark software such as SPEC virt (`http://www.spec.org/virt_sc2013/`). With SPEC virt you spin up a number of VMs and then run different workloads, such as web servers, database servers, and more. At the end, SPEC virt spits out a bunch of numbers you can compare to determine whether XenServer, KVM, or another virtualization platform gives you better performance.

Linux containers (LXC); it is a user-space interface for creating as well as managing system and application containers. LXC is lightweight compared with KVM and, for each hypervisor, you can generally create far more Linux containers than VMs. In an enterprise you might find VMs as well as LXC. A major difference between LXC and KVM is that, with KVM, you run different kernels, one per VM, but with LXC you share the same kernel. LXC is also limited to the same operating system as the hypervisor, but KVM is not; you can install a different operating system on a VM than what's on the hypervisor. The tools for managing LXC are different than the tools for managing KVM. Libvirt, which is a virtualization management library, can be used to manage both KVM VMs and also Linux containers. Libvirt is very flexible and can manage numerous virtualization technologies. An example of LXC is shown in Figure 3-2.

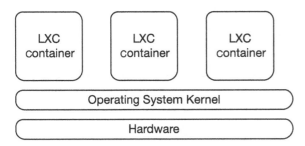

Figure 3-2. *LXC Design*

OpenVZ is also container based, similar to LXC. The choice of using LXC versus OpenVZ can be complicated. LXC has the support of RedHat, so if you are a CentOS or RedHat shop, you might find it easier to get support for LXC versus OpenVZ. Another container-based technology that is rapidly gaining popularity is Docker (`https://www.docker.com/`). Docker can be used for rapid application deployments.

VMware has been the leader in virtualization solutions for more than a decade now. The hypervisors in VMware are Linux based, and the management servers are based on Windows. One advantage of using VMware is that the hypervisor is embedded in some servers, which saves you the trouble of installing a hypervisor. One caveat of VMware and Microsoft virtualization solutions is the cost of licensing. Although both offer free virtualization solutions, their enterprise products are not free.

In the Linux world, XenServer, VMware, and KVM are the leading providers of virtualization. Your choice in an enterprise depends on numerous factors:

- Engineer skill set available

- Installed operating system base

- Internal politics within the organization

- Vendor and partner relations

- Business need

- Technical direction adopted by the enterprise

For instance, if you are running Linux and do not have Windows servers, then it does not make sense to go with Hyper-V; KVM is probably a better choice. On the other hand, if you prefer a mature product with a full-featured graphical user interface and a Linux-based hypervisor, VMware might be a better solution than KVM. One advantage of picking KVM is that it is fully supported by RedHat. XenServer is also fully supported by Citrix; however, it is not as tightly integrated into RedHat or CentOS as KVM is.

Enterprise Architecture

What does it mean to have enterprise architecture? Generally speaking, *enterprise architecture* refers to a multisite design with thousands of physical or virtual servers. A large number of challenges encountered in enterprise design are associated with scale. For instance, if you have to deploy a handful of KVM servers, it is a relatively easier task compared with deploying hundreds of KVM servers.

KVM on its own does not have any enterprise awareness; a lot depends on the management solution you chose for KVM. For instance, if you chose oVirt or RHEVM, both of them support logical data centers that can be used to define different sites and manage them.

KVM Hypervisor Provisioning

KVM can be installed on CentOS using the virtualization collection. Installation is fairly easy; however, the trick is doing the installation on an enterprise scale and in an automated manner. I recommend using Kickstart for this. After you install CentOS using Kickstart, the virtualization group can then be installed as part of postinstallation scripting. For manual installation, the steps in Listing 3-1 show you how to proceed.

Listing 3-1. Manual KVM Installation

```
# Installing the virtualization group
# yum groupinstall "Virtualization"
Loaded plugins: fastestmirror, security
Loading mirror speeds from cached hostfile
Setting up Group Process
Loading mirror speeds from cached hostfile
base/group_gz
| 212 kB     00:00
epel6/group_gz
| 237 kB     00:00
Resolving Dependencies
--> Running transaction check
---> Package hypervkvpd.x86_64 0:0-0.9.el6 will be installed
---> Package qemu-kvm.x86_64 2:0.12.1.2-2.355.0.1.el6_4.9 will be installed
[SNIP]

# Viewing the packages in Virtualization group
# yum groupinfo Virtualization
Loaded plugins: fastestmirror
Setting up Group Process
Loading mirror speeds from cached hostfile
[SNIP]
Group: Virtualization
 Description: Provides an environment for hosting virtualized guests.
 Mandatory Packages:
   qemu-kvm
 Default Packages:
   hypervkvpd
 Optional Packages:
   qemu-guest-agent
   qemu-kvm-tools
```

```
# Creating a virtual machine. In this example, we are using br0, which is a network bridge, and
routed mode. In addition, we are pointing to a local ISO image for installation, and displaying
graphics of the VM using Spice.
# virt-install --connect qemu:///system --name vm1.example.com \
--ram 32768 --vcpus 4 --disk path=/vm1/vm1.example.com.qcow2  \
--network=bridge:br0 --os-type=linux --os-variant=rhel6 \
--cdrom /vm1/iso/CentOS-6.4-x86_64-bin-DVD1.iso \
--graphics spice,password=mypassword -autostart

# Enable libvirt to start automatically.
# chkconfig libvirtd on
# service libvirtd start

# Starting a running VM
# virsh start vm1.example.com

# Stopping a running VM
# virsh shutdown vm1.example.com

# Shutting down a VM forcefully
# virsh destroy vm1.example.com

# Deleting a VM definition
# virsh undefine vm1.example.com
```

Automated KVM Installation

Kickstart can be tuned to support hundreds of hosts at any given time. Out of the box, after you tune TFTP limits, you can easily clone 500 hypervisors at a time. Basically, you configure PXE to boot the hypervisors. After that, install CentOS or RedHat followed by the installation of KVM packages. Listing 3-2 shows a sample PXE Linux configuration file and Listing 3-3 shows a sample Kickstart configuration file.

Listing 3-2. PXE Linux Config

```
default menu.c32
prompt 0
timeout 5

menu title PXE Boot Menu

label 1
  menu label ^1 - Install KVM
  kernel images/centos/6.5/x86_64/vmlinuz
  APPEND text load_ramdisk=1 initrd=images/centos/6.5/x86_64/initrd.img network noipv6
ksdevice=eth0 ks=http://ks/kickstart/ks.cfg i8042.noaux console=tty0

label local
  menu label ^0 - Boot from first hard drive
  com32 chain.c32
  append hd0
```

Listing 3-3. Kickstart Postinstall File

```
# commands sections (required)
bootloader --location=mbr
authconfig --enableshadow
keyboard us
autopart

# optional components
clearpart -all
firewall --disabled
install --url http://ks.example.com/centos/6.4
network --bootproto=static --ip=10.1.1.100 --netmask=255.255.255.0 --gateway=10.1.1.1
--nameserver=10.1.1.10
#packages section (required)
%packages
@Virtualization

# preinstall section (optional)
%pre

# postinstall section (optional)
%post
```

The question is: How do you make Kickstart of KVM enterprise friendly? Setting up a single Kickstart server is not sufficient for an enterprise. Using the reference architecture for Example.com defined later in this chapter, if we have three different sites, with at least 500 hypervisors per site, we need to set up numerous Kickstart servers per site. Also, because PXE is broadcast based, we have to set up IP helpers on routers between different networks of hypervisors. We want to avoid a flat network space for all hypervisors, because it's a bit difficult to manage. An important question to answer is: How many concurrent Kickstarts are you expecting to take place? The solution for a Kickstart architecture is based on your answer. There are numerous ways to devise a solution, and I outline two possibilities in the following sections.

Clustered Kickstart Solution

With this solution we can set up two clusters: one for PXE booting and the other for serving CentOS installation files over HTTP. Per site there will be a pair of clusters. In the cluster, we will have a pair of load balancers and real servers. Instead of using PXE, let's use iPXE (http://ipxe.org/), which supports PXE over HTTP. Another pair of DHCP servers running in primary and secondary mode will serve DHCP. There is no need to run DHCP behind a load balancer because, if you use Internet Systems Consortium (ISC) DHCPD (https://www.isc.org/downloads/dhcp/), primary and secondary modes are supported. The advantage of using a clustered solution is that you can grow on demand while reducing server sprawl. Each site gets a single cluster, and as incoming connections increase, you can increase the amount of real servers behind the load balancers to match the load. IP helpers have to be configured on the routers across the networks of the hypervisors to pass DHCP traffic to the DHCP server. An example is shown in Figure 3-3.

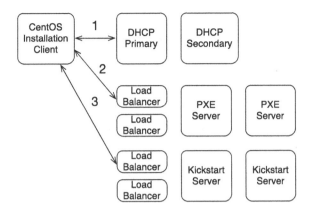

Figure 3-3. *KVM installation in clustered mode*

The boot order of the hypervisors is as follows in BIOS:

- Hard drive
- Network/PXE

During the first boot, because no operating system is installed, the hard drive boot will fail, and a boot is then tried off the network. Because we have configured PXE, the boot continues and the installation can start. The load balancers for the iPXE server and the Kickstart servers can be your enterprise-approved load balancer. HAProxy is a free load balancer (http://www.haproxy.org/) that can be used for the Kickstart server load balancing. HAProxy does not support UDP, so for PXE you may need a UDP-based load balancer, such as the one from F5 networks (https://f5.com/). Listing 3-4 shows a sample DHCPD configuration file when using PXE. Note the class pxeclients.

Listing 3-4. DHCPD Configuration for PXE

```
subnet 10.1.1.0 netmask 255.255.255.0 {
    option domain-name-servers 10.1.1.2;
    option routers 10.1.1.1;
    pool {
        failover peer "failover-partner";
        range 10.1.1.50 10.1.1.250;
        }

class "pxeclients" {
        match if substring(option vendor-class-identifier, 0, 9) = "PXEClient";
        next-server 10.1.1.3;
        filename = "pxelinux.0";
}
```

In the DHCPD configuration example, DHCP IP addresses are leased in the 10.1.1.0/24 subnet. The IP addresses provided will be in the range of 50 to 250. When a server boots, it first gets an IP from the DHCP server, at which point the DHCP server points to the PXE server using the next-server string. The booting server then uses TFTP to contact the iPXE server and download the PXE boot file, from which the server boots. After it boots using the PXE kernel, it can then download the CentOS or RedHat installation file and start the installation. Listing 3-5 shows a DHCPD primary server configuration file; Listing 3-6 shows the secondary DHCPD configuration file.

Listing 3-5. DHCPD Primary Configuration

```
    failover peer "failover-partner" {
        primary;
        address dhcp-primary.example.com;
        port 519;
        peer address dhcp-secondary.example.com;
        peer port 520;
        max-response-delay 60;
        max-unacked-updates 10;
        mclt 3600;
        split 128;
        load balance max seconds 3;
    }

omapi-port 7911;
omapi-key omapi_key;

key omapi_key {
    algorithm hmac-md5;
    secret 0fakekeyfakekeyfakekey==;
}
```

Listing 3-6. DHCPD Secondary Configuration

```
    failover peer "failover-partner" {
        secondary;
        address dhcp-secondary.example.com;
        port 520;
        peer address dhcp-primary.example.com;
        peer port 519;
        max-response-delay 60;
        max-unacked-updates 10;
        load balance max seconds 3;
    }

omapi-port 7911;
omapi-key omapi_key;

key omapi_key {
    algorithm hmac-md5;
    secret 0fakekeyfakekeyfakekey==;
}
```

The primary and secondary configurations are from https://kb.isc.org/article/AA-00502/0/A-Basic-Guide-to-Configuring-DHCP-Failover.html.

Distributed Kickstart Solution

With this solution, instead of having a single cluster per site, you set up numerous DHCP, PXE, and Kickstart servers. The advantage of having a distributed setup is that you avoid the complexity of a cluster, and you can spread the load across different networks in addition to different hosts. How many distributed servers are set up depends on the size of the network. For instance, if hypervisors are distributed across ten networks per site, then you need at least ten Kickstart, DHCP, and PXE servers. The cost of this setup can potentially be more than the cost of setting up a cluster, but you reduce the chance of all of them not being available at the same time. In addition, you do not need IP helpers configured on routers to forward BOOTP DHCP traffic to the servers. One disadvantage of this solution is that you have a lot more hardware to manage. Although, if a particular network's Kickstart is down, only that network is affected. An example of this solution is presented in Figure 3-4. Something to keep in mind is that if you have a large number of networks, this solution may be impractical and you may prefer to go with the clustered solution.

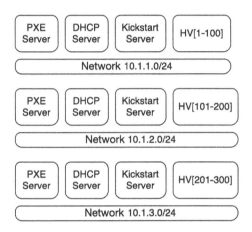

Figure 3-4. *Distributed Kickstart configuration*

VM Provisioning

After you have KVM installed, provisioning of VMs comes into play on an enterprise scale. Using Kickstart is an option for VMs as well, and this works well if you are using bridged networking mode. A big advantage of using VMs is that you can clone them and reduce your provisioning time significantly. Using Kickstart, for instance, might take 20 minutes per VM. On the other hand, deploying VMs from cloned templates might take not more than a few minutes. Listing 3-7 shows how to clone a VM using the virt commands.

Listing 3-7. Cloning a VM

```
# Use virt-sysprep to prepare a turned off virtual machine as a template
# virt-sysprep -d centos.template
Examining the guest ...
Performing "yum-uuid" ...
Performing "utmp" ...
Performing "udev-persistent-net" ...
Performing "sssd-db-log" ...
Performing "ssh-userdir" ...
Performing "ssh-hostkeys" ...
```

```
Performing "smolt-uuid" ...
Performing "script" ...
Performing "samba-db-log" ...
Performing "rpm-db" ...
Performing "rhn-systemid" ...
Performing "random-seed" ...
Performing "puppet-data-log" ...
Performing "pam-data" ...
Performing "package-manager-cache" ...
Performing "pacct-log" ...
Performing "net-hwaddr" ...
Performing "net-hostname" ...
Performing "mail-spool" ...
Performing "machine-id" ...
Performing "logfiles" ...
Performing "hostname" ...
Performing "firstboot" ...
Performing "dovecot-data" ...
Performing "dhcp-server-state" ...
Performing "dhcp-client-state" ...
Performing "cron-spool" ...
Performing "crash-data" ...
Performing "blkid-tab" ...
Performing "bash-history" ...
Performing "abrt-data" ...
Performing "lvm-uuids" ...

# Using the earlier created template, clone a new VM.
# virt-clone -o centos.template -n newclone -f /vm1/newclone.img
Allocating 'newclone.img'          | 8.0 GB      00:09
Clone 'newclone' created successfully.

# Make sure you can see the new cloned virtual machine
# virsh list --all
 Id    Name                          State
----------------------------------------------------
 1     vm1.example.com               running
 2     vm2.example.com               running
 -     centos.template               shut off
 -     newclone                      shut off

# Start the new cloned VM.
# virsh start newclone
Domain newclone started

#Ensure that it is running.
# virsh list
 Id    Name                          State
----------------------------------------------------
 1     vm1.example.com               running
 2     vm2.example.com               running
 3     newclone                      running
```

We have to use virt-sysprep to prepare the image for cloning. virt-sysprep modifies the image and removes certain settings, or unconfigures certain settings that, if left, would conflict on another VM. sysprep stands for system preparation. You can read more about it at http://libguestfs.org/virt-sysprep.1.html.

virt-clone clones the template created from virt-sysprep. There are two types of clones: linked clones and full clones. Linked clones depend on the image from which it was cloned, and the original image cannot be deleted. A full clone, on the other hand, is independent of the image from which it was cloned.

KVM Management Solutions

There are numerous solutions available to manage KVM, and some of them are free whereas others are commercial products. You can find a list of such solutions at http://www.linux-kvm.org/page/Management_Tools. The choices can be split broadly into two categories: one is command line or shell based and the other is graphical or graphical user interface based. oVirt (http://www.ovirt.org/Home) is a very popular open-source software used to manage KVM instances. RedHat has a commercial product built around oVirt called RHEVM, or RedHat Enterprise Virtualization Manager (http://www.redhat.com/products/cloud-computing/virtualization/). A third option is to write your own management using the libvirt API. You can find out more about libvirt at http://libvirt.org/.

Libvirt

Libvirt is a toolkit that support interactions with various virtualization platforms, KVM being one of them. The API for libvirt is extensive and is very useful if you write your own management around KVM. The C library reference for libvirt can be found at http://libvirt.org/html/libvirt-libvirt.html. Numerous language bindings are available for libvirt, such as C#, Java, OCaml, Perl, PHP, Python ,and Ruby. In the following example I use the Python bindings to demonstrate how to write a basic management application for KVM (Listing 3-8). You can find out more information about the bindings at http://libvirt.org/bindings.html.

Listing 3-8. Sample Libvirt Python Code

```
import libvirt
import sys

# Open a read-only connection to the local hypervisor.
conn = libvirt.openReadOnly(None)
if conn == None:
    print 'Failed to open connection to the hypervisor'
    sys.exit(1)

# Get some information about the hypervisor.
hv_info = conn.getInfo()

# Print out the architecture, memory, cores, and speed of the processor.
print 'hv arch {0}'.format(hv_info[0])
print 'hv memory {0}'.format(hv_info[1])
print 'cores in hv {0}'.format(hv_info[2])
print 'Mhz speed of hv CPU {0}'.format(hv_info[3])
```

virsh

virsh is included with KVM and it is a quick and easy way of managing KVM. You can use virsh and skip other management solutions if you prefer simplicity. virsh uses libvirt. However, you have to script around virsh to manage a large number of hypervisors. Some examples of using virsh are shown in Listing 3-9. You can read more about virsh at http://linux.die.net/man/1/virsh.

Listing 3-9. virsh Examples

```
# Given a file called hv.txt, which contains a list of KVM hypervisors, loop through the file and
get a list of VMs running on each hypervisor.

# cat hv.txt
hv1.example.com
hv2.example.com
hv3.example.com

# cat hv.sh
#!/bin/bash

HVLIST=hv.txt
USER=fakeuser

for hv in `cat ${HVLIST}`
do
echo ${hv}
virsh -c qemu+ssh://${USER}@${hv}/system list
done

# When you run hv.sh, below is a sample output you may get.
# ./hv.sh
hv1.example.com
 Id    Name                          State
----------------------------------------------------

 1     vm1.example.com               running
 3     vm2.example.com               running
 4     vm3.example.com               running
hv2.example.com
 Id    Name                          State
----------------------------------------------------

 1     vm4.example.com               running
 3     vm5.example.com               running
 4     vm6.example.com               running
hv3.example.com
 Id    Name                          State
----------------------------------------------------

 1     vm7.example.com               running
 3     vm8.example.com               running
 4     vm9.example.com               running
```

```
# Get information on architecture, CPU, and memory of hypervisor.
# In hv.sh, replace the 'list' command with 'nodeinfo' command
[SNIP]
for hv in `cat ${HVLIST}`
do
echo ${hv}
virsh -c qemu+ssh://${USER}@${hv}/system nodeinfo
done

# ./hv.sh
hv1.example.com
CPU model:              x86_64
CPU(s):                 8
CPU frequency:          3292 MHz
CPU socket(s):          1
Core(s) per socket:     4
Thread(s) per core:     2
NUMA cell(s):           1
Memory size:            16301672 KiB
Hv2.example.com
CPU model:              x86_64
CPU(s):                 8
CPU frequency:          3292 MHz
CPU socket(s):          1
Core(s) per socket:     4
Thread(s) per core:     2
NUMA cell(s):           1
Memory size:            16301672 KiB
Hv3.example.com
CPU model:              x86_64
CPU(s):                 8
CPU frequency:          3292 MHz
CPU socket(s):          1
Core(s) per socket:     4
Thread(s) per core:     2
NUMA cell(s):           1
Memory size:            16301672 KiB
```

Selecting Physical Servers

What kinds of servers are suitable for a virtualization platform? This is a fundamental question to answer to have a successful virtualization platform. This section explores some options, such as custom-built, name brands, Open-Compute, rack and blade severs.

Custom-Built Servers

You can purchase parts and put together your own servers. One advantage of this method is that you have total control over each component of the server, such as hard drive, CPU, memory, network, form factor, and power. The disadvantage is that you have to spend a lot of time making sure the components work together. In addition, you have to maintain spares because parts you select now may go out of production in the future. Your up-front capital expenditure should be low compared with name-brand servers.

Name Brands

Name brands such as Dell, HP, IBM, and others can make your purchasing decision easier relative to custom-built servers. The obvious advantage of choosing this route is that you do not have to worry about getting hardware that has not been tested. In addition, the vendor is responsible for hardware support throughout the life of the support contract; hence, you do not necessarily have to stock up on spare parts. The disadvantage is a higher cost compared with custom-built servers because you pay for the vendor doing integration testing and you pay for support.

Open Compute–Compatible Servers

Open Compute (http://www.opencompute.org/) is a project designed to create hardware at low cost with parts that meet certain specifications. If you purchase hardware that meets the specifications of Open Compute servers, then you can be certain you are getting hardware designed to run at a low cost.

Rack and Blade Servers

Blade servers are very popular for virtualization. The reason for this is that each blade can be a hypervisor, which allows a large number of VMs in a given chassis.

Rack servers can also be used for virtualization; however, you lose the density a blade server provides with respect to the number of VMs you can have in a given rack.

Cisco UCS, or Unified Computing System, is an example of a different type of blade server. Cisco UCS has a controller called the *fiber interconnect* that is used to manage blades in a chassis. Most blade servers do not have an external controller module.

Making Your Choice

Regardless of which platform you pick, some of the features that should be present in your choice are as follows:

- Easy to maintain
- Form factor
- Availability of spare parts
- Low power draw
- Remote console access

When selecting the CPU, the two major players in the market are Intel and AMD. I concentrate on Intel in the following example. Some of the virtualization-specific features that you want to look for in an Intel CPU are

- Intel VT-x
- Intet VT-d
- Intel VT-c

Listing 3-10 shows how to get information about a particular hypervisor using the virsh command.

Listing 3-10. KVM Hypervisor Information

```
# Get version information.
# virsh version
Compiled against library: libvirt 0.10.2
Using library: libvirt 0.10.2
Using API: QEMU 0.10.2
Running hypervisor: QEMU 0.12.1

#View information about a hypervisor.
# virsh sysinfo
<sysinfo type='smbios'>
  <bios>
    <entry name='vendor'>Dell Inc.</entry>
    <entry name='version'>2.2.3</entry>
    <entry name='date'>10/25/2012</entry>
    <entry name='release'>2.2</entry>
  </bios>
  <system>
    <entry name='manufacturer'>Dell Inc.</entry>
    <entry name='product'>PowerEdge T110 II</entry>
    <entry name='version'>Not Specified</entry>
    <entry name='serial'>XXXXXXX</entry>
    <entry name='uuid'>4C4C4544-0034-5210-8054-B7C04F435831</entry>
    <entry name='sku'>Not Specified</entry>
    <entry name='family'>Not Specified</entry>
  </system>
  <processor>
    <entry name='socket_destination'>CPU1</entry>
    <entry name='type'>Central Processor</entry>
    <entry name='family'>Xeon</entry>
    <entry name='manufacturer'>Intel(R) Corporation</entry>
    <entry name='signature'>Type 0, Family 6, Model 58, Stepping 9</entry>
    <entry name='version'>Intel(R) Xeon(R) CPU E3-1230 V2 @ 3.30GHz</entry>
    <entry name='external_clock'>100 MHz</entry>
    <entry name='max_speed'>4000 MHz</entry>
    <entry name='status'>Populated, Enabled</entry>
    <entry name='serial_number'>NotSupport</entry>
    <entry name='part_number'>FFFF</entry>
  </processor>
  <memory_device>
    <entry name='size'>4096 MB</entry>
    <entry name='form_factor'>DIMM</entry>
    <entry name='locator'>DIMM A2</entry>
    <entry name='bank_locator'>BANK 0</entry>
    <entry name='type'>DDR3</entry>
    <entry name='type_detail'>Synchronous Unbuffered (Unregistered)</entry>
    <entry name='speed'>1600 MHz</entry>
    <entry name='manufacturer'>80CE000080CE</entry>
```

```
    <entry name='serial_number'>85DF74FD</entry>
    <entry name='part_number'>M391B5273DH0-YK0</entry>
  </memory_device>
[SNIP]
</sysinfo>
```

Designing KVM Networks

John Burdette Gage from Sun Microsystems once said, "The network is the computer," which is very true. You can have the best storage solution coupled with the best physical hardware, but without a fast network, they are of no use. Most modern networks have at least one or more 10GB network adapters per physical server. When it comes to virtualization with KVM, 10GB is the minimum you should have per network interface. On top of this, the network topology layer is more important. With enterprise networks, the question of having a flat network space is not a consideration.

Open vSwitch (http://openvswitch.org/) is a popular virtual switch that can be used with KVM. The advantage of using Open vSwitch is that it offers flexibility, which KVM networking does not necessarily offer. It is programmatically configurable and it supports numerous features that are enterprise friendly.

KVM supports the following kinds of networking for assigning IP addresses to VMs:

- Network address translation (NAT) virtual networks

- Bridged networks

- Physical device assignment for Peripherel Component Interconnect (PCI)

- Single root input/output virtualization

How many physical network cards should you have on your hypervisors? One possibility is to divide the network interfaces as follows:

- Two in fail-over mode for storage

- Two in fail-over mode for management of KVM

- Two in fail-over mode for VMs

- One for out-of-band Intelligent Platform Management Inteface (IPMI)-based access

An example is shown in Figure 3-5.

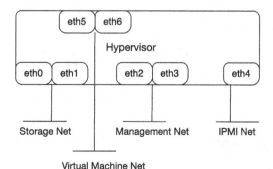

Figure 3-5. *Network interfaces on hypervisor*

Network Address Translation

NAT is generally used with private IP space, RFC 1918, which is 10.0.0.0/8, 172.16.0.0/12 and 192.168.0.0/16. By default, KVM picks IP space in the range of 192.168.122.0/24 for VMs. If you do decide to use NAT, and your hypervisor itself is on a NAT network, then you are, in essence, enabling double NAT for VM access, as shown in Figure 3-6.

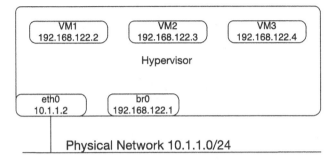

Figure 3-6. *NAT mode*

Bridged Network

In bridged network mode, no NAT is done between the VM and the physical network. The VM behaves as though it is another node on the physical network. If the physical hypervisor is on a NAT network, then the VM shares the same network. The advantage of this is reduced complexity of overall network administration. An example is shown in Figure 3-7.

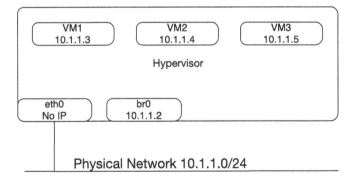

Figure 3-7. *Bridged mode*

A couple of examples of using `virsh` network commands are included in Listing 3-11.

Listing 3-11. KVM Network Commands

```
# View defined networks. By default, KVM creates one network called "default."
# This is the 192.168.122.0/24 network.
# virsh net-list
Name                    State     Autostart   Persistent
--------------------------------------------------
default                 active    yes         yes


# Get information on a given network names.
# Each network is given a unique UUID, and you can see that the default network is active.
# virsh net-info default
Name            default
UUID            f604318f-d3ad-45cb-8e27-d2519d79a3e9
Active:         yes
Persistent:     yes
Autostart:      yes
Bridge:         virbr0
```

Network Bonding

Network bonding allows two interfaces to be in active/active or active/passive mode. The advantage of network bonding is that it provides protection from physical network interface hardware failure. Listing 3-12 shows how a network bonding setup.

Listing 3-12. Networking Bonding Example

```
-bash-3.2$ cat /etc/sysconfig/network-scripts/ifcfg-bond0
DEVICE=bond0
BOOTPROTO=none
ONBOOT=yes
IPADDR=10.1.1.2
NETMASK=255.255.255.0
BONDING_OPTS="mode=1 miimon=80 primary=slave"

-bash-3.2$ cat /etc/sysconfig/network-scripts/ifcfg-eth0
DEVICE=eth0
ONBOOT=yes
BOOTPROTO=none
USERCTL=no
MASTER=bond0
SLAVE=yes
HWADDR=00:E0:81:C5:76:0A

-bash-3.2$ cat /etc/sysconfig/network-scripts/ifcfg-eth1
DEVICE=eth1
ONBOOT=yes
BOOTPROTO=none
USERCTL=no
```

```
MASTER=bond0
SLAVE=yes
HWADDR=00:E0:81:C5:73:36

-bash-3.2$ cat /etc/modprobe.conf
alias eth0 e1000e
alias eth1 igb
alias eth2 igb
alias scsi_hostadapter ahci
alias bond0 bonding
options bond0 miimon=80 mode=1
```

Virtual Local Area Networks

Virtual local area networks (VLANs) help create broadcast domains, thereby making networks more manageable. In a given enterprise, it is common to find numerous VLANs. With regard to using KVM with VLANs, if the VMs are going to be on the same VLAN as the hypervisor, then you do not have to do any additional configuration on the network side of KVM. However, this architecture is not practical, because VMs are going to be on different VLANs. Therefore, the recommended option for enterprises is to trunk the interface going into the KVM hypervisor. Trunking allows numerous VLANs over the same interface. For instance, if the hypervisor network is 10.1.1.0/24, VMs on different networks such as 10.1.2.0/24 or 10.1.3.0/24 can reside on the hypervisor without any networking issues. RedHat or CentOS supports VLANs in the kernel, which is fairly easy to configure. An example is shown in Figure 3-8.

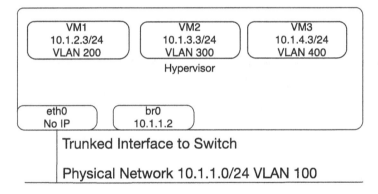

Figure 3-8. *VLAN configuration of VMs*

Open vSwitch

As mentioned earlier, instead of using the built-in networking available with KVM, you can replace it with Open vSwitch, which is far more flexible. Open vSwitch is an in-depth topic, coverage of which is beyond the scope of this chapter. I recommend reading this article—http://git.openvswitch.org/cgi-bin/gitweb.cgi?p=openvswitch;a=blob_plain;f=INSTALL.KVM;hb=HEAD—to start configuring Open vSwitch.

Designing KVM Storage

When it comes to storage, you have to consider the end goal and base your decision on that. If the end goal is to have disposable VMs, with redundancy built in to the application, then having a common, shared storage solution across the KVM hypervisors may not be required. On the other hand, if you are looking for fault tolerance and want to have your VM up even if one or more hypervisors goes down, then shared storage is the way to go.

Without shared storage, when a hypervisor goes down, so do the VMs on that hypervisor. Because the VM image is stored on the hypervisor, or on a storage subsystem that is not shared with other hypervisors, other active hypervisors cannot access the image of the VM and cannot start the VM that is down. You basically have to bring up the hypervisor that crashed, then start the VMs that were running on it.

With shared storage, each of the hypervisors has access to the same VM image file, allowing a VM to come up on any other hypervisor if the host hypervisor crashes.

Another issue to take into consideration when designing storage is whether to boot the hypervisor from a local disk or to use a network boot. Using a network boot eliminates the need for local hard drives and can save money. On the other hand, this solution adds to complexity, because you have to invest in a storage area network that supports network booting.

Without shared storage, each hypervisor has its own disk on which both KVM and the local disk of the VM resides, as shown in Figure 3-9.

Figure 3-9. *KVM without shared storage*

With shared storage, each hypervisor has its own disk on which KVM is installed, and the VMs are stored on the shared storage. The shared storage could be a shared area network (SAN) as shown in Figure 3-10.

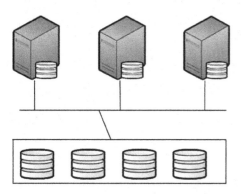

Figure 3-10. *KVM with shared storage*

With shared storage, and no local disk, the hypervisor boots from the SAN, and the VMs are also stored on the SAN, as seen in Figure 3-11.

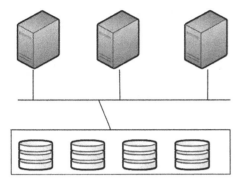

Figure 3-11. *KVM with no local disk and SAN boot*

What kind of shared storage should you use if you do decide that you need the flexibility offered with shared storage? Some of the options available include the following:

- NFS
- iSCSI
- Fiber channel-based LUNs

With NFS, a dedicated NFS server or an NFS appliance is suitable. In enterprise networks, NFS appliances tend to be more prevalent for shared storage of VMs rather than Linux servers dedicated to running NFS. The advantage of the NFS appliance, such as NetApp, is that you are more likely to get faster performance compared with a Linux server running NFS. You cannot boot a hypervisor using NFS alone, but you can use an NFS-mounted partition on the hypervisor to store your VM images.

iSCSI can be used to boot your hypervisor off the network. You can install iSCSI on a Linux box or you can use dedicated storage appliances, such as the Netapp, which supports iSCSI. The iSCSI target will be the storage appliance, and the initiator will be the hypervisor. It is recommended that you use a dedicated network card on your hypervisor if you decide to use iSCSI from which to boot. If you decide not to use iSCSI from which to boot the hypervisor, then you can still use iSCSI to mount a LUN and store your virtual images. You will have to use iSCSI multipath to have the same LUN be visible across other hypervisors.

Image Selection

The kind of VM image you select has an impact on the amount of storage being used and the performance of the VM. A few image types that are available and listed on the man page (`http://linux.die.net/man/1/qemu-img`) include the following:

- Raw
- Qcow2
- Qcow
- Cow
- Vdi
- Vmdk
- Vpc
- Cloop

The most popular ones from the list are Qcow/Qcow2 and Raw. Numerous studies have been done on performance and storage use of one versus the other. Raw images have better performance than Qcow2 images; however, you cannot "snapshot" raw images. One advantage of taking a snapshot of a VM is that you can take a snapshot before a code deployment and, if the deployment does not work out well, you can simply revert to the previous version of the snapshot (Listing 3-13).

Listing 3-13. Snapshot Management

```
# Creating a snapshot
# virsh snapshot-create vm1.example.com
Domain snapshot 1407102907 created

# Viewing a list of snapshots
# virsh snapshot-list vm1.example.com
 Name                 Creation Time               State
------------------------------------------------------------
 1407102907           2014-08-03 14:55:07 -0700 shutoff

# Getting snapshot information
# virsh snapshot-info vm1.example.com --current
Name:           1407102907
Domain:         vm1.example.com
Current:        yes
State:          shutoff
Location:       internal
Parent:         -
Children:       0
Descendants:    0
Metadata:       yes

# View XML information about snapshot
# virsh snapshot-dumpxml vm1.example.com  1407102907
<domainsnapshot>
  <name>1407102907</name>
  <state>shutoff</state>
  <creationTime>1407102907</creationTime>
  <memory snapshot='no'/>
  <disks>
    <disk name='vda' snapshot='internal'/>
    <disk name='hdc' snapshot='no'/>
  </disks>
  <domain type='kvm'>
    <name>vm1.example.com</name>
    <uuid>ba292588-6570-2674-1425-b2ee6a4e7c2b</uuid>
    <memory unit='KiB'>1048576</memory>
    <currentMemory unit='KiB'>1048576</currentMemory>
    <vcpu placement='static'>1</vcpu>
    <os>
      <type arch='x86_64' machine='rhel6.4.0'>hvm</type>
      <boot dev='hd'/>
    </os>
```

```
[SNIP]
  </domain>
</domainsnapshot>

# Revert to a snapshot.
# virsh snapshot-revert vm1.example.com –current

# Delete a snapshot.
# virsh snapshot-delete vm1.example.com --current
```

Domain snapshot 1407102907 deleted

File System Selection

Because VM images are basically files, the question arises: Which file system do you use to place the files? Some of the options are

- Using a file system such as ext3, ext4, XFS, or similar system

- Placing the VM on a Linux Logical Volume Manager (LVM) partition

When using a file system on the hypervisor to place the VM file, there is overhead with respect to accessing the VM. This overhead is not much, but you can potentially get better performance by placing the VM on, say, an unformatted LVM.

Layout of the file system also matters, not only on the hypervisor, but also on the VM. A VM disk partition for a minimal install is shown in Listing 3-14 and Listing 3-15.

Listing 3-14. VM Disk Partition

```
# Disk partition layout
# We reserve 500MB for boot and the rest for an LVM physical volume.
# This is based on an 80GB disk size for a VM.
# parted -l /dev/sda2
Model: XX (scsi)
Disk /dev/sda: 85.9GB
Sector size (logical/physical): 512B/512B
Partition Table: msdos

Number  Start    End     Size    Type     File system  Flags
1       1049kB   538MB   537MB   primary  ext4         boot
2       538MB    85.9GB  85.4GB  primary               lvm
[SNIP]

Using LVM we create on the physical volume.
Size is based on what is left over after allocating 500MB for boot.
# pvs
  PV         VG    Fmt   Attr PSize   PFree
  /dev/sda2  vg0   lvm2  a--  79.50g     0
```

```
# One volume group that covers the entire disk
# vgs
  VG  #PV #LV #SN Attr   VSize  VFree
  vg0   1   4   0 wz--n- 79.50g   0

# I have created logical volumes with names that are self-descriptive.
# lvs
  LV      VG  Attr        LSize  Pool Origin Data%  Move Log Cpy%Sync Convert
  lv_home vg0 -wi-ao---- 20.00g
  lv_root vg0 -wi-ao---- 47.50g
  lv_swap vg0 -wi-ao----  2.00g
  lv_var  vg0 -wi-ao---- 10.00g
```

One distinct advantage of using LVM is that you can grow disk partition on demand. Boot partition cannot be on LVM because the LVM kernel module is not loaded to mount boot in the initrd RAM disk. However, all the other partitions can be LVM partitions. With respect to naming the volume groups, I picked something simple, which is sequential. You can pick whatever suits you. For the sizes of each of the logical volumes, I based it on the VM disk size, which is 80GB. Swap size recommendations from RedHat that apply to CentOS are in Table 3-1.

Table 3-1. *CentOS/RedHat swap recommendations*

RAM installed	Recommended SWAP
2GB or less	Twice installed RAM
>2GB–8GB	Same amount as RAM
>8GB–64GB	Minimum 4GB
>64GB	Minimum 4GB

Listing 3-15. VM File System Layout

```
# cat /etc/fstab

/dev/mapper/vg0-lv_root /      ext4    noatime,nodiratime,relatime      1 1
UUID=141c589e-a255-4cfd-b1bc-8fd337c22cd5 /boot    ext4    defaults      1 2
/dev/mapper/vg0-lv_home /home  ext4    noatime,nodiratime,relatime      1 2
/dev/mapper/vg0-lv_var  /var   ext4    noatime,nodiratime,relatime      1 2
/dev/mapper/vg0-lv_swap swap            swap      defaults      0 0
tmpfs                   /dev/shm        tmpfs     defaults      0 0
devpts                  /dev/pts        devpts    gid=5,mode=620 0 0
sysfs                   /sys            sysfs     defaults      0 0
proc                    /proc           proc      defaults      0 0
```

Virtual Image Optimization

A virtual machine should be optimized to run more efficiently on a KVM hypervisor. Considering that enterprises have a large number of hypervisors and VMs, without optimization, performance may suffer. Changes that should be made on the VM vary from system kernel settings to services. In this section I provide various steps you can take to optimize the image.

When doing CentOS or RedHat installations, select Minimal Install, and nothing else to start with. This strategy reduces the size of the image. Smaller images clone more quickly and, even if you use Kickstart, they install faster. In addition, you reduce your security exposure by having only the minimal set of packages needed.

```
# Configure tuned for virtual guest
# tuned-adm profile virtual-guest
# chkconfig tuned on
```

tuned is a system-tuning daemon that sets various system/kernel parameters based on profiles.

Disable unwanted services. Leaving them enabled slows down the boot process and is a security risk. Here are some services that are potential candidates to be turned off:

```
# for svc in ip6tables cups abrtd abrt-ccpp atd kdump mdmonitor NetworkManager;
do chkconfig $svc off; done
root# for svc in ip6tables cups abrtd abrt-ccpp atd kdump mdmonitor NetworkManager;
do service $svc stop; done
# Disable IPv6 if you are not using it.
# echo "NETWORKING_IPV6=no
IPV6INIT=no" >> /etc/sysconfig/network

# echo "
# Disable IPv6.
net.ipv6.conf.all.disable_ipv6 = 1
net.ipv6.conf.default.disable_ipv6 = 1
" >> /etc/sysctl.conf

# smartd monitors hard drives; no need for that on a VM
root# service smartd stop
root# chkconfig --del smartd

# Allow virsh shutdown to turn of the VM.
# If we do a minimal CentOS install, acpid is not installed by default.
# yum install acpid
# chkconfig acpid on
# service acpid start
```

To access the console of a VM using the virsh console command, you have to redirect the VM console output via the serial console. The following steps show you how to do this:

```
# Getting serial console to work on KVM with RHEL 6 and also with GRUB
# Comment out splashimage and hiddenmenu
# Remove 'rhgb' and 'quiet' from the kernel line
# Add the 'serial' and the 'terminal' line
# Add the last two 'console' parameters on the kernel line
# Now try to access the serial console using 'virsh console <hostname>'

# cat /etc/grub.conf
# grub.conf generated by anaconda
#
# Note you do not have to rerun grub after making changes to this fil.e
# NOTICE:  You have a /boot partition. This means that
```

```
#          all kernel and initrd paths are relative to /boot/, e.g.,
#          root (hd0,0)
#          kernel /vmlinuz-version ro root=/dev/mapper/vg_ns-lv_root
#          initrd /initrd-[generic-]version.img
# boot=/dev/vda
default=0
timeout=10
serial --unit=0 --speed=115200
terminal --timeout=5 serial console
#splashimage=(hd0,0)/grub/splash.xpm.gz
#hiddenmenu
title CentOS (2.6.32-431.el6.x86_64)
        root (hd0,0)
        kernel /vmlinuz-2.6.32-431.el6.x86_64 ro root=/dev/mapper/vg_ns-lv_root rd_NO_LUKS
LANG=en_US.UTF-8 rd_NO_MD SYSFONT=latarcyrheb-sun16 rd_LVM_LV=vg_ns/lv_root crashkernel=auto
KEYBOARDTYPE=pc KEYTABLE=us rd_LVM_LV=vg_ns/lv_swap rd_NO_DM console=tty0 console=ttyS0,115200
        initrd /initramfs-2.6.32-431.el6.x86_64.img
```

Security Considerations

In a virtual environment, where many VMs may be running on a physical hypervisor, the VMs may have applications on them that are not related to one another. VMs are processes like any other process on a hypervisor. In theory, it is possible to break out of a VM and access the hypervisor, and then from there, access another VM. In general, KVM maintainers are pretty quick to address security concerns.

SELinux offers a layer of security for both the hypervisor and the VM. If you do decide to use SELinux, keep in mind there are some changes that need to be made to get KVM working with SELinux.

iptables on both the hypervisor and the VM can protect the hosts at the network layer.

The network design and VM distribution also play a role in security. For instance, some enterprises may choose to have application-specific hypervisors. So, if there are, say, two dozen applications, then there are at least two dozen sets of numerous hypervisors per application. This sort of segregation may offer protection if one or more applications has more security risks than the other application.

Networks, of course, play a huge role. Having a separate management network for the hypervisors, for IPMI management, for storage, and, last, per application networks helps by adding more layers to the security blanket.

Overall, the amount of security has to be balanced with the ease of use. Keep in mind any government or other security standards such as those of the National Institute of Standards and Technology and PCI may have to be followed as well.

Reference Architecture

Based on what we have learned so far in this chapter, let's design the enterprise virtualization strategy for a sample enterprise called Example.com.

The company is an online retailer. A majority of its servers are running Apache for serving its online retail needs. There are also some MySQL database servers that act as the back end for Apache.

The reference architecture consists of an enterprise that has three data centers—one in Oregon (OR), the other in Texas (TX), and the third in Virginia (VA)— seen in Figure 3-12. Each data center has 500 hypervisors, and each hypervisor has ten VMs running on it, for a total of 5000 VMs per site. Across the three sites, there is a total of 15,000 VMs. The VMs are all Linux based, running CentOS 6.5. The hypervisors are running CentOS 6.5 with KVM installed on them.

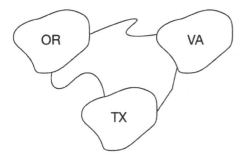

Figure 3-12. *Example.com data center sites*

The hardware of the hypervisors consists of name-brand servers, with seven 10GB network cards, two for the storage network, two for the management network, one for IPMI, and two for the application networks. There are two solid state drives (SSD) based hard drives in each server, both the drives are mirrored, and the drive size is 120GB each. Two CPUs are present on each server; the CPUs are Intel E7-8870 2.4Ghz Xeon, which have 10 cores and 20 threads. Each thread can be allocated as a virtual CPU to a VM for a total of 40 virtual CPUs. With a VM density of ten VMs per hypervisor, we can assign four virtual CPUs to each VM. Each VM needs an average of 32GB of physical memory, for a total memory footprint of 320GB per server. Add to that the overhead of the hypervisor and you need 384GB of physical memory. The server has 12 physical memory sockets; if we stick in 32GB DIMMS, that will give us a total of 384GB of physical RAM, which will suit our needs.

For storage, Example.com uses NetApp NFS filers to store the VM images. Shares from the filers are mounted on the hypervisors. Because each site has 500 hypervisors, the hypervisors are divided into smaller pods of 100 hypervisors each, for a total of 5 pods per site. A pod consists of 100 hypervisors, 1000 VMs, and a filer that is part of a cluster. The cluster has at least two heads and numerous disk shelves. A sample pod is shown in Figure 3-13.

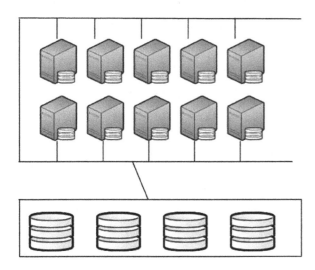

Figure 3-13. *A pod with ten hypervisors and a cluster of NetApp filers*

79

The reason for picking this sort of architecture is based on the type of workload that Example.com has. Workload is pretty consistent across its engineering platform, and as such we can standardize on a VM with four virtual CPUs. In terms of memory use, the Apache instances have been standardized on 32GB of RAM. The reason for this is based on the number of Apache children. The workload is normalized across the VMs; therefore, the number of Apache prefork processes are the same across the different VMs. Assuming each process consumes 20 MB of memory, each VM can support 1200 Apache processes, consuming a total of 24GB of RAM, leaving 8GB of RAM for the operating system and other processes.

For the image type, Example.com is using Qcow2 because we want to be able to snapshot an image, and the raw image type does not support snapshots.

For management, Example.com uses custom-built scripts and programs that use the libvirt Python API

Conclusion

KVM is a robust virtualization solution. With the support of a major Linux vendor such as RedHat, and the open source community, it is rapidly increasing its market share of virtualization. Using one or more of the design techniques shown in this chapter, you can create an enterprise infrastructure that provides stability and is easy to manage.

CHAPTER 4

MySQL, Git, and Postfix

Databases, revision control, and e-mail servers are essential components of an organization's infrastructure. This chapter covers three topics: MySQL, Git, and Postfix. Whether they are hosted in-house or in a public cloud, the choices you make should be well informed and based on technical, business, as well as engineering resources.

MySQL is a very popular open source relational database. It has been around since 1995 and, until recently, was the de facto database for a large number of Linux distributions. When referring to the LAMP architecture, the M stands for MySQL.Git is the leading open source revision control software. Its distributed nature has made it a popular choice among open source developers. It has also gained popularity in its use for infrastructure management.

Postfix has replaced Sendmail as the choice of mail transfer agent (MTA) for a number of Linux distributions. Postfix is fast, secure, and easy to use, and it is well supported.

Database Categories

Databases can be divided into at least the following categories, if not more:

- Relational
- Object
- NoSQL
- Cloud
- Distributed
- NewSQL

Relational databases have been popular for a long time and are by far the most well known. A well-known example of an open source relational database is MySQL. These types of databases store information and the relations among the information components. The software used for relational databases is called a *relational database management system* (RDBMS). A human resources database lends itself very well to be stored in an RDBMS, because employees and their data have a strong relation between them that the database can represent.

Object databases do not store relations; instead, they store objects. Anything that can be stored as an object is a good candidate for object databases. Multimedia applications are ideal candidates for object databases. Content management systems can also use object databases. An example of an object database is db4o (http://www.db4o.com/).

NoSQL databases are good candidates for unstructured data that may not have a strong relation between its components. Also, NoSQL databases can generally handle larger volumes of data compared with an RDBMS. A popular NoSQL database is MongoDB (http://www.mongodb.org/). You can find a list of NoSQL databases at http://nosql-database.org/.

Cloud databases are hosted in public clouds. Google hosts cloud databases such as Google Cloud Storage and Google Cloud Datastore. There are also other cloud databases, such as Amazon DynamoDB, which is a NoSQL database.

Distributed databases store data across a number of instances, and hence they are called *distributed*. An example of an open source distributed database is Cassandra (`https://cassandra.apache.org/`). Distributed databases are alternatives to RDBMSs and object databases for data that is massive in size. For instance, social networking data for millions of users might be a potentially suitable candidate for Cassandra.

NewSQL databases provide the scalability of NoSQL with the atomicity, consistency, isolation, and durability guarantee of RDBMSs. VoltDB (`http://voltdb.com/`) and Clustrix (`http://www.clustrix.com/`) are examples of NewSQL databases.

Picking a Database

There are numerous open source database solutions available. Some of the popular ones include the following:

- MySQL

- MariaDB (a fork of MySQL; very similar to it)

- Cassandra

- PostgreSQL

- MongoDB

- CouchDB

- SQLite

- Redis

There are many other databases. I have listed a few that, in my experience, have a wide installed base. You can view a more complete listing at `https://en.wikipedia.org/wiki/List_of_relational_database_management_systems` and also at `http://www.fromdev.com/2012/07/best-open-source-nosql-database.html`.

A few major commercial databases that run on Linux are

- Oracle (`http://www.oracle.com/index.html`)

- Informix (`http://www-01.ibm.com/software/data/informix/`)

- IBM DB2 (`http://www-01.ibm.com/software/data/db2/`)

The choice of a database should be based on factors such as the following:

- Licensing

- Ease of use

- Support from community

- Commercial support availability

- Type of database required (object, relational, NoSQL)

- Frequency of updates

- Database suitability for application

When designing a human resources application, as mentioned the data is relational in nature—employees have a name, social security number, salary, and other such related information. So, picking a relational database would be appropriate. For multimedia applications, such as photo, video, and art, object databases are more popular, because these media can be stored easily as objects. Cloud databases have the advantage of being managed by the cloud provider; however, your data end up being in the hands of the cloud provider, which may not be ideal in all cases.

Installing MySQL

There are at least two options for installing MySQL:

1. Using the Yellowdog Updater, Modified (YUM) repositories with CentOS/RedHat

2. Downloading source code and compiling on your own

```
# yum install mysql-server
Loaded plugins: fastestmirror
...[SNIP]...
Installed:
  mysql-server.x86_64 0:5.5.39-1.el6.remi
Dependency Installed:
  mysql.x86_64 0:5.5.39-1.el6.remi
Dependency Updated:
  mysql-libs.x86_64 0:5.5.39-1.el6.remi
Complete!
```

You may also notice that if you do a yum install mysql-server, MariaDB is installed instead. Some distributions have deprecated MySQL in favor of MariaDB, which is a drop-in replacement, as explained in the section "Future of MySQL."

```
# yum install mysql-server
Loaded plugins: fastestmirror, security
Setting up Install Process
Package mysql-server is obsoleted by MariaDB-server, trying to install
MariaDB-server-10.0.12-1.el6.x86_64 instead
...[SNIP]...
Installed:
MariaDB-compat.x86_64 0:10.0.12-1.el6
MariaDB-server.x86_64 0:10.0.12-1.el6
Dependency Installed:
  MariaDB-client.x86_64 0:10.0.12-1.el6
  MariaDB-common.x86_64 0:10.0.12-1.el6
Replaced:
  mysql-libs.x86_64 0:5.1.66-2.el6_3
Complete!
```

If possible, use precompiled binaries for MySQL that your Linux distribution provides. It's a lot easier to maintain and manage. However, in case you want to build your own MySQL, you have to download the source code, compile it, and then install the compiled version. MySQL downloads are available from https://dev.mysql.com/downloads/. The MySQL Community Server is a good place to start.

COMPILING MYSQL

Download the latest version. As of this writing, 5.6 is the latest.

```
# wget --no-check-certificate https://dev.mysql.com/get/Downloads/MySQL-5.6/MySQL-5.6.20-1.
el6.src.rpm
--2014-09-10 16:44:06--  https://dev.mysql.com/get/Downloads/MySQL-5.6/MySQL-5.6.20-1.el6.
src.rpm
...[SNIP]...
2014-09-10 16:44:13 (4.72 MB/s) - "MySQL-5.6.20-1.el6.src.rpm" saved [31342030/31342030]

# ls
MySQL-5.6.20-1.el6.src.rpm

# rpm -Uvh ./MySQL-5.6.20-1.el6.src.rpm
   1:MySQL                   ######################################### [100%]
```

Untar the distribution.

```
# cd /usr/local/src
# cp /root/rpmbuild/SOURCES/mysql-5.6.20.tar.gz.
# ls
MySQL-5.6.20-1.el6.src.rpm  mysql-5.6.20.tar.gz
# tar xvfz mysql-5.6.20.tar.gz
mysql-5.6.20/
mysql-5.6.20/Docs/
```

Install cmake and ncurses-devel.

```
# cd mysql-5.6.20
# yum install cmake
Loaded plugins: fastestmirror, security
Loading mirror speeds from cached hostfile
...[SNIP]...
Installed:
  cmake.x86_64 0:2.6.4-5.el6

# yum install ncurses-devel -y
Loaded plugins: fastestmirror, security
Loading mirror speeds from cached hostfile
Setting up Install Process
...[SNIP]...
Installed:
  ncurses-devel.x86_64 0:5.7-3.20090208.el6
```

Run cmake.

```
# cmake.
-- Running cmake version 2.6.4
-- The C compiler identification is GNU
-- The CXX compiler identification is GNU
...[SNIP]...
-- Googlemock was not found. gtest-based unit tests will be disabled. You can run cmake.
-DENABLE_DOWNLOADS=1 to automatically download and build required components from source.
-- If you are inside a firewall, you may need to use an http proxy: export
   http_proxy=http://example.com:80
-- Library mysqlserver depends on OSLIBS -lpthread;m;rt;crypt;dl
-- Configuring done
-- Generating done
-- Build files have been written to: /usr/local/src/MySQL/mysql-5.6.20
```

Run make.

```
# make
Scanning dependencies of target INFO_BIN
[  0%] Built target INFO_BIN
...[SNIP]...
[100%] Building CXX object mysql-test/lib/My/SafeProcess/CMakeFiles/my_safe_process.dir/
safe_process.cc.o
Linking CXX executable my_safe_process
[100%] Built target my_safe_process
```

Install the software after compiling it.

```
# make install
[  0%] Built target INFO_BIN
...SNIP]...
[100%] Built target my_safe_process
Install the project...
-- Install configuration: "RelWithDebInfo"
-- Installing: /usr/local/mysql/./COPYING
...[SNIP]...
-- Installing: /usr/local/mysql/sql-bench/test-wisconsin
```

Add mysql user.

```
# getent group mysql
mysql:x:27:
# useradd -r -g mysql mysql
# getent passwd mysql
mysql:x:495:27::/home/mysql:/bin/bash
# cd /usr/local
# chown -R mysql.mysql mysql/
# pwd
/usr/local
# cd mysql
```

Initialize mysql by bootstrapping the database.

```
# scripts/mysql_install_db --user=mysql
Installing MySQL system tables...2014-09-10 17:25:07 O [Warning] TIMESTAMP with implicit
DEFAULT value is deprecated. Please use --explicit_defaults_for_timestamp server option
(see documentation for more details).
2014-09-10 17:25:07 32087 [Note] InnoDB: Using atomics to ref count buffer pool pages
2014-09-10 17:25:07 32087 [Note] InnoDB: The InnoDB memory heap is disabled
...[SNIP]...

# chown -R root .
```

Change the root password for mysql.

```
# ./bin/mysqld_safe &
# ./bin/mysqladmin -u root password 'new-password'
# ./bin/mysqladmin -u root -h <hostname> password 'new-password'
# cd mysql-test ; perl mysql-test-run.pl
# cp support-files/mysql.server /etc/rc3.d/S90mysql
```

MySQL Failover

MySQL supports master/master and master/slave failover with replication. In master/master mode, writes can occur to one or more of the master servers, and replication keeps track of the updates among them. In master/slave mode, writes have to go to the master; reads can be done on the master as well as the slave.

Figure 4-1 shows a California web server that writes to a MySQL master in CA, and a Texas web server that writes to a master in TX. The CA and TX MySQL servers stay in sync with each other using replication. The CA and TX web servers read the same data from the database. Writes to the database can happen from both web servers.

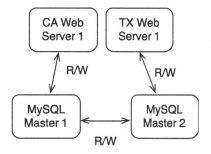

Figure 4-1. *MySQL master/master design*

Figure 4-2 shows a master/slave setup. Writes can happen only to the master database in California. The TX web server reads only from the MySQL slave server in Texas. If writes are needed from the TX web server, we would have to direct them to the CA MySQL server or change the type of MySQL failover from master/slave to master/master. The California master MySQL server sends updates to the MySQL slave in Texas.

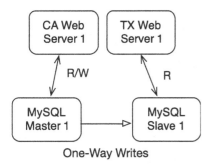

Figure 4-2. *MySQL master/slave design*

MySQL Proxy is another piece of software that is in alpha release at this point. The proxy handles splitting read/writes between two master servers automatically. The proxy is, of course, a single point of failure. Because the software is in alpha release, using it in production may not be suitable. If you decide to use it for nonproduction environments, then set it up as shown in Figure 4-3. The web server is not aware that it is using a proxy, nor does it have to be made aware. Because of the alpha nature of MySQL Proxy, it should be used in noncritical environments only. The scalability of MySQL proxy, and its speed, should be tested before you start using it actively. Ensure the version of MySQL being used is at least version 5.0, so that it works with MySQL Proxy. MySQL Proxy may also be installed on a given MySQL server; however, it is better if it is installed on another server, because in the event that one MySQL server crashes, you do not lose the proxy server with it and you can continue working. Additional information about MySQL Proxy can be obtained at `https://dev.mysql.com/doc/refman/5.0/en/mysql-proxy.html`.

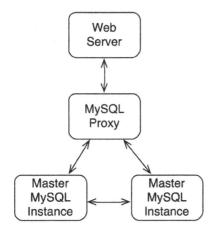

Figure 4-3. *MySQL failover with MySQL Proxy*

Another option is to use HAProxy instead of MySQL Proxy (Figure 4-4). The web server sends all MySQL requests to the HAProxy IP. HAProxy, in turn, checks the availability of both MySQL servers., and forwards the requests to the available MySQL server based on the load-balancing algorithm specified. HAProxy is available at `http://www.haproxy.org/`

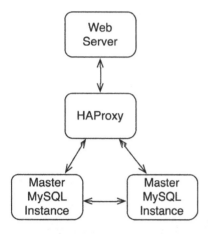

Figure 4-4. *MySQL failover with HAProxy*

MySQL Enterprise Design

Designing an enterprise MySQL installation is challenging. There are at least two different models, if not more, for an enterprise design. One option is to offer MySQL as a service, or database as a service (DBaaS), for everyone in the enterprise (Figure 4-5). One or more teams will manage a few clusters of MySQL database servers, and will provide a database login, password, and server name to which application developers can connect and use. The back-end database, backups, maintenance, and upgrade are all maintained by the team providing the service. The advantage of this model is that it is cost efficient. Maintenance is relatively easier, because it's done at a single point. Individual application teams do not have to worry about setting up their own instances and managing them. Security issues can be resolved more quickly because all corporate MySQL instances are tracked through the team managing them.

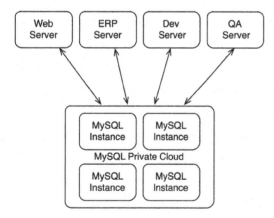

Figure 4-5. *MySQL in-house private cloud (DBaaS) for Web, Enterprise Resource Planning (ERP), Development (Dev) and Quality Assurance (QA)*

Another option is to have individual MySQL database instances per application and let the application owners manage the instances as well as their own data (Figure 4-6). This means that each application ownership team has to have MySQL administration experience.

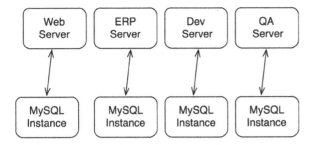

Figure 4-6. *Per-application MySQL servers and no in-house MySQL cloud*

A more robust approach takes per-application instances and makes them redundant. In this case, each team maintains its own database. However the databases are running in master/master or master/slave configuration for failover capabilities (Figure 4-7).

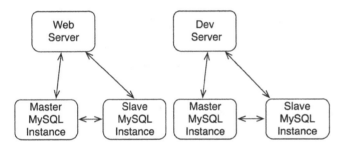

Figure 4-7. *Per-application redundant MySQL servers*

A hybrid model involves both—using DBaaS for small-scale applications and using dedicated instances for large-scale applications (Figure 4-8). Considering the fact that technology is moving toward providing infrastructure as a service, it has become common for enterprises to adopt the DBaaS model.

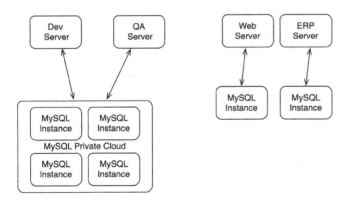

Figure 4-8. *MySQL Hybrid with DBaaS as well as dedicated instances*

The process of setting up MySQL replication can be found at https://dev.mysql.com/doc/refman/5.0/en/replication.html.

Managing MySQL

MySQL comes with command line utilities to manage it. In addition to these utilities, one can also use the following:

- MySQL Utilities, which is an additional set of utilities that helps manage MySQL
  (https://dev.mysql.com/downloads/utilities/)

- MySQL Workbench, which is a graphical user interface to administer, design, and develop
  using MySQL (https://www.mysql.com/products/workbench/)

- Percona Toolkit (http://www.percona.com/software/percona-toolkit)

An enterprise will most likely end up using a combination of these utilities to manage its environment, in addition to perhaps homegrown tools.

Backing up MySQL

A regular backup of MySQL is crucial for business continuity planning. Ideally the backup should be shipped to another location, away from the database. One can even back up the database to a cloud data store. There are numerous types of backups available with MySQL:

- *Cold backup*: when the server has been shut down. This ensures consistency of data.
  This option is usually not possible for a global organization dependent on MySQL for ongoing activities, or for one that has an online presence.

- *Hot backup*: the database table is not locked (in other words, read and writes continues).
  I do not recommend this type of backup, because you can potentially corrupt your backup or miss some important updates to the database.

- *Warm backup*: reads are allowed but writes are blocked. This is a very popular solution because it can be done very quickly while ensuring data consistentency.

A cold backup or warm backup can also take place on a slave server in a master/slave configuration. This allows for continued use of the master database; when the slave is back online, it catches up with the master.

When doing a backup of MySQL, you can either back up the data files themselves, which is considered a raw backup, or you can do a logical backup, which includes SQL statements needed to recreate the schema of the database. My recommendation is to do a logical backup because it's easier to restore. To get a consistent backup, you have a couple of options: one is to do a cold backup; the other is to lock the tables and flush them.

```
mysql>LOCK TABLES tablelist READ;
mysql>FLUSH TABLES tablelist;
```

A number of software utilities can be used to make MySQL backups. Some of them include `mysqldump`, `ibbackup`, and `mysqlhostcopy`. Shown here is an example of using `mysqldump` and the consistent backup copy produced. This exmample is for a small test database called *webapps,* with just one row in it. As you can see in the example, `mysqldump` locks the table for writes before taking the backup.

```
$ mysqldump webapp --user root --password
Enter password:
-- MySQL dump 10.15  Distrib 10.0.12-MariaDB, for Linux (x86_64)
--
-- Host: localhost    Database: webapp
-- ------------------------------------------------------
-- Server version         10.0.12-MariaDB

/*!40101 SET @OLD_CHARACTER_SET_CLIENT=@@CHARACTER_SET_CLIENT */;
/*!40101 SET @OLD_CHARACTER_SET_RESULTS=@@CHARACTER_SET_RESULTS */;
/*!40101 SET @OLD_COLLATION_CONNECTION=@@COLLATION_CONNECTION */;
/*!40101 SET NAMES utf8 */;
/*!40103 SET @OLD_TIME_ZONE=@@TIME_ZONE */;
/*!40103 SET TIME_ZONE='+00:00' */;
/*!40014 SET @OLD_UNIQUE_CHECKS=@@UNIQUE_CHECKS, UNIQUE_CHECKS=0 */;
/*!40014 SET @OLD_FOREIGN_KEY_CHECKS=@@FOREIGN_KEY_CHECKS, FOREIGN_KEY_CHECKS=0 */;
/*!40101 SET @OLD_SQL_MODE=@@SQL_MODE, SQL_MODE='NO_AUTO_VALUE_ON_ZERO' */;
/*!40111 SET @OLD_SQL_NOTES=@@SQL_NOTES, SQL_NOTES=0 */;


--
-- Table structure for table `webservers`
--

DROP TABLE IF EXISTS `webservers`;
/*!40101 SET @saved_cs_client     = @@character_set_client */;
/*!40101 SET character_set_client = utf8 */;
CREATE TABLE `webservers` (
  `name` varchar(255) DEFAULT NULL,
  `location` varchar(32) DEFAULT NULL
) ENGINE=InnoDB DEFAULT CHARSET=latin1;
/*!40101 SET character_set_client = @saved_cs_client */;


--
-- Dumping data for table `webservers`
--

LOCK TABLES `webservers` WRITE;
/*!40000 ALTER TABLE `webservers` DISABLE KEYS */;
INSERT INTO `webservers` VALUES ('web1.example.com','TX');
/*!40000 ALTER TABLE `webservers` ENABLE KEYS */;
UNLOCK TABLES;
/*!40103 SET TIME_ZONE=@OLD_TIME_ZONE */;

/*!40101 SET SQL_MODE=@OLD_SQL_MODE */;
/*!40014 SET FOREIGN_KEY_CHECKS=@OLD_FOREIGN_KEY_CHECKS */;
/*!40014 SET UNIQUE_CHECKS=@OLD_UNIQUE_CHECKS */;
/*!40101 SET CHARACTER_SET_CLIENT=@OLD_CHARACTER_SET_CLIENT */;
/*!40101 SET CHARACTER_SET_RESULTS=@OLD_CHARACTER_SET_RESULTS */;
/*!40101 SET COLLATION_CONNECTION=@OLD_COLLATION_CONNECTION */;
/*!40111 SET SQL_NOTES=@OLD_SQL_NOTES */;

-- Dump completed on 2014-09-13 19:24:23
```

An enterprise backup strategy is a lot easier when MySQL is offered as a DBaaS, because you can take one of the multiple masters in a DBaaS and make a backup with write locks without affecting the applications. If we have a single master server, then the lock table command might cause an application issue for large tables.

Getting Help with MySQL

MySQL support options include the following:

- Commercial support from Oracle (https://www.mysql.com/support/)

- Community forums (http://forums.mysql.com/)

- Documentation (https://dev.mysql.com/doc/)

- Internet Relay Chat (IRC) channel (https://dev.mysql.com/doc/refman/5.0/en/irc.html)

- Mailing list (http://lists.mysql.com/)

- MySQL development project is hosted at https://launchpad.net/mysql, if you want to contribute to the project.

- *Expert MySQL* is a good guide for MySQL (http://www.apress.com/9781430246596)

Future of MySQL

MySQL was owned and operated by a single for-profit company, the Swedish company MySQL AB, until it was purchased by Sun Microsystems in 2008. Sun was later acquired by Oracle in 2009. The open source community viewed the ownership of MySQL by Oracle as inherently a conflict of interest, and has come up with a drop-in MySQL replacement called MariaDB (https://mariadb.org/). The main author of MySQL, Michael "Monty" Widenius, supported splitting up from MySQL into MariaDB. Popular Linux distributions have already switched to providing MariaDB as part of their distribution instead of MySQL. However, MySQL continues to enjoy a large installed base and is still very popular.

Should an enterprise pick MySQL or MariaDB? This question can be best answered by reviewing the enterprise policy on open source software. If an enterprise has a culture of using open source software and agrees with the viewpoint that Oracle ownership of MySQL creates an uncertain future for MySQL, then MariaDB is the right choice. On the other hand, Oracle has, for the past few years, continued the development of MySQL so one could argue that this is sufficient reason for investing in MySQL. As time progresses, there is a possibility that MariaDB will become more different than MySQL.

E-mail in an Enterprise

E-mail plays at least two important roles in an enterprise. One role is the obvious one—communications, both internally and externally. The other is the use of e-mail for infrastructure management. Some examples of using e-mail in infrastructure management include the following:

- For companies that use monitoring tools such as Nagios, e-mail is one way that alerts are delivered.

- E-mail from system services, such as cron, can be collected at a central location and analyzed for troubleshooting.

- Applications on servers can use e-mail gateways for relaying application-specific information.

- Security teams may want to analyze system-related e-mail to determine whether any server or application has been compromised.

Enterprises have different strategies when dealing with mail from servers. Some of these strategies are

- Sending all system-related e-mail to /dev/null and using extensive out-of-band monitoring of services along with SMS-based alerts

- Leaving system-related e-mail on respective systems, having them processed for security, troubleshooting on the system itself, and then pruning as needed

- Having all e-mail from systems be forwarded to an e-mail gateway that then stores and processes the e-mail

As a site reliability engineer, your choice of action should take into consideration at least the following:

- The number of systems you have, because if you manage thousands of servers, receiving e-mail from each of them may not be a practical

- How important system-related e-mail is to you, because you can get the same information that system-related e-mail provides through a comprehensive monitoring architecture

- Configuring MTAs in applications versus relying on system-provided MTA. If the application can send e-mail to a gateway without relying on the system mailer, this option saves you the trouble of configuring e-mail on the servers.

E-mail Solution Strategy

An effective enterprise e-mail solution strategy is crucial for business. There are two main choices when it comes to an e-mail solution:

- Setting up e-mail in-house using open source software or commercial software; an example of this is to use Postfix or Microsoft Exchange

- Using a cloud provider for e-mail, such as Google, Microsoft, or Rackspace

The choice of building in-house or using a public cloud depends on a number of factors. During the decision-making process, spend a lot of time on analyzing the pros and the cons, then make your decision. A few things to keep in mind are the following:

- Any regulations an organization is subject to that would prevent it from hosting e-mail in a cloud provider

- Cost of the cloud solution versus an in-house solution (for instance, Gmail for Work is around $5 per person per month at list price)

- Whether an existing solution is in-house, because the effort to migrate to the cloud might be too painful

- Client access methods for cloud e-mail providers (for example, if your users want to sync e-mail/calendar with their smartphone)

Hosted e-mail providers are numerous and the cost varies tremendously. Many of them provide e-mail, calendar, and a smartphone sync feature. Exchange hosting is also very popular, and there are numerous Microsoft partners that provide hosted Exchange accounts. Some of the options for hosted e-mail are:

- Google Gmail for Work (https://www.gmail.com/intl/en/mail/help/about.html)

- Hosted Exchange (https://office.microsoft.com/en-us/)

- Rackspace-hosted e-mail (http://www.rackspace.com/email-hosting/webmail/)

Having your e-mail in a public cloud is very convenient. A few advantages of using hosted e-mail are

- No capital expenditure on hardware or software

- Engineering staff not required to maintain mail infrastructure

- Total cost of ownership for hosting can be less than in-house infrastructure

Not everything is rosy with having your e-mail in a public cloud. Disadvantages of hosted e-mail include the following:

- Your e-mail security is in the hands of someone else.

- Recurring operational cost may be higher than an in-house solution.

- Not all e-mail requirements, such as archiving, may be available with hosting providers.

- Loss of Internet connectivity from the corporate office may result in loss of e-mail access as well.

Enterprise Mail Transfer Agents

A MTA is software that transfers mail between servers. A mail user agent is software that end users use to download and read e-mail. The choice of MTAs is huge; some of more popular ones include the following:

- Sendmail

- Postfix

- Qmail

- Apache James

- Exim

Sendmail used to be the default MTA on CentOS until CentOS 6.x was released, at which time Postfix became the default MTA. When deciding to pick an MTA for your organization, keep the following few items in mind:

- Open source or commercial?

- If open source, do you need commercial support?

- How active is the end user community?

- How quickly are security holes plugged?

- What is the release cycle of the product like?

- Does the MTA meet the technical needs of speed and reliability for your organization?

Postfix Enterprise Design

The most basic Postfix design is to have direct mail delivery for each server that needs it, for both outbound and inbound mail delivery. The advantages of such a design are as follows:

- It is simple, if the number of servers receiving incoming mail is less than a handful. No routing complications are encountered because each server handles its own mail, or mail for the domain it is responsible for.

- It is independent. One server is not dependent on the other; changes can be made on one server without affecting the other.

- It is fast. Because routing is more direct and is not proxied, mail is delivered quickly.

The disadvantages of such as design include the following:

- It is not scalable. Beyond a handful of servers, it can be difficult to manage.

- It is not secure. Each server that handles mail has to have an open port from the Internet. Therefore, the server is vulnerable to attacks from the Internet.

- It is difficult to maintain. Each server has to be updated individually and managed individually.

Although the direct mail design is simple, it is not popular for large enterprises because it allows for multiple points of entry into the enterprise (Figure 4-9).

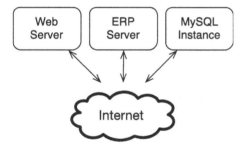

Figure 4-9. *Postfix with direct outbound and inbound mail delivery*

Another approach is to have a single point of entry and exit for mail into the enterprise. This is a more common approach. The advantages of this approach are as follows:

- It's easy to maintain because there is a single choke point.

- The monitoring of e-mail traffic is simple because all traffic goes through one gateway.

- Reporting is accurate because there is only one entry/exit.

- Security is enhanced because there is only one server open to the Internet for mail.

- The cost is reduced because fewer mail servers are needed, which also reduces the cost of licensing, if using commercial solutions.

This solution is more popular than the direct delivery one because of the numerous advantages over direct mail delivery (Figure 4-10). Enterprises can also use dedicated antispam and antivirus solutions such as the one from Barracuda networks (`https://www.barracuda.com/`) or Mailfoundry (`http://www.mailfoundry.com/`). For open source solutions, one can set up a server running SpamAssassin (`https://spamassassin.apache.org/`) and ClamAV (`http://www.clamav.net/index.html`).

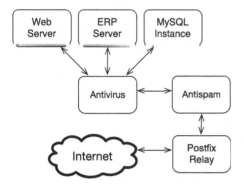

Figure 4-10. *Postfix with internal antivirus, antispam, and outbound and inbound relay*

Another approach is to use a third-party vendor, such as Websense (`https://www.websense.com/content/websense-email-security-products.aspx`) to handle antispam and antivirus (Figure 4-11). The advantages of this solution are the following:

- There is no hardware or software to maintain.

- Updates to antispam and antivirus definitions are automatic.

- The power of the cloud is leveraged with autoscaling.

- Your network is protected by only allowing the cloud provider to have access to it.

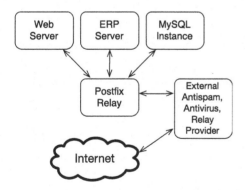

Figure 4-11. *Postfix with external hosted antispam, antivirus, and outbound and inbound relay*

Installing Postfix

Postfix is the default MTA on CentOS/RedHat, so it's present on most server installs, unless you remove it.

Installing using yum is straightforward. Simply run yum install postfix.

```
# yum install postfix -y
Loaded plugins: fastestmirror
...[SNIP]...
--> Running transaction check
---> Package postfix.x86_64 2:2.6.6-6.el6_5 will be installed
--> Finished Dependency Resolution
...[SNIP]...
Installed:
  postfix.x86_64 2:2.6.6-6.el6_5
Complete!
```

If you want a different version than the one in your yum repository, then first download the version.

```
# wget http://mirrors-usa.go-parts.com/postfix/source/official/postfix-2.10.3.tar.gz
--2014-09-11 23:40:37-- http://mirrors-usa.go-parts.com/postfix/source/official/postfix-2.10.3.tar.gz
...[SNIP]...
2014-09-11 23:40:39 (3.42 MB/s) - "postfix-2.10.3.tar.gz" saved [3828808/3828808]
```

Untar and make to compile.

```
# tar xvfz postfix-2.10.3.tar.gz
postfix-2.10.3/
...[SNIP]...
postfix-2.10.3/README_FILES/XFORWARD_README
```

```
# make
make -f Makefile.in MAKELEVEL= Makefiles
...[SNIP]...
gcc -Wmissing-prototypes -Wformat -Wno-comment  -g -O -I. -I../../include -DLINUX2 -o tlsproxy
tlsproxy.o tlsproxy_state.o ../../lib/libtls.a ../../lib/libmaster.a ../../lib/libglobal.a ../../
lib/libutil.a -ldb -lnsl -lresolv
cp tlsproxy ../../libexec
```

make install to install. This will install with the prefix /, so it replaces your system Postfix.

```
# make install
set -e; for i in src/util src/global src/dns src/tls src/xsasl src/milter src/master src/postfix
src/fsstone src/smtpstone src/sendmail src/error src/pickup src/cleanup src/smtpd src/local src/
trivial-rewrite src/qmgr src/oqmgr src/smtp src/bounce src/pipe src/showq src/postalias src/postcat
src/postconf src/postdrop src/postkick src/postlock src/postlog src/postmap src/postqueue src/
postsuper src/qmqpd src/spawn src/flush src/verify src/virtual src/proxymap src/anvil src/scache
src/discard src/tlsmgr src/postmulti src/postscreen src/dnsblog src/tlsproxy; do \
        (set -e; echo "[$i]"; cd $i; make 'CC=gcc -Wmissing-prototypes -Wformat -Wno-comment '
update MAKELEVEL=) || exit 1; \
        done
...[SNIP]...
Editing /etc/postfix/master.cf, adding missing entry for tlsproxy unix-domain service
```

Configuring Postfix

There are many hundreds of configuration options with Postfix. I outline a few of the common ones from /etc/postfix/main.cf file.

Domain Name to Use for Outbound Mail

Set this option to be the domain name you want for your outbound mail. By default, this option uses the hostname for outbound e-mail. The option also specifies the domain appended to an unqualified recipient address.

```
#default value is:
#myorigin = $myhostname
#myorigin = $mydomain

#we are going to send outbound mail as originating from example.com
mydomain = example.com
myorigin = $mydomain
```

Domain Name for which to Receive E-mail

This option specifies the domain name for which Postfix receives e-mail. By default, Postfix receives e-mail for the hostname only. For a domain mail server change the value to include the domain name.

```
#default value
mydestination = $myhostname, localhost.$mydomain, localhost

#we are going to change it so that we can receive email for example.com
mydestination = $myhostname, localhost.$mydomain, localhost, $mydomain
```

Networks from which to Allow Relay

By default, Postfix allows clients on the local subnet of the Postfix server to use it as a relay—in other words, those networks defined in the $mynetworks configuration parameter. Change this to include all your networks within the organization that should be allowed to send e-mail using this Postfix server.

```
#default value
#mynetworks_style = class
#mynetworks_style = subnet
#mynetworks_style = host
#mynetworks = 168.100.189.0/28, 127.0.0.0/8
#mynetworks = $config_directory/mynetworks
#mynetworks = hash:/etc/postfix/network_table

#change the default values to be your network, assuming your network is 10.0.0.0/8
mynetworks = 10.0.0.0/8

#another way of accomplishing the above is:
mynetworks_style = class
```

```
#if you want to forward e-mail only from the Postfix host:
mynetworks_style = host

#if you want only the Postfix server subnet to forward e-mail via the Postfix server:
mynetworks_style = subnet
```

Relay Mail to Destinations

Postfix forwards e-mail only to authorized domains when the mail is from clients outside the authorized network. You can specify which domains can be the recipient domains for unauthenticated senders using the relay_domains parameter.

```
#default value is:
#relay_domains = $mydestination

#if you do not want to forward e-mail from strangers, then change it as follows (recommended for
outgoing mail servers, not for incoming):
relay_domains =

#if you want to forward e-mail from strangers to your domain:
relay_domains = $mydomain
```

Delivery Method

Mail is delivered directly by Postfix using the mail exchanger (MX) record of the recipient. You may not want this feature because it may be better to forward to an outside mail-hosting provider who filters outbound mail as well.

```
#default value is:
#relayhost = $mydomain
#relayhost = [gateway.my.domain]
#relayhost = [mailserver.isp.tld]
#relayhost = uucphost
#relayhost = [an.ip.add.ress]

#change the value to be
relayhost = external.mail.provider.ip.address
```

Reporting Trouble

Another value that you probably want to define is to whom to send e-mail in the case of any problems. The postmaster email address is specified in /etc/aliases and not in /etc/postfix/main.cf.

```
#default value is:
$ grep -i postmaster /etc/aliases
mailer-daemon:  postmaster
postmaster:     root

#change to an e-mail address in your org that is an alias for the team responsible for Postfix
postmaster:     email-admins@example.com
```

Using NAT

If the Postfix server is using NAT (in other words, it is in a private IP space), and it is receiving e-mail addresses to a public IP address, you need to specify this as well.

```
#default value is:
#proxy_interfaces =
#proxy_interfaces = 1.2.3.4

#change it to your external IP address to which e-mail is sent
proxy_interfaces = your.public.email.server.ip.address
```

Logging

Postfix logging is done via Syslog in /etc/rsyslog.conf. The default generally sends all mail logs to /var/log/maillog, which is a good place to store your mail logs.

```
#default value is:
mail.* -/var/log/maillog
```

E-mail Protocols

After Postfix has been set up, the next issue to address is how you give clients access to e-mail. When it comes to client access, some of the popular protocols include

- IMAP

- POP (also known as POP3)

In general, direct delivery to a destination server in an organization is avoided, to keep things simple; instead, the application server pulls e-mail from a mailbox server. The application servers can use one or more of the protocols, such as IMAP or POP. Instead of application servers, you can also have end users use these protocols to access their mailbox. IMAP is defined in RFC 3501 (http://tools.ietf.org/html/rfc3501) and has more features than POP. POP is defined in RFC 1939 (https://www.ietf.org/rfc/rfc1939.txt) and has been around for a long time.

If you have application servers that need to pull e-mail, a potential design that could assist is shown in Figure 4-12. Both the mail delivery agent (MDA) and the mail submission agent (MSA) can be Postfix servers. The MDA is the agent that delivers mail to mailbox; the MSA accepts e-mail from a mail user agent.

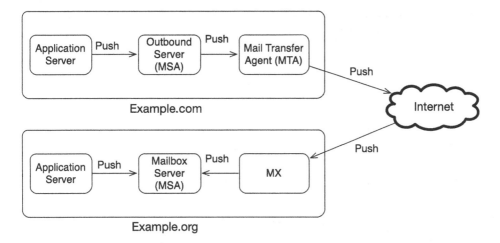

Figure 4-12. *Application servers using e-mail*

For the MSA, there are numerous options, including

- Dovecot (`http://www.dovecot.org/`)

- Courier (`http://www.courier-mta.org/imap/`)

- Cyrus (`https://www.cyrusimap.org/`)

Each of these MSA options is open source and free. All of them support thousands of mailboxes and can help you manage your e-mail environment with ease.

Getting Help with Postfix

There are numerous options for Postfix support. The online documentation is excellent and, as with any open source free software, the user community is your best option for getting help after reading the documentation. A few online help options include:

- Mailing lists (`http://www.postfix.org/lists.html`)

- IRC channel (`http://irc.lc/freenode/postfix/irctc@@@`)

- Online documentation (`http://www.postfix.org/documentation.html`)

Revision Control in an Enterprise

Revision control has many uses in an enterprise infrastructure. The traditional approach was to use revision control for source code management. However, revision control can play an important role in infrastructure management as well. For instance if BIND is being used in the environment, then BIND configuration can be stored in Git. Configuration for software such as Postfix and other software such as OpenVPN, iptables, and Hadoop can also be stored in revision control. Configuration management tools such as Puppet and Salt easily integrate with Git as well.

A large number of open source software source code is stored in Git. One advantage of using Git in an enterprise is that collaboration with the Internet community becomes a lot easier. A few major open source projects that are using Git include

- Linux kernel

- OpenStack

- OpenVZ

- GNOME

- Yum

A more complete list is found at `https://git.wiki.kernel.org/index.php/GitProjects`.

Revision Control Management Choices

There is a large number of revision control software available, both in the open source world and in the commercial world. Some of the open source code management options available include the following:

- CVS (`http://www.nongnu.org/cvs/`)

- Git (`http://git-scm.com/`)

- Mercurial (`http://mercurial.selenic.com/`)

- Apache Subversion (`https://subversion.apache.org/`)

Commercial revision control software that is popular and runs on Linux includes

- BitKeeper (`http://www.bitkeeper.com/`)

- Rational ClearCase (`http://www-03.ibm.com/software/products/en/clearcase`)

- Perforce (`http://www.perforce.com/`)

A more complete list is found at `https://en.wikipedia.org/wiki/Comparison_of_revision_control_software`. Your choice of which software to use should depend on the following:

- Integration with any continuous integration and continuous deployment software that you may be using

- Compatibility with infrastructure software that you may be using, such as Puppet/Salt

- Cost of the software

- Whether you need commercial support

- Different operating system support that may be needed

- Ease of use

- How quickly bugs are fixed in the software

- Knowledge base of engineers in the organization

Why Git?

Git is fundamentally different than other revision control software. Some of the ways that Git is different are as follows:

1. Git maintains snapshots of the file system, instead of just differences.

2. Nearly every operation in Git is local and does not require connectivity to a remote Git server.

3. Git uses checksum of files before it stores the file, and references the file using that checksum.

Of these three differences, the most important aspect of Git that makes it an ideal candidate for infrastructure management is that you can continue to use Git even when you cannot connect to a remote repository. Because you cannot assume the network between servers is always reliable, we have to ensure that the Git repositories on your servers function independently, and that they do not cause a problem with your services if they are unable to reach the Git server. The distributed nature of Git makes it ideal for infrastructure use. Git was developed by Linus Torvalds, the founder of Linux, which also helps in its popularity.

Installing Git

Git open source is easy to install. As with most open source software, you can use the yum repository from your Linux distribution or you can download and compile the software. The easiest route is to use the yum repository.

INSTALLING GIT

The easiest way to install Git is to use yum.

```
# yum install git
Loaded plugins: fastestmirror
Loading mirror speeds from cached hostfile
...[SNIP]...
Setting up Install Process
Resolving Dependencies
--> Running transaction check
---> Package git.x86_64 0:1.7.1-3.el6_4.1 will be installed
--> Processing Dependency: perl-Git = 1.7.1-3.el6_4.1 for package: git-1.7.1-3.el6_4.1.x86_64
--> Processing Dependency: perl(Git) for package: git-1.7.1-3.el6_4.1.x86_64
--> Running transaction check
---> Package perl-Git.noarch 0:1.7.1-3.el6_4.1 will be installed
--> Finished Dependency Resolution
Dependencies Resolved
...[SNIP]...
Installed:
  git.x86_64 0:1.7.1-3.el6_4.1
Dependency Installed:
  perl-Git.noarch 0:1.7.1-3.el6_4.1
Complete!
```

If you would rather use the source code, then install the dependencies first.

```
$ sudo yum install curl-devel expat-devel gettext-devel openssl-devel zlib-devel -y
Loaded plugins: fastestmirror
Loading mirror speeds from cached hostfile
...[SNIP]...
Updated:
  libcurl-devel.x86_64 0:7.19.7-37.el6_5.3 openssl-devel.x86_64 0:1.0.1e-16.el6_5.15
Dependency Updated:
  curl.x86_64 0:7.19.7-37.el6_5.3 libcurl.x86_64 0:7.19.7-37.el6_5.3
openssl.x86_64 0:1.0.1e-16.el6_5.15
Complete!
```

Download Git.

```
# wget https://github.com/git/git/archive/master.zip
--2014-09-10 12:22:46-- https://github.com/git/git/archive/master.zip
...[SNIP]...
2014-09-10 12:22:48 (3.37 MB/s) - "master.zip" saved [6192829/6192829]
```

```
# unzip master.zip
Archive:  master.zip
0c72b98f31bf6eabd75be565a08ffcf0d8e74b1f
...[SNIP]...
git-master/RelNotes -> Documentation/RelNotes/2.2.0.txt
```

Run make.

```
# make prefix=/usr/local all
GIT_VERSION = 2.1.0.GIT
...[SNIP]...
GEN bin-wrappers/test-subprocess
GEN bin-wrappers/test-svn-fe
GEN bin-wrappers/test-urlmatch-normalization
GEN bin-wrappers/test-wildmatch
GEN git-remote-testgit
```

Install Git.

```
# make prefix=/usr/local install
    GEN perl/PM.stamp
    SUBDIR perl
...[SNIP]...
```

Setting up a Git Server

It is common practice to set up a Git server to streamline Git repositories. The steps involved in creating a Git server include the following:

1. Dedicate a server to Git.

2. Install Git.

3. Create a git user.

4. Copy your secure shell (SSH) public keys into authorized keys for git user.

5. Initialize a bare repository on the server.

6. Clone the repository from your desktop.

7. Check in files in the repository.

8. Push the repository back to the server.

```
# yum install git -y
# useradd git
# su - git
$ mkdir .ssh
$ cd .ssh
$ cat <your-ssh-public-key> >> authorized_keys
$ cd $HOME
$ mkdir postfix.git
$ cd postfix.git
$ git --bare init
$ exit
# su - <your-user-name>
$ git clone git@localhost:/home/git/postfix.git
$ touch myfile
$ git add myfile
$ git commit -am "initial commit"
$ git push origin master
```

Git Enterprise Design

Planning a Git enterprise deployment can be a complex task. The simplest design is that of a single Git server that hosts all Git repositories (Figure 4-13). Clients clone from this single Git server, and push to it as well. In case an enterprise has numerous geographically dispersed locations, this solution might be challenging to implement because there is only one server for many location. It may work out if the network connections between the sites are reliable and fast, and Git is not used frequently at the remote sites.

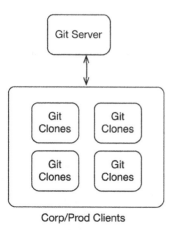

Figure 4-13. *A single Git server*

A more realistic solution is that of having multiple Git repositories—say, one per site—and keep those repositories in sync (Figure 4-14). Clients clone and push to the server in their site. The advantage of this solution is that it is faster than the previous solution. In addition, it is more reliable. The disadvantage is that you have to manage keeping the Git master repositories in sync between different sites.

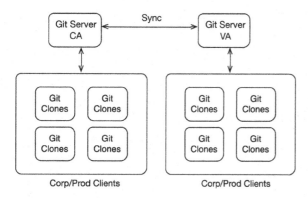

Figure 4-14. *Multisite Git servers*

Another solution is to use hosted Git—say, with GitHub.com (Figure 4-15). This option allows you to maintain all repositories with GitHub, and different sites can pull directly from GitHub.com. You will pay for this expense, but you have no hardware or software to maintain, and GitHub takes cares of all authentication as well as upgrades for you. Other services such as Bitbucket (https://bitbucket.org/), GitLab (https://about.gitlab.com/) and Atlassian Stash (https://www.atlassian.com/software/stash) are viable alternatives to GitHub.com.

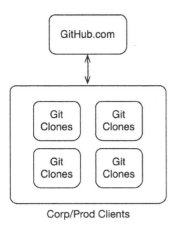

Figure 4-15. *Hosted Git*

Git Protocols

Git signs commits with a GNU Privay Guard (GPG) key to confirm the authenticity of the author/tools. The protocols used to access Git are as follows:

- *Local*: The local protocol works on a local machine, not remotely. If you have a shared file system that can be accessed across all the clients that need Git, this might be an option. An advantage of this is that it is simple to set up.

- *SSH*: A very common and secure way of using Git is to use SSH, which gives you an authenticated and encrypted connection to a Git server. The disadvantage of this method is that you cannot share unauthenticated repositories, so perhaps it is not ideal for public projects that want to share repositories. If you set up SSH keys for users in the git user directory in $HOME/.ssh/authorized_keys, then you can use SSH password-less authentication, which is very easy to administer.

- *Git*: There is a special daemon that comes with Git; it listens on port 9418. It does not provide any authentication; however, it is very fast. You generally do not want to enable a push on a repository that is shared using this protocol because of the lack of authentication.

- *HTTP/S*: The advantage of using HTTP is that you can leverage your existing installed Apache or other web server infrastructure. HTTP is also very convenient and fast, plus you can use secure sockets layer certificates. You have to enable a Git hook to use HTTP, and other than that there is no other configuration. You simply place the Git directory in a path served by your web server.

```
# using local protocol from the directory /gitrepos
$ git clone file:///gitrepos/project.git
or
$ git clone /opt/git/project.git

# using ssh protocol from git@example.com and cloning project.git
$ git clone ssh://git@git.example.com:project.git
```

```
# this example uses the git protocol on
$ git clone git://git.example.com/gitproject.git
$ git clone https://git.example.com/project.git
```

Getting Help with Git

Git has become very popular in the recent past because it is fairly easy to find support for it. Some available support options include

- Mailing list (http://git-scm.com/community)

- IRC (http://git-scm.com/community)

- Documentation (http://git-scm.com/documentation)

- When using GitHub, additional support options, which include commercial support (https://enterprise.github.com/support)

- *Pro Git*, is a very useful book on Git (http://www.apress.com/9781484200773)

Conclusion

There are three extremely powerful platforms for managing data: MySQL for database, Git for source code and configuration data, and Postfix for e-mail. Each of them is an essential component of a successful Linux infrastructure. Used together, they can act as business enablers and become an essential part of your business strategy.

CHAPTER 5

■ ■ ■

Configuration Management with Puppet

If you are managing more than a dozen Linux systems, configuration management is a must. Without configuration management, updating system configuration files and deploying applications can become very challenging. This chapter is about using Puppet configuration management software to deploy and support Linux systems in an enterprise.

Legacy Solutions

Operations engineers use various methods to deploy and maintain systems:

1. Shell scripts to deploy applications. After an operating system (OS) is installed, shell scripts are used to push applications to servers and to configure them. This can be done using Kickstart postinstall scripts. The cons of such an approach are the following:

    *   Custom scripts have to be developed per application.

    *   Knowledge transfer between author and maintainer of scripts has to occur frequently.

    *   The script may not be flexible enough to support changes in applications and may require a rewrite when applications are upgraded.

    *   Lack of unit testing may result in bugs.

2. OS image-based deployment—having an OS image configured with the application preinstalled. This method has gained popularity with cloud-based virtual machine deployments. Challenges with this method are as follows:

    *   You need a separate image for each application.

    *   Maintaining consistency across the image version is challenging.

    *   Each time a change has to be made, a new image has to be created.

3. Application deployment using software packages. This method uses packages, such as RPMs on RedHat to deploy applications and their configuration files. Issues with this option include the following:

    *   Even minor changes require new packages.

    *   Different operating systems use different packages, creating more work in a diverse OS environment.

    *   Deployment time increases because of the complexity of maintaining packages.

4. Manual installation of applications. This is the old-school method—using tools such as scp and rsync to deploy applications and settings. It can be a very linear process; other drawbacks are as follows:

- It is nearly impossible to scale.

- Consistency not guaranteed across nodes.

Each of the four methods mentioned have been around for many years in the industry. None of them have met the needs of an enterprise, and all have been plagued with issues. Configuration management resolves many of these issues.

What Is Configuration Management?

Configuration management is a broad term, that relates to products and software. In the information technology/operations world, configuration management can imply OS configuration, application management and deployment, and product management.

Configuration management can be defined as the process that maintains consistency across the design, development, deployment and maintainance of a product.

Software configuration management can be divided into six core functional areas:

1. *Source code management*: related to source code; how to manage different versions, access, life cycle; and so on

2. *Build engineering*: related to building of source code, how to integrate different branches to produce a build that can be tested and deployed, and so on

3. *Environment configuration*: related to compile and runtime dependencies, how best to integrate different dependencies in the environment, and so on

4. *Change control*: related to managing changes in the code, who is allowed to do them, how often they happen, and so on

5. *Release engineering*: related to packaging the build and making it ready for deployment

6. *Deployment*: related to deploying the actual, released software and managing the steps involved in this process

The focus of this chapter is on OS configuration management, which includes

- Managing system configuration files on Linux, such as /etc/rsyslog.conf, /etc/sshd/ssh_config, and /etc/hosts

- Using configuration management for deploying applications, such as Apache web server or FTP server

- Managing users—for instance, in /etc/passwd

Configuration Management Requirements

Any given configuration management solution should have at least a few of the qualities outlined here:

- Policy enforcement

- Fast updates

- Security

- Encryption

- Merging of updates

- Rollback

- Dry run

- Reporting

- Rolling updates

- Modular

- Easy to use

An organization's information technology policies should be translated using the configuration management system (CMS) into rules that can then be applied to a system. For instance, if all systems are required to disable remote root login, then, using the CMS, you should be able to enforce this policy.

Updates should be "fast enough" on systems. If a user account needs to be removed from systems, it should be removed within a reasonably acceptable amount of time. The time period itself is dependent on the needs of the organization. Puppet, by default, runs every 30 minutes; however, you may prefer to change updates it to two hours or 15 minutes or some other interval based on how soon you want updates pushed out.

Security is essential because using a CMS can potentially affect all the servers in an organization. The CMS should not provide any information to clients who do not need the information. Any application configuration should be stored securely so that it cannot be misused.

Communication between the client and server should be encrypted. Any communication between the various components of the CMS should be encrypted if it traverses the network. If public/private key encryption is being used, private keys should be stored securely.

Local changes on clients should be allowed, per policy, with the ability to merge these changes with the master. Some CMSs can be prescriptive and may overwrite local changes; this feature may be warranted. At the same time, however, there must be a way to incorporate local changes without policy violation.

Rollback is a crucial component of CMS. An unwarranted change can wreak havoc on an organization's system. Rollback implies being able to go back to a previous version of configuration. For instance, if the CMS stores all configuration in Git, you should be able to go back to a previous revision of the configuration stored in Git.

Dry run enables you to stage changes in the environment. If a secure shell (SSH) setting is being changed, a dry-run option should let you know which file is being changed and the contents being changed, without actually making the change.

Reporting can help you with asset discovery and asset reconciling. It can also be used for software inventory. If a bug is discovered in a version of Apache, using CMS reporting you can figure out how many systems have the affected version of Apache. You can then stage the changes needed to secure Apache and roll them out using the CMSs.

Rolling updates allows you to make changes incrementally. If an organization has 10,000 nodes, it's not prudent to make a change on all 10,000 at the same time. Rolling updates allows you to make changes on a smaller subset. If the update works, you can then roll it out to a larger subset until all clients have been reached.

Modularity implies the system is not monolithic. Monolithic systems can be difficult to upgrade. Also, if a monolithic system crashes, then all components of the CMS may crash. Modular systems allow plug-and-play technologies and hence make it easier to manage and update. For instance, if a CMS uses message-queuing technology, then being able to use more than one type of message-queuing software might help in performance improvement. Some of the options may include ActiveMQ, ZeroMQ, and RabbitMQ.

A CMS that is easy to use is an often-overlooked issue. CMSs can be very complex, so it's important that the implementation be simple enough to reduce barriers to learning. Some CMSs use YAML for storing configuration, whereas others might use some other markup language. Puppet uses its own declarative scripting language for storing configuration information. Administration must also be easy; if there are a lot of moving parts, then it's difficult to manage the CMS.

CMS Options

A few popular CMSs are

- Puppet (`http://puppetlabs.com/`)

- Chef (`http://www.getchef.com/chef/`)

- CFEngine (`http://cfengine.com/`)

- SaltStack (`http://www.saltstack.com/`)

- Bcfg2 (`http://bcfg2.org/`)

- Ansible (`http://www.ansible.com/home`)

Which solution to pick should be based on some of the factors outlined in the prevision section.

CFEngine is written in C. CFEngine has been around the longest. It was first released in 1993. CFEngine is available under GPLv3 and commercial open source license. Bcfg2 was released initially in 2004. It is written in Python and is available under the Berkeley Software Distribution (BSD) license. Puppet is written in Ruby, and includes an open source version as well as a commercial solution. Puppet is available under Apache license from v2.7.0 onward, and under GNU General Public License (GPL) before that version. Puppet was released initially in 2005. Chef is written in Ruby and Erlang, and is licensed under Apache. Chef was released in 2009. SaltStack is written in Python and is available under the Apache license. Salt is new to the field compared with some of the other options, 2011 is the first year that Salt was released. Ansible was released initially in 2012. It is written in Python and is available under the GPL license. .

When picking a CMS system, some things to keep in mind are the following:

- If you have a strong preference for a particular programming language, then stick with the CMS written in that language. You may find it easier to extend the CMS and to resolve any bugs in it.

- The license under which the various CMSs are offered *does* matter. GPLv3 is different than Apache, which is different than BSD. Your organization might have a policy on which open source licenses are allowed in the company, so make sure you check with your legal department.

- Commercial versions of some CMSs are identical to the open source versions, whereas for others the commercial version has more features. For instance, with Puppet, the Puppet Console, the Web user interface, is available only with the Enterprise commercial version.

- SaltStack uses YAML for its configuration language; however, Puppet uses its own. This might be a consideration as well if you have a strong preference for a particular configuration language. Configuration language is different than the language in which the program is written.

Commercial Versus Open Source

Puppet has an enterprise version that costs money, and a free version. A few differences between them are outlined in Table 5-1.

Table 5-1. *Puppet Enterprise Versus Open Source*

Feature	Open source	Enterprise
Puppet Console graphical user interface	No	Yes
Puppet–supported modules	No	Yes
Role-based access control	No	Yes
Commercial technical support	No	Yes
VMware provisioning	No	Yes
Configuration management, user accounts	Yes	Yes
Amazon, Google Compute Engine (GCE) provisioning	Yes	Yes

The choice of which version to go with can be confusing. My recommendation is to download the open source version and try it out. If you have difficulties, then refer to the documentation and the user community. Beyond that, if you still need help, then you may be a suitable candidate for the Enterprise version. Based on the list price of Puppet, a 1000-node deployment with standard support can cost $93,000 annually for Puppet Enterprise. This is the list price and discounts may be available. Additional details can be found at `http://puppetlabs.com/puppet/enterprise-vs-open-source` for the differences between the two. For updated pricing, refer to `http://puppetlabs.com/puppet/how-to-buy`.

Understanding Puppet

Puppet is based on client–server model. Figure 5-1 gives an overview of the communication between the client and the server. In step 1, the client contacts the server. This communication uses encryption. The client provides "facts" about itself to the server. The server then looks in its configuration repository—Git, for instance—for rules to apply to the client. It compiles these rules in a catalog and, in step 3, sends them to the client. The client applies the catalog and, in step 4, reports back to the server.

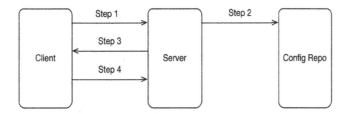

Figure 5-1. *Puppet communication between client and server*

Puppet Facts

Puppet facts are information pieces about the server on which it is running. The Puppet client using the Puppet `facter` command collects Puppet system details before sending them to the server. A sample of Puppet facts is shown in Listing 5-1.

Listing 5-1. Puppet Facts

```
# facter
architecture => x86_64
augeasversion => 1.0.0
boardmanufacturer => Dell Inc.
boardproductname => XXXX
domain => example.com
facterversion => 1.6.18
fqdn => web.example.com
hardwareisa => x86_64
hardwaremodel => x86_64
hostname => web
id => root
interfaces => em1,lo
ipaddress => X.X.X.X
ipaddress_lo => 127.0.0.1
is_virtual => false
kernel => Linux
kernelmajversion => 2.6
kernelrelease => 2.6.32-431.17.1.el6.x86_64
kernelversion => 2.6.32
macaddress => XX:XX:XX:XX:51:DF
macaddress_em1 => XX:XX:XX:XX:51:DF
...[SNIP]...
swapsize => 7.81 GB
timezone => PDT
type => Main Server Chassis
uptime => 31 days
uptime_days => 31
uptime_hours => 764
uptime_seconds => 2752287
virtual => physical
```

Puppet facts are extremely useful in writing Puppet code. They can be referenced in Puppet code as top-scope variables, which means outside any class definition, type definition, or node definition. In other words, Puppet facts are global variables. A sample fact reference is shown in Listing 5-2.

Listing 5-2. Puppet Fact in Code

```
if $hostname == 'web' {
        #some code here
}
```

You can also write your own custom facts. Facts are snippets of Ruby code that are distributed from the master to the clients. Custom facts that are needed by a module can be stored in <MODULEPATH>/<MODULE>/facts.d/ when using pluginsync. Another way to store facts is in the environment variable FACTERLIB, which refers to a path. Last, you can use the Ruby $LOAD_PATH variable in which to store facts. On most systems, it is /usr/lib/ruby/site_ruby/<version>/facter.

Facts have two parts to them: their name and the code. Facter.add('fact_name') is the way to set the name. Next follows the code, which is specified as setcode. Facts normally return a single string; however, they can also return a hash or an array. These are called *structured facts*. You don't have to do anything special for a structured fact.

■ **Note**   Structured facts are not enabled by default and are only supported in Puppet 3.3 and greater.

To enable structured facts, in a master/client setup, the `stringify_facts` variable must be set to `false` in `puppet.conf`. This should be set in both the master and agent `puppet.conf` file. On the master, it can be in the `[master]` section or in the `[main]` section. On the slave, it can be in the `[main]` or `[agent]` section.

Two custom facts are shown in Listing 5-3. In the first case we are adding a custom fact called `perlpath`. The path returns the location of Perl on the system. In the second case we are returning an array that contains network interfaces.

Listing 5-3. Custom Fact

```
#Case 1
Facter.add(:perlpath) do
  setcode do
    'which perl'
  end
end

#Case 2
Facter.add(:int_array) do
  setcode do
    interfaces = Facter.value(:interfaces)
    int_array = interfaces.split(',')
    int_array
  end
end
```

Puppet Catalog

The Puppet server has to compile a catalog and send it back to the client after the client has contacted the Puppet master. Building the catalog is a four-step process:

1. Retrieve the node object

2. Set variables from the node object, from facts, and from the certificate

3. Evaluate the main manifest

4. Evaluate classes from the node object

So, exactly what does the Puppet agent provide to the server? The Puppet agent provides:

- Its hostname, which is almost always the certname—for instance, `/production/catalog/www.example.com`

- The agent certificate

- Agent facts

- The environment requested, which is embedded in the request URL (`production` is default)

After these data have been provided, it is up to the master to create a catalog. The catalog is a set of instructions for the client to execute. For instance, a catalog might ask the Puppet client to install Apache and configure it in a particular way.

Additional resources on facts and catalogs are available from the following sources:

- List of core Puppet facts (`https://docs.puppetlabs.com/facter/latest/core_facts.html`)

- Writing your own custom facts
  (`https://docs.puppetlabs.com/facter/latest/custom_facts.html`)

- Write structured facts

  (`https://docs.puppetlabs.com/facter/latest/fact_overview.html#writing-structured-facts`)

- Understanding Puppet catalog

  (`https://docs.puppetlabs.com/puppet/latest/reference/subsystem_catalog_compilation.html`)

Puppet Resources

Puppet resources are the building blocks of Puppet. A resource is defined as single entity that can be managed using Puppet. For instance, a user is a resource. Some other single resources are

- A user account, such as `ftp`

- A network service, such as `sshd`

- A software package, such as `httpd`

- A directory, such as `/home/ftp`

- A file, such as `/home/ftp/.ssh/authorized_keys`

Each resource is of a specific type; for instance, the user `ftp` is a resource of type `user`. The software package `httpd` is of type `package`. Resources also have attributes. Attributes are specific to resource type. A user resource might have an attribute called `uid`, and a file resource may have an attribute called `mode`. There are also some common attributes across resource types; one would be the `namevar` attribute, which specifies the name of the resource. When adding user `admin`, the namevar is `admin`.

A few common resources are shown in Listing 5-4.

RESOURCE TYPES LISTING 5-4

In this example, we add a user called admin; the resource type is user. The user type has many attributes, which we are defining. One attribute is ensure, the values for which can be {present, absent, role}. present indicates the user should be present on the system—in other words, add the user if missing. absent ensure means remove the user if present on the system. The uid, gid, shell, and home attributes are self-explanatory. managehome is an attribute that tells Puppet to create the user's home directory, because Puppet does not do this by default.

```
user { "admin":
    ensure      => present,
    uid         => '2000',
    gid         => '100',
    shell       => '/bin/bash',
    home        => '/home/admin',
    managehome => true,
}
```

cron is another resource type that can be managed. In this example, we are managing the resource logrotate—the namevar is logrotate.

```
cron { logrotate:
    command => "/usr/sbin/logrotate",
    user => root,
    hour => 1,
    minute => 0
}
```

For installing a package, we use the package resource type.

```
package { 'openssh-server':
    ensure => installed,
}
```

Installing a custom /etc/ssh/sshd_config file using the file resource is shown next. We can use the notify attribute to notify the ssh service after we install the file. This action causes the ssh service to be restarted. For the source of the file, we are specifying the Puppet file store.

```
file { '/etc/ssh/sshd_config':
    source  => 'puppet:///modules/sshd/sshd_config',
    owner   => 'root',
    group   => 'root',
    mode    => '640',
    notify  => Service['sshd'], # sshd will restart whenever we edit this file.
    require => Package['openssh-server'],
}
```

If we need to ensure that a service is running when the system starts, we use the `service` attribute.

```
service { 'sshd':
    ensure => running,
    enable => true,
    hasstatus => true,
    hasrestart => true,
}
```

The format of a resource *does* matter. It can be broken down into

- Type—in the case of service, it is `type` service

- An open curly brace

- The title of the type—in this case, it is `sshd`

- A colon

- A set of attributes, with a key value pair in the format of `=>`, with the attributes separated by a comma

- An end curly brace

Not all attributes of a resource are required; some values can be left out, in which case Puppet picks default values. For instance, when creating a file resource, if you omit the mode, Puppet, by default, picks the mode 0644. When creating a directory resource, if you omit the mode, Puppet picks the default mode 0755.

The resource abstraction layer is responsible for implementing resources on the different OSs; it consists of the resource types and providers. Providers are platform specific—in other words, OS specific. When adding a user, CentOS might use `useradd`, but Debian might use `adduser`. As a Puppet maintainer, you do not have to concern yourself with the actual syntax the underlying platform uses. In Puppet, you specify the user as a resource, and Puppet handles the rest.

Additional reading resources include

- A cheat sheet that shows the most common resources and their use (`https://docs.puppetlabs.com/puppet_core_types_cheatsheet.pdf`)

- Understanding the resource abstraction layer (`https://docs.puppetlabs.com/learning/ral.html`)

- Viewing all the available resource types (`https://docs.puppetlabs.com/references/latest/type.html`)

Puppet Manifests

Puppet instructions or programs are called *manifests*. Manifests are generally stored in files with the `.pp` extension. We learned about resources earlier and manifests are actions with resources. Listing 5-5 shows a manifest that can be used to add a file to a system with Puppet. When a manifest contains a resource, we say the resource is being declared.

Listing 5-5. A Puppet Manifest

```
#this file is called manifest.pp
file { "motd":
        path    => '/etc/motd',
        ensure  => present,
        mode    => 0640,
        content => 'Authorized users only!',
}
```

Manifests can be applied, as in using the command puppet apply <manifest-name> individually, or they can be part of the Puppet manifest directory. The directory is, by default, /etc/puppet/manifest. Listing 5-6 shows the application of a Puppet manifest that changes /etc/motd, based on the Listing 5-5.

Listing 5-6. Puppet Manifest Application

```
## First, check the contents of /etc/motd
# cat /etc/motd
This is an initial motd

## Create a Puppet manifest that changes /etc/motd
# cat /etc/puppet/manifests/motd.pp
file { 'motd':
        path    => '/etc/motd',
        ensure  => present,
        mode    => 0640,
        content => 'Authorized users only!',
}

## Run Puppet in local mode, using the 'apply' Puppet command
# puppet apply /etc/puppet/manifests/motd.pp
notice: /Stage[main]//File[motd]/content: content changed
'{md5}dd41045e84f18dea33427f8d1e0d21ec' to
'{md5}ab98686fda944143765f6efbcb59c105'
notice: Finished catalog run in 0.04 seconds

## New changes are reflected in /etc/motd
# cat /etc/motd
Authorized users only!
```

■ **Note** A Puppet manifest is very particular about colons and commas. If you miss any of them, you get syntax errors similar to Could not parse for environment production: Syntax error at 'ensure'; expected '}' at /etc/puppet/manifests/motd.pp:3 on node web.example.com'.

The contents of a Puppet manifest can be conditional statements, variables, functions, and other forms of logic as well. A conditional statement that sets /etc/motd based on the OSs is shown in Listing 5-7.

Listing 5-7. A conditional statement

```
## Using the 'facter' command view the value of 'osfamily'
# facter osfamily
RedHat


## Conditional manifest using the facter 'osfamily' to change '/etc/motd'
# cat /etc/puppet/manifests/motd.pp
if $osfamily == 'RedHat' {
        file { 'motd':
                path    => '/etc/motd',
                ensure  => present,
                mode    => 0640,
                content => 'RedHat users only!',
        }
}


## Check the syntax using the 'parser' functionality of Puppet
# puppet parser validate /etc/puppet/manifests/motd.pp


## Check the /etc/motd before making a change
# cat /etc/motd
This is an initial motd


## Apply the manifest using the 'apply' function
# cat /etc/motd
Authorized users only!# puppet apply /etc/puppet/manifests/motd.pp
notice: /Stage[main]//File[motd]/content: content changed '{md5}ab98686fda944143765f6efbcb59c105' to
'{md5}5f87968e2b5271c3622cd12b271bb7a3'
notice: Finished catalog run in 0.05 seconds


## Check the motd after applying Puppet changes, and it shows 'RedHat' users only
# cat /etc/motd
RedHat users only!
```

Relationships in Puppet Manifests

There are four different metaparameters that define the relationship between resources in Puppet:

1. require

2. before

3. subscribe

4. notify

■ **Note**   The order of resources in a manifest does not determine the order of execution. Puppet builds a dependency graph based on the resources, which then determines the order of execution.

In Listing 5-8, each of the metaparameters is explained further. require means the referenced resource must be applied before the resource that requires it. For instance, with SSH, we need the openssh package to be present before the service is started, so we require the package.

Listing 5-8. Resource Metaparameters

```
## REQUIRE
package { 'openssh':
  ensure    => present,
}

service { 'sshd':
  ensure    => running,
  enable    => true,
  require   => Package['openssh'],
}

## BEFORE
package { 'openssh':
  ensure    => present,
  before    => Service['sshd'],
}

service { 'sshd':
  ensure    => running,
  enable    => true,
}

## SUBSCRIBE
file  { '/etc/sshd/sshd_config':
  ensure    => present,
  source    => 'puppet:///modules/ssh/sshd_config',
}

service { 'sshd':
  ensure    => running,
  enable    => true,
  subscribe => File['/etc/ssh/sshd_config'],
}

## NOTIFY
file  { '/etc/sshd/sshd_config':
  ensure    => present,
  source    => 'puppet:///modules/ssh/sshd_config',
  notify    => Service['sshd'],
}

service { 'sshd':
  ensure    => running,
  enable    => true,
}
```

before ensures the resource is applied before the referenced resourced. In the sample code snippet, we are saying that before the service sshd is started, we have to install the openssh package. In this case, there are two ways of ensuring openssh package is present before attempting to start the service. One way is to use the require metaparameter; the other is to use the before metaparameter. You can use either of these options to get the job done. No method is better than the other; it's your preference.

subscribe and notify have similar relationships as require and before. notify sends a notification to the resource requested if a change occurs in the resource. For instance, when the sshd_config file changes, we ask Puppet to notify the sshd service so it can be restarted. Another way of handling this is to tell the sshd service to subscribe to the sshd_config file, so that when we notice any changes to it, we restart the service.

To summarize, if a resource such as sshd is dependent on another resource, such as /etc/sshd/sshd_config file, then in the definition of sshd you can use the metaparameter subscribe so that any time there is a change in the config file, sshd is made aware of the change. Or, in the definition of the sshd_config file, you could use the metaparameter notify, so that each time sshd_config is change, it informs the sshd service.

Similarly, if a service such as sshd requires a package such as OpenSSH, then you can use the metaparameter require in the sshd definition or you can use the metaparameter before in the OpenSSH configuration file definition.

Additional reading resources that might be helpful include:

- Puppet manifest documentation

  (https://docs.puppetlabs.com/learning/manifests.html)

- Relationships and ordering in Puppet

  (https://docs.puppetlabs.com/puppet/latest/reference/lang_relationships.html)

Puppet Modules

Modules are directories that contain configuration information. Modules have predefined structures. An example module is openssh, which not only installs OpenSSH on a client, but also configures it. Modules can be shared easily with others. Numerous modules are available on Puppet Forge (https://forge.puppetlabs.com/). Before creating your own module, check to see if an existing module works for you. An important issue with modules is being able to trust them, because they can be written by anyone. There are certain modules that are in the Puppet Labs name space; perhaps those may be more trustworthy than other modules.

Modules allow autoloading of classes, file serving for templates and files, and autodelivery of custom Puppet extensions. The location of modules is specified in the Puppet configuration file:

```
[master]
modulepath = /etc/puppet/modules
```

Puppet modules use classes. A Puppet class is a collection of code that references some resources. Classes have to be defined and then declared. Defining a class is done using the term class. To declare the class, you use the term include. Without declaring a class, you are not using it. An example of defining a class and using it follows:

```
#define a class called ssh
class ssh {
    package {  'openssh-clients':
        ensure  =>  present,
    }
}
```

```
#declare the ssh class, which causes it to be invoked
node 'www.example.com' {
  include ssh
}
```

The default storage location of a module is /etc/puppet/modules. Modules are directory trees. If we were to create a module for myapp (Listing 5-9), then in /etc/puppet/modules, you would expect to find a directory called myapp. Under that directory would be five other directories: manifests, templates, files, tests, and facts.d. In each of these directories are files relating to the specific module component. The init.pp file is where it all begins, because it contains the module class. Templates are in the templates directory for any configuration you may have. The files directory stores any files the module might install, and they are accessible with the path puppet:///modules/myapp/index.html. tests also contains init.pp and is used by Puppet to test the module if you so wish. If you have any custom facts that this app shares, they would be stored in facts.d directory.

Listing 5-9. myapp Module Directory Structure

```
- myapp
  - manifests
    - init.pp
  - templates
    - app.erb
  - files
    - index.html
  - tests
    - init.pp
  - facts.d
    - myapp.rb
```

You can read more about modules at

- https://docs.puppetlabs.com/guides/module_guides/bgtm.html

- https://docs.puppetlabs.com/pe/latest/quick_writing_nix.html

- https://docs.puppetlabs.com/puppet/3.6/reference/modules_fundamentals.html

Hiera

Hiera is a key-value data store that is external to Puppet but can be called from Puppet. The advantage of using Hiera is that you can separate code from data. This feature makes it a lot easier to read code and reuse code. To understand Hiera more completely, let's take a look at code with Hiera and without Hiera.

```
class ntp {
  if ( $::environment == 'development' ) {
    $ntpserver = '10.1.1.100'
  } else {
    $ntpserver = '10.1.2.100'
  }

class { 'ntp::client':
    server => $ntpserver,
}
```

We have two different NTP servers: 10.1.1.100 and 10.1.2.100. Based on the environment, we want to assign the appropriate NTP server. If the number of sites or environments increases, the `if..else` statement has to accommodate each of them by adding more `..else` statements.

Using Hiera, we can simplify the code to look like this:

```
class { 'ntp::client':
    server => hiera('ntpserver','us.pool.ntp.org')
}
```

In Hiera, you can then place the different NTP servers, and Puppet will pick based on the appropriate value. You can read more about Hiera at `https://docs.puppetlabs.com/hiera/1/puppet.html`.

Puppet Style Guide

The Puppet style guide is a list of best practices when writing Puppet code. There are more than a dozen recommended guidelines, and I list some of them here. The rest are available for your reading pleasure at the sites mentioned at the end of this section. Writing Puppet code may occur in manifests or when designing modules.

Commonality

Any large enterprise will have hundreds if not thousands of lines of Puppet code. Going through the code may be a routine job for a Puppet administrator, which brings us to our first principle: Make Puppet code as easy to read as possible. Don't assume that complex code is a sign of your Puppet skills. I try to write Puppet code in a way that a beginner Puppet practitioner is able to understand.

Although inheritance can be helpful, when possible try to avoid a deep nested inheritance that makes it difficult to trace. Within a module itself, inheritance is fine; however, if you try to inherit from another module, this makes things more complicated. A way around this is to parameterize classes.

```
#good case of inheritence
class database { ... }
class database::mysql  inherits database { ... }
class database::oracle inherits database { ... }

#bad case of inheritence
class database inherits server { ... }
class mysql inherits nagios { ... }
class oracle inherits linuxlvm { ... }
```

Using external node classifiers (ENCs) is OK, but don't require your module to have an ENC. An ENC is an external script or application that tells Puppet which classes a node is supposed to have. ENCs do not have to be written in Ruby.

Classes should not declare other classes they need; instead, allow class dependency to fail if the needed class is not present. The reason for this is as that you want classes declared as close as possible to the node scope.

Module Metadata

Every module should have metadata associated with it. Metadata are generally stored in the `metadata.json` file. Some of the items to include in metadata are as follows:

```
name 'my-ssh-module'
version '1.0'
author 'Your-Name'
summary 'SSH module for CentOS'
description 'This module enables you to manage SSH on CentOS v6.x and above'
license 'Apace 2.0'
project_page 'http://www.example.com'
dependency 'name-of-other-modules'
```

General Formatting

Proper formatting of Puppet code can make it very easy to read if done appropriately. Some recommendations are as follows:

- Use two-space soft tabs; do not use literal tab characters.

- Do not use trailing white space and do not exceed the 80-character line width.

- Align fat comma arrows (=>) within blocks of code.

- Comments should use #, not // or /*.

- Strings should use single quotes unless specifying variables. For variable interpolation, use double quotes. On the other hand, variables that stand on their own do not need quoting.

- The ensure attribute should be listed first for a resource if required.

- Group logical pieces of code together, rather than type of code

```
## Good code
# This is a comment using a single #
# Using double quotes for interpolation
# Also using braces for interpolation
" /etc/security/${file}.conf"
"${::sshmodule} requires ${another_module}"
# Proper spacing
user admin {
  ensure  => present,
  uid     => 2000,
}

## Bad code
// Trying a comment
" /etc/security/$file.conf"
"$::sshmodule requires $another_module"
# Improper spacing
  user admin {
      uid=>2000,
      ensure=>present,
}
```

Additional reading:

- Puppet style guide (`https://docs.puppetlabs.com/guides/style_guide.html`)

- External node classifiers (`https://docs.puppetlabs.com/guides/external_nodes.html`)

Puppet Config Files

The main configuration file for Puppet is `puppet.conf`. This file's usual location is `/etc/puppet`. The file consists of at least three sections: main, master, and agent.

The main section applies to both master and clients. The master section is only needed on the Puppet master, and the agent section is only needed on the Puppet client. A very basic `puppet.conf` can look like:

```
$ sudo cat /etc/puppet/puppet.conf
[main]
  server = puppet.example.com
  report = true
  pluginsync = true
  certname = puppet.example.com
  logdir = /var/log/pe-puppet
  rundir = /var/run/pe-puppet
  modulepath = /etc/puppet/modules

[master]
  dns_alt_names = puppet,puppet.example.com

[agent]
```

Many of the options in the file are self-explanatory. The server value should point to the Puppet server name. `report = true` lets the client know to report its status to the Puppet master. `pluginsync` asks the master to distribute custom facts to the clients. You can read more about it at `https://docs.puppetlabs.com/guides/plugins_in_modules.html`. `logdir` and `rundir` define where Puppet sends its log and where Puppet runs from. `modulepath` defines the location of all modules.

In the master section, the `dns_alt_names` parameter specifies the alternate domain name server names for the server. In our case it's just `puppet` and `puppet.example.com`.

The agent section is blank because we don't have any specific items to identify here. Some of the items of the agent are already in the `[main]` section.

Reporting

By default, Puppet client reports to the Puppet master. This information can be stored in various ways. PuppetDB (`https://docs.puppetlabs.com/puppetdb/latest/`) is one way you can store reporting information. Additional options include both open source tools and also commercial software.

PuppetDB can store the following information:

- The most recent facts from every node

- The most recent catalog for every node

- Optionally, 14 days (configurable) of event reports for every node

Puppet Enterprise Console is available with the Enterprise edition of Puppet (`https://docs.puppetlabs.com/pe/latest/console_accessing.html`). Puppet Console is easy to use and has a lot of features that make it a possible option. The caveat with Puppet Console is its cost; the list price for Enterprise is quite high.

Foreman is a very popular Puppet reporting open source tool (`http://theforeman.org/`). Foreman is more than just a reporting tool, however; it is a full provisioning ecosystem. Some of the features of Foreman as listed on its web site are

- Discover, provision, and upgrade your entire bare-metal infrastructure

- Create and manage instances across private and public clouds

- Group your hosts and manage them in bulk, regardless of location

- Review historical changes for auditing or troubleshooting

- Extend as needed via a robust plug-in architecture

- Build images (on each platform) automatically per system definition to optimize deployment

Puppetboard (`https://github.com/nedap/puppetboard`) is primarily a web interface to PuppetDB.

Puppet Dashboard has been around for a while as well, although it does not have an install base as large as Foreman. You can find out more about it at `https://github.com/sodabrew/puppet-dashboard`.

Additional reading about reporting is available at `http://puppetlabs.com/blog/when-puppet-reports-part-1`.

Certificate Management

Puppet master and client communicate securely using encryption. This encryption is done with the help of certificates. Both the master and client have a certificate. When a client contacts the master, it presents its certificate request to the master. As a Puppet administrator, you have two options. One option is to set up autosigning, in which case the master automatically accepts the client certificate request. The other option is a more manual process, in which you, as a Puppet administrator, have to sign the client certificate. For safety, manual signatures might be OK; however, some enterprises chose to enable autosigning for the sake of convenience.

The Puppet server is normally the Certificate Authority (CA) server as well. For additional security you can create another CA server and get Puppet to use that instead of having the CA server on the same server as the Puppet server.

You do not need to purchase certificates for Puppet because Puppet generates its own, and does not require a public key infrastructure that it can use.

To list the client certificates from the Puppet server, run the following:

```
# puppet cert list --all
+ "puppet.example.com"  (SHA256) 84:68:8B:32:BE:F8:CA:1D:09:80:E7:38:5D:36:EE:46:9A:DC:...
+ "www.example.com"     (SHA256) AA:A2:7A:EE:1B:FA:80:65:2C:97:DD:EB:5B:E1:FD:60:AA:DD:...
+ "mysql.example.com"   (SHA256) 06:B4:C4:8B:C2:7E:97:27:03:57:FF:55:69:C1:2F:1D:7A:FC:...
```

If you want to enable autosigning of certificate requests by the server, then in /etc/puppet/autosign.conf, type in the either the individual hostnames for which you want autosigning enabled, or the wildcard for the domain:

```
# cat /etc/puppe/autosign.conf
*.example.com
```

If you have autosigning disabled, then after you install each Puppet client, on the server you must sign the certificate request of the client manually:

```
# puppet cert sign web.example.com
notice: Signed certificate request for web.example.com
notice: Removing file Puppet::SSL::CertificateRequest agent1.localdomain at '/etc/puppet/ssl/ca/
requests/web.example.com'
```

■ Note Time has to be synchronized between the server and client for Puppet to work, because certificate-based authentication and encryption are time sensitive. Make sure you have NTP installed and enabled on both master and client.

Additional reading is available at

- `http://projects.puppetlabs.com/projects/1/wiki/certificates_and_security`
- `https://docs.puppetlabs.com/references/3.5.1/man/cert.html`

Puppet Hardware Requirements

Puppet client is very lightweight and can be installed on most systems. Puppet server, on the other hand, is heavyweight and has restrictions on the hardware on which it can run effectively. The minimum requirement as of this writing is a dual-core processor with 1GB RAM. Realistically, this will not be enough if you have more than a hundred nodes. For instance, if you have 1000 nodes, you should get at least a quad-core processor with minimum of 8GB RAM. This number might be different for you, depending on the following factors:

- How often clients check in
- The complexity of your manifests
- How many modules you have installed
- The number of resources being managed by Puppet

A single Puppet master cannot serve an enterprise with thousands of nodes effectively. You should plan on having multiple Puppet masters per few thousand clients. For instance, if you have two sites, California and Texas, and 5000 Puppet clients at each site, with 1000 resources being managed, including users, files, services, software packages, and all other Puppet resources, you might want to consider a minimum of six Puppet servers, three at each site. The three at a given site should be behind a load balancer, and each of them should have at least a single quad-core processor with 32GB RAM. This is just an example to show how you can provision hardware for Puppet; actual number and hardware varies based on the sites, Puppet clients. and resources being managed. For further information on system requirements for Puppet, refer to `https://docs.puppetlabs.com/puppet/latest/reference/system_requirements.html`.

Puppet Software Requirements

Two kinds of software are available for Puppet: one is the official package repository and the other is if a third party has provided packages for a particular distribution. If you are using popular Linux distributions, you are better off using the Puppet package repository because the code there is tested and supported by Puppet. You can view the availability of the official Puppet packages at https://docs.puppetlabs.com/guides/puppetlabs_package_repositories.html.

Puppet Open Source supports the following OSs as of this writing:

- RedHat 5, 6, 7, and compatible OSs, such as CentOS and Oracle Linux

- Debian and Ubuntu 6, 7, 10.04, 12.04, and 14.04

- Fedora 19 and 20

- Suse Linux Enterprise Server, 11 and higher

- Gentoo Linux

- Mandriva Corporate Server 4

- ArchLinux

- FreeBSD 4.7 and higher

- OpenBSD 4.1 and higher

Puppet also requires Ruby; your Ruby version might determine the compatibility of Puppet. The version of Ruby chosen has an impact on compatibility and performance. The newer versions of Puppet run faster on later versions of Ruby. Table 5-2 includes a Ruby compatibility chart.

Table 5-2. *Puppet Enterprise Versus Open Source*

Ruby version	Puppet 2.7	Puppet 3.x
2.1.x	No	3.5 and higher supported
2.0.x	No	3.2 and higher supported
1.9.3 (p392)	No	Supported
1.9.2	No	No
1.9.1	No	No
1.8.7	Yes	Yes

Additional information about software requirements for Puppet can be found at https://docs.puppetlabs.com/guides/platforms.html.

Installing Puppet

Puppet installation can be done in at least the following different ways:

- Most Linux distributions include Puppet in their repositories. For CentOS, if you install the EPEL repositories, you can download Puppet.

- Puppet Labs maintains its own YUM repositories, which can also be used to download Puppet (https://docs.puppetlabs.com/guides/puppetlabs_package_repositories.html).

- You can download source code for Puppet and compile it (https://github.com/puppetlabs)

- Puppet provides binaries that can be downloaded and installed.

- Amazon Machine Image includes Puppet.

Using EPEL

Enable the EPEL repositories for CentOS 6. I include the Remi repository here because it's useful to have:

```
$ wget http://dl.fedoraproject.org/pub/epel/6/x86_64/epel-release-6-8.noarch.rpm
$ wget http://rpms.famillecollet.com/enterprise/remi-release-6.rpm
$ sudo rpm -Uvh remi-release-6*.rpm epel-release-6*.rpm
```

Ensure that the repositories have been installed:

```
$ ls -1 /etc/yum.repos.d/epel* /etc/yum.repos.d/remi.repo
/etc/yum.repos.d/epel.repo
/etc/yum.repos.d/epel-testing.repo
/etc/yum.repos.d/remi.repo
```

Edit the Remi repository configuration file:

```
$ sudo vim /etc/yum.repos.d/remi.repo
```

Change the enabled value from zero to one for Remi:

```
name=Les RPM de remi pour Enterprise Linux $releasever - $basearch
#baseurl=http://rpms.famillecollet.com/enterprise/$releasever/remi/$basearch/
mirrorlist=http://rpms.famillecollet.com/enterprise/$releasever/remi/mirror
enabled=1
gpgcheck=1
gpgkey=file:///etc/pki/rpm-gpg/RPM-GPG-KEY-remi
failovermethod=priority
```

Using Puppet Labs Repository

Install the Puppet Labs repository for CentOS 6. If you need it for another OS, refer to https://yum.puppetlabs.com/:

```
$ sudo rpm –Uvh https://yum.puppetlabs.com/puppetlabs-release-el-6.noarch.rpm
```

Using YUM

After the repositories are installed, you can now install the server and client portion:

```
$ sudo yum install puppet puppet-server facter -y
```

If you want to install the client on another host:

```
$ sudo yum install puppet faceter -y
```

Installing via rubygems

Another way is to use Ruby to install Puppet:

```
# yum install rubygems -y
# gem install puppet facter
```

Modular Architecture

A typical enterprise has thousands of nodes, and having an optimized Puppet configuration is crucial for a successful deployment of Puppet. The speed at which Puppet catalogs can be compiled and applied to clients determines how fast you can push changes out and how often. For instance, if it takes one minute to apply a Puppet configuration on a server if manifests are structured in one way, versus 30 seconds in another way, then the organization should evaluate its manifests. An optimized Puppet run speed depends on how you lay out your manifest structure and the number of resources managed.

One possible way of architecting Puppet is to break down Puppet manifests into smaller components. Puppet execution starts in the file site.pp. In site.pp you can classify nodes based on type, using hostnames for example. Listing 5-10 shows an entry in site.pp for Git servers. The hostname is in the format git01.example.com. In this example we instruct Puppet that, if the facter provided by the client shows the client name to be in this format, move execution to the module called role and, in the module, look at git.pp file.

Listing 5-10. site.pp file

```
# Git server
node /^git\d+\.example\.com$/ {
  include ::role::git
}
```

The directory tree structure for the role module is shown in Listing 5-11.

Listing 5-11. Directory tree structure for modular architecture

```
tree /etc/puppet/modules/
├── role
│   ├── manifests
│   │   ├── git.pp
│   │   ├── mysql.pp
│   │   ├── apache.pp
...[SNIP]...
```

```
# tree /etc/puppet/manifests/
/etc/puppet/manifests/
└── site.pp
```

The workflow of Puppet in this modular architecture is shown in Figure 5-2, starting from site.pp and ending with the mysql module, in this case.

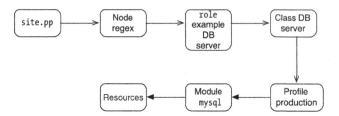

Figure 5-2. *Puppet Enterprise architecture*

In addition to dividing up the manifests using roles and profiles, designing a modular architecture entails having numerous Puppet masters in front of a load balancer for failover, as seen in Figure 5-3.

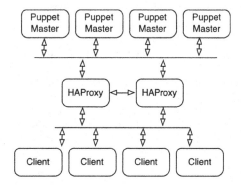

Figure 5-3. *Fault-tolerant Puppet*

HAProxy (http://www.haproxy.org/) is an open source load balancer that can be used for Puppet fault tolerance. Alternatives are not use to HAProxy and instead use nginx (http://nginx.org/) or Apache, as shown in Figure 5-4.

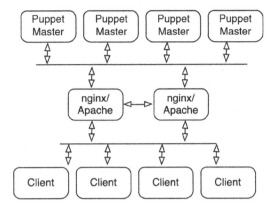

Figure 5-4. *Puppet high availability using nginx/Apache*

■ **Caution**   Puppet Open Source comes with a basic Ruby's WEBrick library web server. This will not work for more than ten clients. You should replace it with Apache Passenger.

For a cross-site modular architecture—between, say, California (CA) and Texas (TX), simply replicate the pod architecture as seen in Figure 5-5.

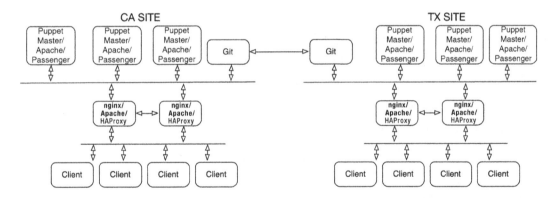

Figure 5-5. *Cross-site Puppet modular architecture*

If you want to use caching on the load balancer, use nginx. HAProxy and Apache are not suitable as caching solutions for Puppet 3.x.

Additional resources include:

- Apache/Passenger with Puppet (`https://docs.puppetlabs.com/guides/passenger.html`)

- Role- and profile-based deployment (`http://www.craigdunn.org/2012/05/239/`)

- Scaling Puppet (`https://docs.puppetlabs.com/guides/scaling.html`)

- Multiple Puppet masters (`https://docs.puppetlabs.com/guides/scaling_multiple_masters.html`)

- Passenger (`https://github.com/phusion/passenger`)

Putting It All Together

Resources, manifests, classes, dependencies, and a lot of other terminology can make Puppet confusing. This section simplifies the process of putting it all together by providing a step-by-step guide on where to get started.

Step 1: Install Puppet master on a server.

Step 2: Install Puppet client on the same server.

Step 3: Create a `site.pp` file in `/etc/puppet/manifests`.

Step 4: In the `site.pp` file, have a single resource, such as adding a user.

Step 5: Modify the `/etc/puppet/puppet.conf` file and set up the master/agent.

Step 6: Run `puppet agent -tv`.

Step 7: Approve the client certificate on the server.

Step 8: Install a single module in `/etc/puppet/modules`.

Step 9: Use the module to add another manifest in `/etc/puppet/manifests`.

Step 10: Use roles to create different groupings in manifests.

Step 11: Use roles to create actual roles in the `role` module.

Step 12: Create a `profile` module.

Step 13: Define a profile to be used in `role`.

Step 14: Test again with `puppet agent -tv`.

Step 15: If things work out OK, then you can start adding more Puppet clients and adding more manifests.

There are numerous troubleshooting steps outlined in Chapter 10 with regard to Puppet. Refer to them if you get stuck with an error.

Where to Get Help

Puppet has been around for many years; the knowledge base for Puppet is extensive. Some available options for support include the following:

- *Pro Puppet* published by Apress is an excellent guide on Puppet
  (`http://www.apress.com/9781430260400`)

- The Puppet Users Google Group (`https://groups.google.com/forum/#!forum/puppet-users`)

- The Puppet IRC channel (`https://webchat.freenode.net/?channels=puppet`)

- Puppet Enterprise customer support (`http://puppetlabs.com/services/customer-support`)

- Puppet Q&A (`http://ask.puppetlabs.com/questions/`)

- Puppet documentation (`https://docs.puppetlabs.com/`)

- Puppet Open Source home page (`http://puppetlabs.com/puppet/puppet-open-source`)

- Puppet FAQ (`https://docs.puppetlabs.com/guides/faq.html`)

Conclusion

Puppet is very powerful configuration management software. Using it can make your life a lot easier if you manage more than a dozen systems. The end user community is very active in Puppet. Every year there is PuppetConf, which hosts training and other sessions of interest. After you start using Puppet and become comfortable with it, you should look into contributing to the Puppet community. Writing modules is an easy way to give back to the community.

With the advent of the cloud infrastructure, you can use Puppet to deploy to Amazon, Google Cloud, Rackspace, and perhaps other cloud providers as well. From provisioning to management, Puppet can be your friend.

CHAPTER 6

■ ■ ■

Apache for Enterprise-Level Fault Tolerance

Web services are the foundation of applications hosted on the Internet. This chapter covers the Apache HTTP Server, which is run on a majority of Internet web sites. The Apache Software Foundation (ASF) is discussed briefly, followed by an in-depth analysis of HTTP and then of Apache HTTP. The HTTP load balancer HAProxy is studied, and a brief summary of the failover software Keepalived is provided.

Apache Software Foundation

The ASF consists of more than 150 open source projects. These projects range in categories such as database, HTTP, mail, big data, build management, and many more. Some of their more popular projects include the following:

- Apache Hadoop (`https://hadoop.apache.org/`)

- Apache CouchDB (`https://couchdb.apache.org/`)

- Apache HTTP Server (`https://httpd.apache.org/`)

- Apache Traffic Server (`https://trafficserver.apache.org/`)

- Apache Tomcat (`https://tomcat.apache.org/`)

You can view the Apache projects page at `https://projects.apache.org/` for a complete listing of all Apache projects. An enterprise that believes in open source software can benefit greatly from Apache projects. When building a Linux infrastructure, using ASF supported software can do the following for you:

- Reduce the cost of doing business

- Give you access to high-quality software

- Keep your organization plugged in to the open source software movement

Consider donating to the ASF if you use their software. ASF is volunteer run and its infrastructure needs our financial support for them to provide the framework under which open source free software flourishes.

Additional resources can be found at

- ASF web site (`https://www.apache.org/`)

- Listing of ASF projects (`https://projects.apache.org/`)

- Donate to ASF (`https://www.apache.org/foundation/contributing.html`)

Understanding HTTP

HTTP is a transactional TCP-based protocol. There are at least three different methods of HTTP communication between a client and a server:

1. *Traditional method*: With this method the client opens a connection, sends a single request, receives a response, and then closes the connection.

    ```
    Open->Request1<-Response1<-Close
    Open->Request2<-Response2<-Close
    ```

2. *Keep-alive*:- A single connection is opened, content length is decided between the server and the client, and, for the duration of the content length, the connection is open with sequential requests and responses.

    ```
    Open->Request1<-Response1->Request2<-Response2<-Close
    ```

3. *Pipelining*: The connection is opened between the client and the server, and numerous requests are sent at the same time. Not all HTTP servers support this method, because it requires the HTTP server to keep track of request order and response order.

    ```
    Open->Request1->Request2<-Response1<-Response2<-Close
    ```

Apache HTTP Server supports all three methods. Keep-alive is enabled by default, and if a browser uses pipelining, then Apache supports it. Figure 6-1 shows the difference between request and response with and without pipelining (https://en.wikipedia.org/wiki/HTTP_pipelining#mediaviewer/File:HTTP_pipelining2.svg).

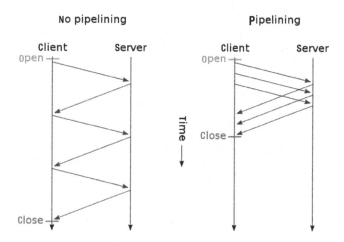

Figure 6-1. *HTTP with and without pipelining*

HTTP Headers

HTTP headers are part of request and response in an HTTP conversation. Listing 6-1 shows some common headers. Headers are in both a request and a response. Lines that you see beginning with > are part of the request header; lines that begin with < are part of the response header. Many of the headers are self-explanatory. For instance, the User-Agent header is part of the request, and it specifies the software that is connecting to the web server. In this case, because the Linux curl command is being used, the User-Agent is curl/7.37.1.

Similarly, the response header contains items that are mostly obvious to understand. For example, Date lists the date. Another example is the HTTP version, which is 1.1, followed by the response code, 200. There is also a cookie that Google is returning with Set-Cookie:. You can read more about HTTP headers at http://www.w3.org/Protocols/rfc2616/rfc2616-sec14.html.

Listing 6-1. HTTP Headers

```
$ curl -s -I -v www.google.com | egrep '^>|^<'
* Rebuilt URL to: www.google.com/
* Hostname was NOT found in DNS cache
*   Trying 74.125.239.147...
* Connected to www.google.com (74.125.239.147) port 80 (#0)
> HEAD / HTTP/1.1
> User-Agent: curl/7.37.1
> Host: www.google.com
> Accept: */*
>
< HTTP/1.1 200 OK
< Date: Mon, 17 Nov 2014 05:25:20 GMT
< Expires: -1
< Cache-Control: private, max-age=0
< Content-Type: text/html; charset=ISO-8859-1
< Set-Cookie: PREF=ID=0bc84cc1a616136e:FF=0:TM=1416201920:LM=1416201920:S=ayPF-9wOyv5Qgxx4;
  expires=Wed, 16-Nov-2016 05:25:20 GMT; path=/; domain=.google.com
< Set-Cookie: NID=67=ezWHuu1mNYXg2I_JleI3Mwuirzt8ETbv8RZiyfqMp3sMkBNFJMdbgSFPmCk36QUmFvYwC46bOLEyCbJ
  uzvpjBsQwuASOw4JHxkA3y-f35D3uGTW83S4hI1AcbiHARi1-; expires=Tue, 19-May-2015 05:25:20 GMT; path=/;
  domain=.google.com; HttpOnly
< P3P: CP="This is not a P3P policy! See http://www.google.com/support/accounts/bin/answer.
  py?hl=en&answer=151657 for more info."
* Server gws is not blacklisted
< Server: gws
< X-XSS-Protection: 1; mode=block
< X-Frame-Options: SAMEORIGIN
< Alternate-Protocol: 80:quic,p=0.01
< Transfer-Encoding: chunked
<
* Connection #0 to host www.google.com left intact
```

HTTP Method

HTTP methods are included in HTTP headers and provide a way for the client to request information from the server. There are eight HTTP methods:

1. HEAD: Used for validating links, verifying accessibility, and checking for any recent modifications.

2. GET: Used to get information from the server; contains a message body when the server responds.

3. POST: Used to upload data to a web server.

4. PUT: Similar to POST, with the difference being PUT identifies the resource that handles the data, and it should be applied only to that resource.

5. CONNECT: Used for proxy that can switch dynamically to a tunnel.

6. DELETE: Use to request that the identified resource be deleted.

7. OPTIONS: Used to request communication options from the server by the client.

8. TRACE: Used for diagnostics and testing.

Additional information about HTTP methods can be found at http://www.w3.org/Protocols/rfc2616/rfc2616-sec9.html.

HTTP Response

HTTP response is similar to HTTP request (made with the HTTP method). A sample response is shown in Listing 6-2.

Listing 6-2. HTTP Response

```
$ curl -IL  http://172.16.127.212
HTTP/1.1 200 OK
Date: Wed, 12 Nov 2014 06:53:03 GMT
Server: Apache/2.4.10 (Unix)
Last-Modified: Mon, 11 Jun 2007 18:53:14 GMT
ETag: "2d-432a5e4a73a80"
Accept-Ranges: bytes
Content-Length: 45
Content-Type: text/html
```

The anatomy of a HTTP response line is as follows:

- A version tag: HTTP/1.1

- A status code: 200

- A reason: OK

The status code is always three digits and is of the following types:

- 1xx: informational message (100, 101)

- 2xx: OK, content is following (200, 206)

- 3xx: OK, no content is following (302, 304)

- 4xx: error caused by client (401, 403, 404)

- 5xx: error caused by server (500, 502, 503)

Role of Apache HTTP Server

This chapter is mostly about the Apache HTTP Server Project found at https://httpd.apache.org/. Commonly known as Apache or HTTPD, it is the most widely used web server on the Internet (http://news.netcraft.com/archives/2014/02/03/february-2014-web-server-survey.html). Throughout this chapter, when I say Apache, I am referring to Apache HTTP Server.

Apache 1.0 was released in December 1995 and, as of this writing, is at version 2.4. This chapter covers version 2.4. Besides the most obvious use of a web server, Apache can help with other applications as well, such as forward proxy, reverse proxy, caching server, and more.

Installing Apache HTTP Server

As with most other open source software, you can install Apache using the yum repository on CentOS/RedHat or you can download the source code, compile, and install it. If installed using yum, the configuration files are in /etc/httpd. If you compile Apache, the default destination is /usr/local/apache2. Listing 6-3 shows how to install Apache HTTP Server.

Listing 6-3. Installing Apache HTTP Server

First, install the yum development tools group so that you have a compiler and make tools.

```
# yum groupinstall 'Development Tools'
```

Next, install APR, which is Apache Portable Runtime Project. For Apache 2.4.10, you need APR 1.5.X.

```
# cd /usr/local/src
# wget http://www.eng.lsu.edu/mirrors/apache//apr/apr-1.5.1.tar.gz
# tar xvfz apr-1.5.1.tar.gz
# cd apr-1.5.1
# ./configure
# make
# make test
# make install
```

You also need APR-Util, which is part of APR.

```
# cd /usr/local/src
# wget http://apache.spinellicreations.com//apr/apr-util-1.5.4.tar.gz
# tar xvfz apr-util-1.5.4.tar.gz
# cd apr-util-1.5.4
# ./configure --with-apr=/usr/local/apr/
# make
# make test
# make install
```

In addition, you need the Perl-compatible regular expression library, or PCRE.

```
# cd /usr/local/src
# wget http://sourceforge.net/projects/pcre/files/pcre/8.36/pcre-8.36.tar.gz/download -O pcre-8.36.
tar.gz
# tar xvfz pcre-8.36.tar.gz
# cd pcre-8.36
# ./configure
# make
# make test
# make install
```

Last, you compile and install Apache.

```
# wget http://mirror.nexcess.net/apache//httpd/httpd-2.4.10.tar.gz
# tar xvf httpd-2.4.10.tar.gz
# cd httpd-2.4.10
# ./configure --with-pcre=/usr/local/bin/pcre-config
# make
# make install
```

Start Apache using apachectl.

```
# /usr/local/apache2/bin/apachectl -k start
```

Use curl to access the web server. In this case, it's 172.16.127.212. If you see "It works!," your web server is ready!

```
$ curl http://172.16.127.212
<html><body><h1>It works!</h1></body></html>
```

Configuring Apache HTTP Server

Apache is configured via numerous text-based configuration files. Because we compiled Apache and installed it in a default location, the configuration directory is /usr/local/apach2/conf and the configuration file itself is /usr/local/apach2/conf/httpd.conf. If you are using the version of Apache installed using yum, then the location of the configuration directory is /etc/httpd/conf and the file for configuration is /etc/httpd/conf/httpd.conf.

Best practices include adding any additional configuration settings for Apache HTTP in individual configuration files for an application that you install. These application-specific HTTP configuration files should be in /etc/httpd/conf.d for the yum-installed version; for your compiled version, the default location is /usr/local/apache2/conf/extra. You can change the location of this using the httpd.conf directive Include conf.d/*.conf or by adding Include extra/*.conf. Any files placed in the conf.d or the extra directory and ending with the *.conf extension are read as Apache configuration files and are merged with the httpd.conf configuration file.

There are numerous configuration options available in Apache HTTP. A few of them are explained in this section.

> ServerRoot: Specifies the location of Apache configuration files. For yum-installed Apache it is /etc/httpd. Because I compiled Apache HTTP and installed it in the default location, it is /usr/local/apache2.

> Listen: Specifies on which port Apache should listen.

> DocumentRoot: Lists the path in which Apache looks to serve files. If you request http://www.example.com/help.html, then help.html has to be a file in the DocumentRoot directory.

> VirtualHost: Settings specific to a virtual host.

You don't necessarily have to modify the default settings of Apache; it works out of the box. Simply start writing to DocumentRoot, and Apache serves those files. The tweaks that need to occur are in relation to the multiprocessing module, which is explained in the next section.

A sample httpd.conf can be viewed at https://github.com/syedaali/configs/blob/master/http-vanilla.conf. For more information, refer to https://httpd.apache.org/docs/2.4/configuring.html.

Apache Multiprocessing Modules

Apache HTTP Server is compiled with support for multiprocessing modules (MPMs). There are three kinds of MPMs:

1. *Worker*: Worker uses multiple child processes with many threads each, one connection per thread. For sites that have a lot of connections per Apache server, worker is a good choice because it can handle a lot of connections with a low memory footprint.

2. *Event*: Similar to worker MPM, but Event can handle more simultaneous requests than worker because it passes off some processing work to supporting threads, freeing up the main thread to accept more connections. When compiling, the Apache HTTP event MPM is picked by default if the system supports threads.

3. *Prefork*: Prefork uses multiple child processes with one thread each. It consumes more memory than event or worker, because one process per connection is required. It is, however, easier to debug on systems that have poor thread debugging support. Prefork can also be used with non-thread safe modules.

You can figure out which MPM Apache is using with the command curl -s http://<server-name>/server-info | html2text | egrep '^\s+MPM Name:'. If the server-info module is not loaded, then follow the instructions in the next section to turn it on so that you can query the loaded module in real time. Another way of finding out with which modules Apache was compiled is to run the command /usr/local/apache2/bin/httpd -l. The -l option does not list the dynamically loaded modules, just the ones with which Apache was compiled. Listing 6-4 shows a sample output of getting MPM information.

Listing 6-4. Apache MPM Information

```
## Figure out which MPM is currently loaded in running Apache HTTP instance
# curl -s  http://localhost/server-info | html2text | egrep '^\s+MPM Name:'
  MPM Name: event

## View the static modules Apache was compiled with; in our case, the event module is static
# /usr/local/apache2/bin/httpd  -l
Compiled in modules:
  core.c
  mod_so.c
  http_core.c
  event.c

## List static AND shared modules
# /usr/local/apache2/bin/httpd  -M
Loaded Modules:
 core_module (static)
 so_module (static)
 http_module (static)
 mpm_event_module (static)
...[SNIP]...
```

If Apache HTTP was compiled only with one MPM and you want to change the MPM, then you have to recompile Apache HTTP. To make Apache load MPM as a dynamic shared object, or DSO, when running the configure command, as shown earlier in the chapter, add the --enable-mpms-shared=all option, as shown in Listing 6-5.

Listing 6-5. Compiling Apache with MPM as a DSO

```
## Compiling Apache with MPM as a DSO
# ./configure --enable-mpms-shared=all --with-pcre=/usr/local/bin/pcre-config --with-apr=/usr/local/
apr
# make
# make install

## Verifying after installation that there is no static MPM loaded
# /usr/local/apache2/bin/httpd -l
Compiled in modules:
  core.c
  mod_so.c
  http_core.c

## If we attempt to start Apache HTTP without configuring a DSO MPM, we get an error
# /usr/local/apache2/bin/apachectl start
AH00534: httpd: Configuration error: No MPM loaded.

## Uncomment the httpd-mpm line in /usr/local/apache2/conf/httpd.conf file
Include conf/extra/httpd-mpm.conf

## Add the mpm module line in /usr/local/apache2/conf/httpd.conf file
LoadModule mpm_event_module modules/mod_mpm_event.so
```

You can switch between the event, prefork, and worker modules with the single LoadModule line. Listing 6-6 shows how to switch between the modules. The file that is being modified is /usr/local/apache2/conf/httpd.conf.

Listing 6-6. Switching between MPM

```
## Worker
LoadModule mpm_worker_module modules/mod_mpm_worker.so

## Prefork
LoadModule mpm_prefork_module modules/mod_mpm_prefork.so

## Event
LoadModule mpm_event_module modules/mod_mpm_event.so

## Verify running module
# curl -s  http://<server-name>/server-info | html2text | egrep '^\s+MPM Name:'
  MPM Name: prefork
```

Always restart Apache HTTP after changing the module, and verify the module is loaded with the command curl -s http://<server-name>/server-info | html2text | egrep '^\s+MPM Name:'.

■ **Note**   By default, Apache HTTP compiles a static multiprocessing event module if the system supports threads, and thread-safe polling—specifically, the kqueue and epoll functions.

Monitoring Apache HTTP Server

There are two configuration options that you should enable to get more information from Apache HTTP: The first one is server-status and the second one is server-info.

To enable server-status in the /usr/local/apache2/conf/httpd.conf file, uncomment the line Include conf/extra/httpd-info.conf. Edit the /usr/local/apach2/conf/extra/httpd-info.conf file and ensure the following:

1. The two server-status and server-info Location directives are uncommented, as seen in Listing 6-7.

2. Change the Require lines in the Location directive and add your domain as well as the network range. If you want, you can use only one of the directives: domain or network range. It is highly recommended in a production site to restrict access to server-info and server-status, because the information available can be used to exploit Apache.

3. Uncomment the ExtendedStatus On line and, last, restart Apache HTTP.

Listing 6-7. Apache HTTP server-info and server-status

```
# grep -iv '^#' conf/extra/httpd-info.conf
<Location /server-status>
    SetHandler server-status
    #Require host .example.com
    #Require ip 127
</Location>

ExtendedStatus On

<Location /server-info>
    SetHandler server-info
    #Require host .example.com
    #Require ip 127
</Location>

#/usr/local/apache2/bin/apachectl restart
```

After you have completed the tasks in Listing 6-7, you can access both the server-status and server-info URL with http://<server-name>/server-status or http://<server-name>/server-info. Both of these give you very useful information about Apache HTTP to help you monitor Apache HTTP. A sample of the information displayed is presented in Listing 6-8.

Listing 6-8. Apache HTTP Server Info

```
curl -s http://`hostname`/server-status | html2text
****** Apache Server Status for dlmgr002-ota.va3.svcmot.com ******
  Server Version: Apache/2.2.15 (Unix) DAV/2 mod_ssl/2.2.15 OpenSSL/1.0.0-fips
  Server Built: Aug 13 2013 17:29:28
===============================================================================
  Current Time: Sunday, 16-Nov-2014 21:35:24 UTC
  Restart Time: Sunday, 16-Nov-2014 03:11:01 UTC
  Parent Server Generation: 3
  Server uptime: 18 hours 24 minutes 22 seconds
  Total accesses: 87412 - Total Traffic: 87.3 GB
  CPU Usage: u837.98 s256.39 cu0 cs0 - 1.65% CPU load
  1.32 requests/sec - 1.3 MB/second - 1.0 MB/request
  27 requests currently being processed, 328 idle workers
```

Apache HTTP Benchmarking

After you have Apache HTTP Server installed and configured, you should benchmark it to determine whether it can perform under load. Benchmarking helps you accomplish the following:

- Figure out how many maximum connections a server can handle

- Identify any network issues that may reside server side

- Give you an idea of throughput for Apache HTTP

There are at least three programs that let you load-test Apache:

1. *HTTP ab*: A simple-to-use HTTP 1.0–based tool that can help do rapid load testing (`https://httpd.apache.org/docs/2.4/programs/ab.html`)

2. *Apache JMeter*: A more complex Java–based tool for comprehensive Apache HTTP Server benchmarking (`https://jmeter.apache.org/`)

3. *curl-loader*: C-based HTTP/HTTPS load-testing software (`http://curl-loader.sourceforge.net/`)

Listing 6-9 shows you how to use HTTP ab.

Listing 6-9. Using Apache ab

To use ab, install `httpd-tools` if it is not already installed. Then, let's make 20,000 connections to a web server, 200 at a time, and measure the response time.

```
# yum install httpd-tools
# ab  -n 20000 -c 200  http://web2/
Benchmarking web2 (be patient)
Completed 2000 requests
Completed 4000 requests
Completed 6000 requests
Completed 8000 requests
Completed 10000 requests
Completed 12000 requests
Completed 14000 requests
Completed 16000 requests
Completed 18000 requests
Completed 20000 requests
Finished 20000 requests


Server Software:        Apache/2.4.10
Server Hostname:        web2
Server Port:            80

Document Path:          /
Document Length:        45 bytes

Concurrency Level:      200
Time taken for tests:   9.499 seconds
Complete requests:      20000
Failed requests:        0
Write errors:           0
Total transferred:      5780000 bytes
HTML transferred:       900000 bytes
Requests per second:    2105.39 [#/sec] (mean)
Time per request:       94.994 [ms] (mean)
Time per request:       0.475 [ms] (mean, across all concurrent requests)
Transfer rate:          594.20 [Kbytes/sec] received
```

```
Connection Times (ms)
              min   mean[+/-sd] median    max
Connect:        0    20 170.3      0     6999
Processing:     0    68 128.8     61     6293
Waiting:        0    68 128.8     61     6292
Total:         42    88 221.7     62     7293
```

```
Percentage of the requests served within a certain time (ms)
  50%      62
  66%      62
  75%      63
  80%      63
  90%      64
  95%      66
  98%     277
  99%    1061
 100%    7293 (longest request)
```

Although there is a lot of data in the output of ab, some items of interest include the following:

- Time taken for tests is 9.499 sec

- Requests per second is 2105.39 #/sec (mean)

- The longest request took 7293 msec

- The transfer rate is 594.20Kbytes/sec

When we check the number of outgoing TCP connections using the ss command, we can see the client making 200 connections. Before ab was started there were 13 connections; while ab was running that number jumped to 213 connections.

```
# ss -s | grep TCP
TCP:   20 (estab 2, closed 7, orphaned 0, synrecv 0, timewait 6/0), ports 28
4        2
TCP      13        8         5
```

During the ab run, the number of connections jumped to 213.

```
# ss -s | grep TCP
TCP:  220 (estab 160, closed 7, orphaned 0, synrecv 0, timewait 6/0), ports 236
4        2
TCP      213      208        5
```

This test was run without using keep-alive. ab supports HTTP 1.0 with keep-alive. Using the -k option, we can make 20,000 connections, 200 at a time.

Tuning Apache HTTP

Out of the box, Apache HTTP performs well; however, you will find that you can get more out of Apache by tuning it. This section explains some of the options you can use to squeeze more performance out of Apache.

Hardware

Apache is constrained by the amount of physical RAM and the CPU processing power in a system. This is one case when bigger is better. The more CPU and RAM you have, the more Apache HTTP children you can fork or the more threads you can create to serve more connections. An Apache server should not be swapping out the process, because this greatly reduces performance. Calculate the amount of memory each child process takes and multiply that by the maximum number of Apache HTTP children allowed. The solution is the minimum amount of RAM needed just for Apache, not including other processes and the operating system.

Network throughput is also very important to the performance of Apache HTTP. If your HTTP server has multiple network interfaces, the network bandwidth capacity of Apache HTTP increases. For busy sites, 10GB network interfaces should be considered. Also, have redundant multiple network interfaces and bond them using Linux network interface controller (NIC) bonding to give you failover as well as increased capacity.

Software

Use the latest version of Apache to get more out of your HTTP process. In general, newer versions of Apache have performance improvements over the previous versions, or bug fixes that might add significant value to your current environment.

Modules

Apache HTTP provides a lot of modules, and many of them are loaded by default. You can get a listing of all modules loaded in the server by querying `server-info`, as seen in Listing 6-10.

Listing 6-10. Querying Apache for Loaded Modules

```
# curl -s http://localhost/server-info?list | html2text
****** Apache Server Information ******
  Server Module List
      core.c
      event.c
      http_core.c
      mod_access_compat.c
      mod_alias.c
      mod_auth_basic.c
      mod_authn_core.c
      mod_authn_file.c
      mod_authz_core.c
      mod_authz_groupfile.c
      mod_authz_host.c
      mod_authz_user.c
      mod_autoindex.c
      mod_dir.c
      mod_env.c
      mod_filter.c
```

```
mod_headers.c
mod_info.c
mod_log_config.c
mod_mime.c
mod_reqtimeout.c
mod_setenvif.c
mod_so.c
mod_status.c
mod_unixd.c
mod_version.c
================================================================================
```

Some of these modules may not be needed and should be removed. To figure out what a module does, read the documentation for the module at https://httpd.apache.org/docs/2.4/mod/. To disable a module in /usr/local/apache2/conf/httpd.conf, comment out the line that begins with LoadModule <modulename> for the module you want to disable and then restart Apache HTTP with the command /usr/local/apache2/bin/apachectl restart.

Modifying MPM Configuration

Apache HTTP default is configured to accept a certain number of client connections when installed with default settings. For the event-based MPM, you can comfortably increase the MaxRequestWorkers connection to fit within the amount of memory of your server. Listing 6-11 shows the default settings for event-based MPM. If you want to increase the number of concurrent connections Apache can handle for event-based MPM, increase the value of MaxRequestWorkers. Multiplying the value of ServerLimit with ThreadsPerChild derives the MaxRequestWorkers value. You should also increase the value of ServerLimit if you increase MaxRequestWorkers. ServerLimit defaults to 16; if you do not find it in the httpd-mpm.conf file, add it in for clarity.

Apache HTTP starts a single parent process, which then spawns the number of servers specified in StartServers. In Listing 6-11, this is one parent, followed by three processes. Each of these processes then spawn MinSpareThreads, which in this case is 75. In addition to MinSpareThreads, one more thread is spawned that is a listener thread for listening to connections and passing them to processing threads.

MaxSpareThreads is the upper limit of spare threads, after which Apache starts to kill threads to keep them under MaxSpareThreads. MaxConnectionsPerChild is the number of connections a child can serve, after which the child is killed and a new child is spawned. This might help if you have memory leaks in web applications. Setting this value to zero lets Apache know there is no need to kill a thread after a certain limit of connections served.

There is a limit in code of 20,000 for ServerLimit for the event and worker MPMs. For prefork, the limit is 200,000. If you want to go beyond this limit per server, you have to change the value of MAX_SERVER_LIMIT in the source code and recompile.

Listing 6-11. Event MPM Defaults

```
## From /usr/local/apache2/conf/extra/httpd-mpm.conf

# event MPM
# StartServers: initial number of server processes to start
# MinSpareThreads: minimum number of worker threads which are kept spare
# MaxSpareThreads: maximum number of worker threads which are kept spare
# ThreadsPerChild: constant number of worker threads in each server process
# MaxRequestWorkers: maximum number of worker threads
# MaxConnectionsPerChild: maximum number of connections a server process serves
# before terminating
```

```
<IfModule mpm_event_module>
    ServerLimit              16
    StartServers              3
    MinSpareThreads          75
    MaxSpareThreads         250
    ThreadsPerChild          25
    MaxRequestWorkers       400
    MaxConnectionsPerChild    0
</IfModule>
```

You can use the command pstree to look at the number of processes and threads Apache HTTP would create. When ServerLimit is 3, MinSpareThreads is 3, and you see output similar to that shown in Listing 6-12. You would have a parent process; the process ID in this example is 65427, which then spawns three children: 65428, 65429, and 65430. Each of the children have a listening thread and a minimum number of threads, three in this case. The reason there is one "extra" thread per process is to handle to incoming connections and pass them to "worker" threads.

Listing 6-12. pstree with the Event MPM

```
httpd(65427)-+-httpd(65428)-+-{httpd}(65486)
             |                |-{httpd}(65487)
             |                |-{httpd}(65488)
             |                |-{httpd}(65489)
             |-httpd(65429)-+-{httpd}(65460)
             |                |-{httpd}(65461)
             |                |-{httpd}(65462)
             |                |-{httpd}(65463)
             `-httpd(65430)-+-{httpd}(65434)
                             |-{httpd}(65435)
                             |-{httpd}(65436)
                             |-{httpd}(65437)
```

The worker MPM is very similar to the event-based MPM. As such, the settings seem similar. Listing 6-13 shows the defaults for the worker MPM.

Listing 6-13. Worker MPM Defaults

```
# worker MPM
# StartServers: initial number of server processes to start
# MinSpareThreads: minimum number of worker threads that are kept spare
# MaxSpareThreads: maximum number of worker threads that are kept spare
# ThreadsPerChild: constant number of worker threads in each server process
# MaxRequestWorkers: maximum number of worker threads
# MaxConnectionsPerChild: maximum number of connections a server process serves
# before terminating
```

```
<IfModule mpm_worker_module>
    ServerLimit             16
    StartServers             3
    MinSpareThreads         75
    MaxSpareThreads        250
    ThreadsPerChild         25
    MaxRequestWorkers      400
    MaxConnectionsPerChild   0
</IfModule>
```

The prefork MPM is a bit different than event and worker because it spawns processes and not threads. Instead of the default 75 threads for event and worker, prefork starts with a StartServers value of 5. MaxRequestWorkers is less than for event and worker MPMs and is listed at 250, compared with 400 for event and worker. Processes are more expensive than threads, and as such you need more resources to do the same task. Listing 6-14 shows the defaults for the prefork MPM.

Listing 6-14. Prefork MPM Defaults

```
# prefork MPM
# StartServers: number of server processes to start
# MinSpareServers: minimum number of server processes that are kept spare
# MaxSpareServers: maximum number of server processes that are kept spare
# MaxRequestWorkers: maximum number of server processes allowed to start
# MaxConnectionsPerChild: maximum number of connections a server process serves
# before terminating
<IfModule mpm_prefork_module>
    ServerLimit             16
    StartServers             5
    MinSpareServers          5
    MaxSpareServers         10
    MaxRequestWorkers      250
    MaxConnectionsPerChild   0
</IfModule>
```

Configuration

There are configuration options as well, they should be tuned to help speed up Apache HTTP. Some of these options are listed here:

- HostnameLookups Off is present. It reduces the name lookup queries that Apache has to perform, thereby making Apache faster.

- Avoid using Options SymLinksIfOwnerMatch, because since this results in two lstat calls for directories and files. Use FollowSymLinks to avoid the twice lstat penalty.

- Specify AllowOverride None To save Apache the trouble of checking the .htaccess file.

- Avoid content negotiation, and use specifics such as DirectoryIndex index.cgi index.pl index.html.

- Use mod_cache to speed up serving of pages.

- Verify that ExtendedStatus off is present.

There is additional information about performance tuning at `https://httpd.apache.org/docs/current/misc/perf-tuning.html`.

Enabling keep-alive

Enabling `keep-alive` reduces the time it takes clients to download content from your web server. `keep-alive` is on by default in Apache. The directive that controls it is `KeepAlive On`. Some advantages of using `keep-alive` are as follows:

- Less CPU/memory use on the server because of fewer connections

- Reduced network congestion because one TCP connection transfers more than one HTTP object

- Reduced latency in subsequent requests from client because they use the same TCP connection

- HTTP pipelining of requests

In the previous section on Apache benchmarking, you learned about using HTTP ab to do Apache benchmarking. By default, HTTP ab does not use `keep-alive`. Listing 6-15 runs the same test that was run in Listing 6-9, but with `keep-alive` enabled.

Listing 6-15. HTTP ab with `keep-alive` Enabled

The `-k` option tells ab to use `keep-alive`.
```
# ab -k  -n 20000 -c 200  http://web2/
...[SNIP]...

Benchmarking web2 (be patient)
Completed 2000 requests
Completed 4000 requests
Completed 6000 requests
Completed 8000 requests
Completed 10000 requests
Completed 12000 requests
Completed 14000 requests
Completed 16000 requests
Completed 18000 requests
Completed 20000 requests
Finished 20000 requests

Server Software:        Apache/2.4.10
Server Hostname:        web2
Server Port:            80

Document Path:          /
Document Length:        45 bytes
```

```
Concurrency Level:      200
Time taken for tests:   4.114 seconds
Complete requests:      20000
Failed requests:        502
   (Connect: 0, Receive: 0, Length: 502, Exceptions: 0)
Write errors:           0
Keep-Alive requests:    19498
Total transferred:      6337489 bytes
HTML transferred:       877410 bytes
Requests per second:    4861.57 [#/sec] (mean)
Time per request:       41.139 [ms] (mean)
Time per request:       0.206 [ms] (mean, across all concurrent requests)
Transfer rate:          1504.40 [Kbytes/sec] received

Connection Times (ms)
              min  mean[+/-sd] median   max
Connect:        0    1  18.8      0    1001
Processing:     0   39  85.6     11    1233
Waiting:        0   32  70.1     10    1233
Total:          0   40  88.4     11    1241

Percentage of the requests served within a certain time (ms)
   50%     11
   66%     15
   75%     19
   80%     57
   90%     96
   95%    145
   98%    345
   99%    478
  100%   1241 (longest request)
```

Comparing the output of ab when using keep-alive (as shown in Listing 6-15) versus when not using keep-alive (as shown in Listing 6-9), you should note the tremendous improvement in performance with keep-alive, as shown in Table 6-1.

Table 6-1. Comparing HTTP Response Time with keep-alive and without keep-alive

Metric	Without **keep-alive**	With **keep-alive**
Time taken for tests (sec)	9.499	4.114
Requests per seconds	2105.39	4861.57
Longest request (msec)	7293	1241
Transfer rate (KB/sec)	594.20	1504.4

For additional information, see

- https://httpd.apache.org/docs/2.4/misc/perf-tuning.html

- http://www.w3.org/Protocols/HTTP/Performance/Pipeline.html

- https://en.wikipedia.org/wiki/HTTP_persistent_connection

Apache Reverse Proxy

Reverse proxy mode is when Apache HTTP acts as a transparent proxy and the client is not aware the request is going through a proxy server. Reverse proxy is also known as *gateway mode*. Figure 6-2 shows an example of a reverse proxy.

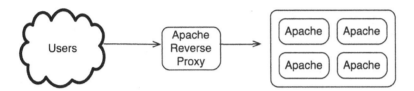

Figure 6-2. *Apache reverse proxy*

Reverse proxy is useful if you have real servers behind a firewall and you do not want to give direct access to them from the Internet. You can place an Apache HTTP reverse proxy in the demilitarized zone (DMZ) and then, through the proxy, provide access to the real servers.

To use reverse proxy mode, you have to use mod_proxy. This module provides basic proxy services. If you want to use a load-balancing feature as well, then you have to include mod_proxy_balancer.

Reverse proxy is activated using the ProxyPass directive of Apache. As an alternative, you can use the [P] flag with the RewriteRule directive.

Apache HTTP also allows you to use it as a load balancer with reverse proxy, similar to HAProxy, although HAProxy is more full featured and probably a better choice. You can put Apache HTTP Server in front of application web servers such as Jetty (http://www.eclipse.org/jetty/) and get better performance.

Let's review an example to understand reverse proxy more completely. Assume you manage a site such as www.example.com and you have a web server that hosts documentation for the site. The documentation server is called docs.example.com. When users visit www.example.com/help, you want to redirect them to docs.example.com. To do this, first you have to enable the mod_proxy.so and mod_proxy_http.so modules. Then you have to add the ProxyPass or the ProxyPassMatch directive in the Apache HTTP configuration file and restart Apache HTTP, as shown in Listing 6-16. ProxyPassReverseCookieDomain and ProxyPassReverseCookiePath are present to enable Apache HTTP Server cookie handling when doing reverse proxy.

Using reverse proxy is preferred over using rewrite rules, unless you have extensive rewrite rules that make more sense when using the rewrite module.

Listing 6-16. Apache HTTP Reverse Proxy

```
## On www.example.com, in /usr/local/apache2/conf/httpd.conf file, uncomment the lines:
LoadModule proxy_module modules/mod_proxy.so
LoadModule proxy_http_module modules/mod_proxy_http.so

## In /usr/local/apache2/conf/httpd.conf file, add a line such as:
Include conf/extra/httpd-proxy.conf

## Create a file called /usr/local/apache2/conf/extra/httpd-proxy.conf with contents:
ProxyPass /help http://docs.example.com/
ProxyPassReverse /help http://docs.example.com/
ProxyPassReverseCookieDomain docs.example.com www.example.com
ProxyPassReverseCookiePath / /help

## Instead of using ProxyPass, you can also use ProxyPassMatch. The difference between the two ## is
that ProxyPassMatch supports regular expressions and ProxyPass does not. You only need to ## use one
of them and not both.
ProxyPassMatch /help http://docs.example.com/
```

Additional documentation is available for the following:

- mod_proxy (https://httpd.apache.org/docs/2.4/mod/mod_proxy.html)

- mod_proxy_balancer (https://httpd.apache.org/docs/2.4/mod/mod_proxy_balancer.html)

- ProxyPass (https://httpd.apache.org/docs/2.4/mod/mod_proxy.html#proxypass)

- RewriteRule (https://httpd.apache.org/docs/2.4/mod/mod_rewrite.html#rewriterule)

Apache Forward Proxy

Forward proxy servers sit between a client and origin server. To access the origin server, the client sends a request to the forward proxy naming the origin server as the target. The proxy fetches the data from the origin server and gives it to the client. Forward proxies can be used to connect intranet users to the Internet, if you want to avoid direct Internet access from the intranet. Figure 6-3 shows an example of a forward proxy.

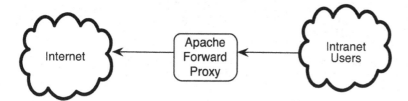

Figure 6-3. *Apache forward proxy*

Listing 6-17 shows how to set up a forward proxy. There are two directives that must be provides: `ProxyRequests` and `ProxyVia`. `ProxyVia` controls the `Via:` HTTP header. There are four options for this header: on, off, full, and block. For security purposes, it is recommended to restrict who can use the proxy server by using the `Require` directive. Without a restriction, anyone can use the proxy server.

The clients also have to configure proxy settings on their systems. If they are using the Firefox browser, then they have to go in the advanced networking setting in Firefox and add an HTTP proxy pointing to the Apache forward proxy.

Listing 6-17. Apache HTTP Forward Proxy

```
ProxyRequests On
ProxyVia On

<Proxy *>
  Require ip 10.0.0.0/255.0.0.0
</Proxy>
```

For additional documentation, refer to

- https://httpd.apache.org/docs/2.4/mod/mod_proxy.html

- https://httpd.apache.org/docs/2.4/mod/mod_proxy.html#proxyvia

- https://httpd.apache.org/docs/2.4/mod/mod_proxy.html#proxyrequests

Apache with Python

There are numerous options when it comes to using Python programs with Apache:

- A common gateway interface (CGI) is the oldest method of running Python with Apache. The Python library that enables CGI is `cgitb`. CGI is not the best way of running Python with Apache because each CGI request starts a new Python interpreter, making it slow for large load situations (https://docs.python.org/2/library/cgi.html).

- The `mod_python` module embeds the Python interpreter with Apache. Unlike CGI, a new Python interpreter is not started with each request. However, each Apache child process starts its own embedded Python interpreter. Programs written with `mod_python` are not portable to other web servers (http://modpython.org/).

- Two Apache modules, `mod_fastcgi` and `mod_fcgid`, try to overcome the limitations of `mod_python`. Instead of embedding the interpreter with Apache, they create a separate, long-running Python process. There is still a module in Apache that communicates with the long-running Python process (http://www.fastcgi.com/drupal/node/2 https://pypi.python.org/pypi/scgi).

- The module `mod_wsgi` (where WSGI stands for web server gateway interface) is used by Python frameworks to allow Python programs to run in web servers (https://code.google.com/p/modwsgi/).

- WSGI servers such as Gunicorn and Cherry are replacements for Apache, although you can put Apache in front of them (http://gunicorn.org/ and http://www.cherrypy.org/).

- Python Frameworks such as Django and Zope can be deployed with Apache when running Python (https://www.djangoproject.com/ http://www.zope.org/).

For additional information, see the following:

- Python web servers (https://docs.python.org/2/howto/webservers.html)

- PEP 333 for WSGI (http://legacy.python.org/dev/peps/pep-0333/)

HAProxy

HAProxy is an open source load balancer often used with Apache. A typical configuration of HAProxy with Apache HTTP is shown in Figure 6-4.

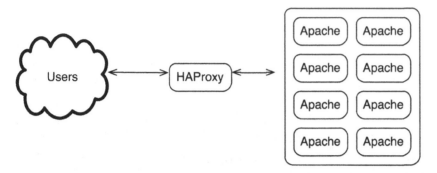

Figure 6-4. *HAProxy with Apache HTTP*

To install HAProxy, run sudo yum install haproxy. The configuration of HAProxy is stored in /etc/haproxy/haproxy.cfg.

HAProxy configuration can be done three ways: through command line parameters to HAProxy, through global section of the haproxy.cfg file, and through the proxy section of the same file. A sample configuration is shown in Listing 6-18.

Listing 6-18. haproxy.cfg Sample File

The global section defines options for the entire file. We are specifying that HAProxy use syslog to which to send logs, using the local2 facility. local2 should be configured in syslog.conf. We also specify that HAProxy should run as user haproxy and group haproxy in a chroot environment. The maxconn directive limits the number of connections to 4000; we can increase this as needed. Keep in mind that the ulimit should be increased to 2 × maxconn + nbproxies + nbservers + 1.

```
global
    log         127.0.0.1 local2
    chroot      /var/lib/haproxy
    pidfile     /var/run/haproxy.pid
    # use su haproxy --shell /bin/bash --command "ulimit -n" to get haproxy ulimit
    maxconn     4000
    user        haproxy
    group       haproxy
    daemon
    stats socket /var/lib/haproxy/stats
```

Default values apply to the proxy section, which consists of listen, frontend, backend, and defaults. Instead of repeating them in each proxy section, we can specify them once in the default section, and the listen, frontend, and backend sections inherit these values.

```
defaults
    mode                    http
    log                     global
    option                  httplog
    option                  dontlognull
    option http-server-close
    option forwardfor       except 127.0.0.0/8
    option                  redispatch
    retries                 3
    timeout http-request    10s
    timeout queue           1m
    timeout connect         10s
    timeout client          1m
    timeout server          1m
    timeout http-keep-alive 10s
    timeout check           10s
    maxconn                 3000

listen frontend
  bind *:80
  balance  roundrobin
  stats enable
  stats uri /haproxy?stats
  option  tcplog
  server web1 172.16.127.211:80  check
  server web2 172.16.127.212:80 check
```

You must have noticed that there are two maxconn statements. One is in the global section and the other is in the proxy section. The global value applies to all connections that HAProxy handles. The maxconn statement in the default section is for the proxy statement.

An alternative way of specifying real servers in the haproxy.cfg file is show in Listing 6-19. Instead of using one listen statement, we replace it with frontend and backend. The net effect is the same; however, using frontend and backend gives you the additional flexibility of doing layer 7 load balancing.

Listing 6-19. HAProxy with frontend and backend Configuration

```
frontend http-in
    bind *:80
    default_backend servers

backend servers
  balance  roundrobin
  stats enable
  stats uri /haproxy?stats
  server web1 172.16.127.211:80  check
  server web2 172.16.127.212:80 check
```

A sample HAProxy stats page is seen in Figure 6-5.

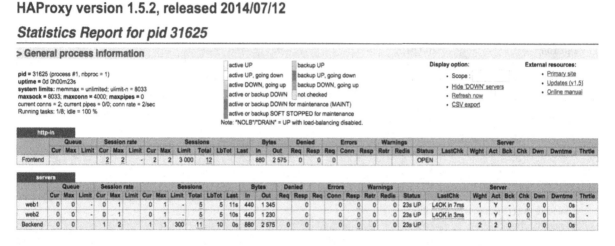

Figure 6-5. *HAProxy stats page*

■ **Note**   Before applying a configuration change, test it with sudo haproxy -f /etc/haproxy/haproxy.cfg -c. This test lets you know if there is a syntax error in your configuration file without restarting HAProxy.

Additional documentation is available at

- `http://www.haproxy.org/`
- `http://www.haproxy.org/download/1.5/doc/configuration.txt`

HAProxy Load-Balancing Algorithms

HAProxy supports numerous load-balancing algorithms, some of them include the following:

- `roundrobin`, with weights: Changing the weight of a server dynamically changes the connections to it. This is the default algorithm used if none is specified. A maximum of 4095 real servers are supported with `roundrobin`.

- `static-rr`: This algorithm is similar to `roundrobin`, except that changing the weight has no dynamic effect.

- `leastconn`: The server with the least number of connections is preferred for new connections.

- `first`: As the name implies, the first available server is used until `maxconn` is reached, then the next one is used.

- source: The source IP address is hashed and divided by the total weight of the running servers to designate which server receives the request (from the HAProxy docs).

- uri: This algorithm hashes either the left part of the uniform resource identifider (URI) (before the question mark) or the whole URI (if the whole parameter is present) and divides the hash value by the total weight of the running servers. The result designates which server receives the request (from the HAProxy docs).

There are other load-balancing algorithms that HAProxy supports, such as url_param, hdr, and rdp-cookie. Refer to the documentation of HAProxy for more information about them.

HAProxy Management

The easiest way to manage HAProxy is through the Unix socket that HAProxy provides. To enable it in /etc/haproxy/haproxy.cfg in the global section, add a line such as stats   socket /var/lib/haproxy/stats and restart HAProxy. Download and install socat with the command yum install socat. After installing socat you can use it to connect to the HAProxy management socket, as show in Listing 6-20.

Listing 6-20. Managing HAProxy through Sockets

```
$ grep -i socket /etc/haproxy/haproxy.cfg
  stats   socket /var/lib/haproxy/stats

$ sudo yum install socat -y

# echo "show info" | socat stdio /var/lib/haproxy/stats
Name: HAProxy
Version: 1.4.24
Release_date: 2013/06/17
Nbproc: 1
Process_num: 1
Pid: 21664
Uptime: 30d 16h17m41s
Uptime_sec: 2650661
Memmax_MB: 0
Ulimit-n: 8023
Maxsock: 8023
Maxconn: 4000
Maxpipes: 0
CurrConns: 11
PipesUsed: 0
PipesFree: 0
Tasks: 18
Run_queue: 1
node: haproxy.example.local
description:
```

Keepalived

Keepalived is a Linux–based router that supports the Virtual Router Redundancy Protocol (VRRP). It is often used in conjunction with HAProxy to provide redundancy, because HAProxy does not provide any redundancy on its own. Figure 6-6 shows a typical configuration of HAProxy and Keepalived.

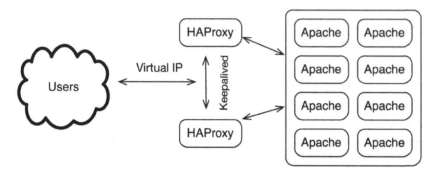

Figure 6-6. *HAProxy with Keepalived*

One of the HAProxy servers is a Keepalived master; the other is a Keepalived slave. Listing 6-21 shows a master/slave configuration.

Listing 6-21. Keepalived Master/Slave Configuration

Install Keepalived.

```
# yum install keepalived -y
```

/etc/keepalived/keepalived.conf has the following contents on the master:

```
global_defs {
   notification_email {
     admin@example.com
   }
   notification_email_from keepalived@example.com
   smtp_server 10.1.1.100
   smtp_connect_timeout 30
   router_id LVS_DEVEL
}

vrrp_script check_haproxy {
    script    "/sbin/service haproxy status"
    interval 2
    fall 2
    rise 2
}
```

```
vrrp_instance VI_1 {
    state MASTER
    interface eth0
    virtual_router_id 51
    priority 101
    advert_int 1
    authentication {
        auth_type PASS
        auth_pass 1111
    }
    virtual_ipaddress {
        10.1.1.30
    }
    track_script {
        check_haproxy
    }
}
```

/etc/keepalived/Keepalived.conf has the following contents on the backup server:

```
global_defs {
    notification_email {
      admin@example.com
    }
    notification_email_from keepalived@example.com
    smtp_server 10.1.1.100
    smtp_connect_timeout 30
    router_id LVS_DEVEL
}

vrrp_script check_haproxy {
    script    "/sbin/service haproxy status"
    interval 2
    fall 2
    rise 2
}

vrrp_instance VI_1 {
    state MASTER
    interface eth0
    virtual_router_id 51
    priority 101
    advert_int 1
    authentication {
        auth_type PASS
        auth_pass 1111
    }
```

```
    virtual_ipaddress {
        10.1.1.30
    }
    track_script {
        check_haproxy
    }
}
```

Additional documentation is available at

- http://www.keepalived.org/

- http://datatracker.ietf.org/wg/vrrp/documents/

Keepalived in Action

Listing 6-22 shows Keepalived in action. There are two HAProxy servers; one is called haproxy and is the master. The IP address of the master is 172.16.127.210. The other server is called haproxy1 and it has the IP address of 172.16.127.213; it is also the backup server. They both have HAProxy installed and configured. The Virtual IP address value is 172.16.127.214. When the master is online, it owns the virtual IP address. When we stop the haproxy service on the master, the backup server takes over the virtual IP address.

Listing 6-22. Keepalived in Action

Ensure the service haproxy is running.

```
# service haproxy status
haproxy (pid  2435) is running...
```

Check the IP address of the master Keepalived host. Its IP address is 172.16.127.210. The virtual floating IP address is 172.16.127.214.

```
# ip addr show | egrep '^\s+inet\s+'
    inet 127.0.0.1/8 scope host lo
    inet 172.16.127.210/24 brd 172.16.127.255 scope global eth0
    inet 172.16.127.214/32 scope global eth0
```

On the backup host, ensure the service haproxy is running.

```
# service haproxy status
haproxy (pid  2341) is running...
```

Check the IP address of the backup Keepalived host. We only see a single IP for the interface: 172.16.127.213.

```
# ip addr show | egrep '^\s+inet\s+'
    inet 127.0.0.1/8 scope host lo
    inet 172.16.127.213/24 brd 172.16.127.255 scope global eth1
```

On the master, we stop haproxy service.

```
# service haproxy stop
```

When we check /var/log/messages on the master, we see the virtual IP address being removed.

```
Nov 19 13:48:07 haproxy Keepalived_vrrp[2471]: VRRP_Script(check_haproxy) failed
Nov 19 13:48:07 haproxy Keepalived_vrrp[2471]: VRRP_Instance(VI_1) Entering FAULT STATE
Nov 19 13:48:07 haproxy Keepalived_vrrp[2471]: VRRP_Instance(VI_1) removing protocol VIPs.
Nov 19 13:48:07 haproxy Keepalived_vrrp[2471]: VRRP_Instance(VI_1) Now in FAULT state
Nov 19 13:48:07 haproxy Keepalived_healthcheckers[2470]: Netlink reflector reports IP 172.16.127.214
removed
```

On the backup, we check /var/log/messages and determine whether it is picking up the virtual IP address of 172.16.127.214.

```
Nov 19 13:48:07 haproxy Keepalived_vrrp[2366]: VRRP_Instance(VI_1) Transition to MASTER STATE
Nov 19 13:48:08 haproxy Keepalived_vrrp[2366]: VRRP_Instance(VI_1) Entering MASTER STATE
Nov 19 13:48:08 haproxy Keepalived_vrrp[2366]: VRRP_Instance(VI_1) setting protocol VIPs.
Nov 19 13:48:08 haproxy Keepalived_vrrp[2366]: VRRP_Instance(VI_1) Sending gratuitous ARPs on eth1
for 172.16.127.214
Nov 19 13:48:08 haproxy Keepalived_healthcheckers[2365]: Netlink reflector reports IP 172.16.127.214
added
```

On the backup host, when we check the IP address, we notice the floating IP address of 172.16.127.214 now belongs to the backup.

```
# ip addr show | egrep '^\s+inet\s+'
    inet 127.0.0.1/8 scope host lo
    inet 172.16.127.213/24 brd 172.16.127.255 scope global eth1
    inet 172.16.127.214/32 scope global eth1
```

Getting Help

Apache has been around for many years, and documentation on it is easy to find. Listed here are some ways of getting additional help:

- Apache documentation (https://httpd.apache.org/docs/current/)

- Books on Apache (http://www.amazon.com/Apache-Books/lm/2P2M3GSM1NKR8)

- Apache mailing list (https://httpd.apache.org/lists.html)

- IRC (#httpd channel on irc.freenode.net)

Conclusion

In this chapter I gave a brief introduction to the ASF and also explained the HTTP protocol. After that we looked at how to install Apache and configure it, and how to enhance Apache performance. Last, we examined HAProxy and Keepalived. Using these tools, you can build a fault-tolerant enterprise infrastructure. The load-balancing, proxy, failover, caching, and serving functions help you build a redundant infrastructure that increases uptime.

CHAPTER 7

■ ■ ■

Monitoring with Nagios and Trend Analysis with Cacti

Monitoring is perhaps one of the most important pieces of infrastructure management. When systems go down, monitoring should alert the site reliability engineers (SREs) so they can investigate the service affected and try to bring the system back online. After that, a root cause analysis should be conducted and actions should be taken to prevent similar issues in the future. Ideally, monitoring will alert about issues before they cause a service outage.

Trend analysis is being able to view historical and current metrics on a given application or a system. Trend analysis can help in troubleshooting and capacity planning. Looking at memory use over a period of a week or more helps to profile applications and plan for future upgrades and performance enhancements.

This chapter is about what to monitor and how to monitor in infrastructure using open source software—specifically, *Nagios*. It also covers trend analysis using another open source software called *Cacti*.

What to Monitor

What to monitor is a perpetual question that operation teams ask. To help arrive at a decision about what to monitor, consider some of these issues:

- Critically of the application

- The service-level agreement

- Resources needed to monitor

Production applications, those that generate revenue, should be monitored to the extent that is needed to ensure maximum uptime. If an application has a service-level agreement, then monitoring should help in maintaining the agreement. In addition, keep in mind the resources needed to monitor your infrastructure, because having alerts pop up all over the place but not having enough engineers to respond causes pager fatigue in engineers.

System Monitors

With regard to Linux systems, there are a number of services that can be monitored and a number of metrics that can be tracked. Some of them are listed here:

- *CPU busy/free*: If a CPU is close to 100% busy, perhaps it is time to add more processing power to the system. It is common practice to set warnings for 80% CPU busy, and critical alerts for 100% CPU busy percentages.

- *Memory free/used*: Both physical memory and swap space should be monitored. One possible threshold for memory use is: if memory is used more than 80%, then send a warning alert; if used at 100%, send a critical alert.

- *Disk used/free*: Monitoring available disk space can help prevent file systems from getting full. Thresholds similar to CPU/memory can be used, with 80% and 95% for warning and critical alerts, respectively.

- *Network use*: Depending on the bandwidth of the network, you might want to set alerts for warning/critical thresholds. Using the 80%/100% rule is standard practice.

Application Monitors

Along with system monitors, application monitors can help detect trouble spots with applications. Monitoring and metrics should be factored into an application design itself; they should not be an afterthought. If you are building a web application, having the web application keep track of its key metrics and outputting them to a log file or perhaps through an API helps in monitoring and tracking the application. The status page for Apache consists of useful metrics that can be used for monitoring Apache. An example page is located at https://www.apache.org/server-status. Listed here are some metrics that can be monitored for Apache:

- *Number of Apache processes running*: This number should match at least the MinSpareServers and not more than ServerLimit if using the prefork.c module.

- *Number of clients connected*: This number should be less than MaxClients. If equal to MaxClients, then perhaps a warning alert should be triggered so that additional Apache instances can be spun up.

- *URL*: This metric accesses web pages through Apache and ensures the pages are served within an expected time frame.

How to Monitor

After "what to monitor" has been decided, the next step is to figure out how to monitor. The "how" can be done in at least three different ways:

1. Active checks

2. Passive checks

3. SNMP based

Active checks are those that are initiated by the monitoring platform. If you have a Nagios server and it reaches out to the client to perform a test, it is considered an active check. The advantages of active checks are the following:

- *Easy to manage*: Because all checks are centralized on a server, upgrades are easy to do. Also, setting up monitoring is relatively easy because you have to configure the server only.

- *Helps simplify firewall rules*: Clients being monitored have to trust a single server or a cluster of servers, and allow incoming checks, which reduces the number of firewall rules.

The disadvantages of centralized active checks are as follows:

- They place a lot of load on the centralized server as the number of clients grows.

- Active checks may not be able to monitor non-network based processes on the clients unless they are exposed via the network.

Passive checks are those the monitoring agents submit to the monitoring server. The server does not reach out to the clients; instead, the clients check in with the server periodically. Advantages of passive checks are

- Easier to scale than active checks, because clients submit checks to the server

- More secure because non-network processes are not exposed to the network and can submit their status to the server.

Disadvantages of passive checks include

- Inability to control clients from the server, because the server cannot initiate any checks

- A flooded server as the number of clients increases.

SNMP (`https://en.wikipedia.org/wiki/Simple_Network_Management_Protocol`), or Simple Network Management Protocol, is another way to monitor your infrastructure. SNMP can do both active and passive checks, and is detailed in the next section.

SNMP

SNMP is a mechanism for managing devices on IP networks. The fact that you can use it to monitor devices is a huge plus. A large number of network devices such as routers, switches, firewalls, and printers support SNMP. In addition, Linux systems also support SNMP. The most popular implementation of SNMP on Linux is Net-SNMP (`http://www.net-snmp.org/`). There are three versions of SNMP: v1, v2c, and v3. Both IPv4 and IPv6 are supported by SNMP. There is a rich command line interface available to work with SNMP on Linux systems.

Understanding SNMP

SNMP operates at layer 7 of the Open Systems Interconnection (OSI) model and is a client–server-based protocol. SNMP uses two ports—161 and 162—and it can use both TCP as well as UDP. Port 162 is used for `snmptrap` and port 161 for `snmp`. When the master needs to contact the client, it does so on port 161 of the client. When the client needs to send a trap to the master, it does so on port 162 of the master.

When used with transport-laser Security or with datagram transport-layer security, the master contacts the agent on port 10161 and the agent sends traps to the master on port 10162.

As mentioned, there are three different versions of SNMP: v1, v2c and v3. Version 1 was the initial version; it supported UDP and not TCP. Authentication occurred via a community string that was sent in clear text across the network. Although still used, it is better to avoid this version because of its inherent security issues with sending an authentication string in clear text across the network.

Version 2 added more functionality and added security to v1. However, v2 was not widely accepted; instead, it was replaced by v2c, which removed some of the difficult-to-use security features of v2. Version 2 and v2c are not backward compatible with version 1.

Version 3 is the current version of SNMP. It includes encryption, message integrity, and authentication. For an enterprise, v3—if supported by the network devices—is the one that should be used because it is the only version that supports encryption.

Installing Net-SNMP

The easiest way to install Net-SNMP is via YUM repo. The two packages that you need at a minimum are `net-snmp-libs` and `net-snmp`. Version 5.7.2.1 of Net-SNMP is the latest version as of the writing of this chapter.

Configuring Net-SNMP

There are two configuration files for SNMP and both are located in the `/etc/snmp` directory. The first file is `/etc/snmp/snmpd.conf`, which is the SNMP agent configuration file. The other file is `/etc/snmp/snmptrapd.conf`, which controls how incoming traps should be handled. The `snmptrapd.conf` file is needed only on the master designed to receive traps. The `snmpd.conf` file is needed on all agents that respond to SNMP queries and send traps.

■ **Note**   If you have iptables running, make sure you allow port 161 UDP/TCP inbound to the servers running the SNMP agent software from the polling server. You can use the commands in Listing 7-1 to enable inbound SNMP connections.

Listing 7-1. iptables Rule for Inbound SNMP

```
# iptables -I INPUT -m state --state NEW -m tcp -p tcp --dport 161 -j ACCEPT
# iptables -I INPUT -m state --state NEW -m udp -p udp --dport 161 -j ACCEPT
```

You can start off with a very basic snmpd.conf and add more configuration options as you go along. Listing 7-2 shows a working `snmpd.conf`.

Listing 7-2. Sample snmpd.conf

```
# cat snmpd.conf
##### SNMP Configuration Versions 1 and 2 #####
##### Community String #####
com2sec notConfigUser 172.16.127.0/24 public

##### Security Name #####
group notConfigGroup v1 notConfigUser
group notConfigGroup v2c notConfigUser

##### View of Tree #####
view all included .1 80

#####
access notConfigGroup "" any noauth exact all none none
rwuser snmpuser
```

The file is based on using SNMP v1, v2c, and v3 as well. For v3, the username is snmpuser and the password as seen in Listing 7-3 is notarealpassword.

Listing 7-3. Useful SNMP-Related Commands

To view the directories where snmpd looks for management information bases (MIBs), run

```
# snmptranslate -Dinit_mib .1.3 2>&1 |grep MIBDIR
init_mib: Seen MIBDIRS: Looking in '/root/.snmp/mibs:/usr/share/snmp/mibs' for mib dirs ...
```

To view the different SNMP object identifiers (OID) that can be read or set from an agent:

```
$ snmpwalk -c public <ipaddress-of-agent>
```

To view the UCD-SNMP-MIB::memory OIDs:

```
$ snmpwalk -v1 -c public 172.16.127.212 UCD-SNMP-MIB::memory
UCD-SNMP-MIB::memIndex.0 = INTEGER: 0
UCD-SNMP-MIB::memErrorName.0 = STRING: swap
UCD-SNMP-MIB::memTotalSwap.0 = INTEGER: 4095996 kB
UCD-SNMP-MIB::memAvailSwap.0 = INTEGER: 4095996 kB
UCD-SNMP-MIB::memTotalReal.0 = INTEGER: 1914428 kB
UCD-SNMP-MIB::memAvailReal.0 = INTEGER: 1705492 kB
UCD-SNMP-MIB::memTotalFree.0 = INTEGER: 5801488 kB
UCD-SNMP-MIB::memMinimumSwap.0 = INTEGER: 16000 kB
UCD-SNMP-MIB::memBuffer.0 = INTEGER: 34432 kB
UCD-SNMP-MIB::memCached.0 = INTEGER: 82616 kB
UCD-SNMP-MIB::memSwapError.0 = INTEGER: noError(0)
UCD-SNMP-MIB::memSwapErrorMsg.0 = STRING:
```

To add an SNMP v3 user, use the net-snmp-create-v3-user command.

```
# net-snmp-create-v3-user
Enter a SNMPv3 user name to create:
snmpuser
Enter authentication pass-phrase:
notarealpassword
Enter encryption pass-phrase:
  [press return to reuse the authentication pass-phrase]

adding the following line to /var/lib/net-snmp/snmpd.conf:
   createUser snmpuser MD5 "notarealpassword" DES
adding the following line to /etc/snmp/snmpd.conf:
   rwuser snmpuser
```

SNMP MIB

SNMP MIB is a collection of hierarchically organized information about a particular device. There are numerous MIBs available based on devices. In the Linux world, you should get really comfortable with the host resource MIB because it gives you a lot of valuable information about a Linux system. Some of the things that you can get from the MIB are the following:

- `HOST-RESOURCES-MIB::hrSystem`: general information relating to uptime, number of users, and number of running processes

- `HOST-RESOURCES-MIB::hrStorage`: file system use and memory data

- `HOST-RESOURCES-MIB::hrDevices`: processors, network devices, and file systems

- `HOST-RESOURCES-MIB::hrSWRun`: running processes

- `HOST-RESOURCES-MIB::hrSWRunPerf`: memory and CPU statistics on the process table from `HOST-RESOURCES-MIB::hrSWRun`

- `HOST-RESOURCES-MIB::hrSWInstalled`: RPM Package Manager (RPM) database listing for installed packages

Monitoring Software

There is a lot of choice when it comes to open source monitoring software. Some of the options available are listed here, with the latest release as of the writing of this chapter:

1. Nagios: latest release, August 2014 (`http://www.nagios.org`)

2. Zabbix: latest release, November 2014 (`http://www.zabbix.com`)

3. openNMS: latest release, November 2014 (`http://www.opennms.org`)

4. Munin: latest release, October 2014 (`http://munin-monitoring.org`)

5. Ganglia: latest release, August 2014 (`http://ganglia.info`)

The question of which one to pick for your environment should be answered by taking into consideration factors such as

- Ease of use

- Experience your team has with the given software

- Active end user community for the software

- Release history

You can also download and install this software into your environment and test it before making a decision.

Cloud-Based Monitoring

With the advent of cloud computing, there are now solutions available in the cloud as well. Such online-hosted solutions have a server in the cloud, and you download and install agents in your network that then report into the cloud. One advantage of such a solution is that you do not have to maintain a server infrastructure for monitoring. A few such cloud providers are

- LogicMonitor (http://www.logicmonitor.com/)

- Pingdom (https://www.pingdom.com/)

- DotCom Monitor (https://www.dotcom-monitor.com/)

- Server Density (https://www.serverdensity.com/)

In addition to using an agent-based monitor, some of these companies also support agentless monitoring. This will help in monitoring your external web sites from different geographic regions for latency and availability.

Understanding Nagios

Nagios is based on client–server model. In the earlier How to Monitor section, I outlined three types of checks that can be used in infrastructure monitoring: active, passive, and SNMP based. Nagios supports all three types. The following steps will help you get started with Nagios:

1. Install Nagios on the server.

2. Configure the server.

3. Install the Nagios plug-in on the client.

4. Add the client to the server.

To monitor services and applications, Nagios uses plug-ins. For instance, there is a plug-in called check_ssh that can be used to check whether secure shell (SSH) is running on a particular host.

Commercial Versus Community Edition

There are two versions of Nagios; one is the commercial version known as Nagios XI and the other is Nagios Core. Some of the differences between the two versions are presented in Table 7-1.

Table 7-1. *Comparing Nagios Core and Nagios XI 2014*

Feature	Nagios XI	Nagios Core
Infrastructure monitoring	Yes	Yes
Alerting	Yes	Yes
Advanced reporting	Yes	No
Customizable user interface	Yes	No
Advanced distributed monitoring	Yes	No
Send/receive SNMP traps	Yes	No
Third-Party ticketing integration	Yes	No

Additional information about Nagios is available at:

- Comparing Nagios XI 2014 and Nagios Core (http://assets.nagios.com/handouts/ nagiosxi/Nagios-XI-vs-Nagios-Core-Feature-Comparison.pdf)

- Nagios Core, free edition (http://www.nagios.com/products/nagioscore)

- Nagios XI 2014 (http://www.nagios.com/products/nagiosxi/)

Installing the Nagios Server

As with most other software, you can download and compile Nagios, or simply install the packages. The most convenient solution for CentOS/RedHat is to install using yum, as shown in Listing 7-4.

Listing 7-4. Installing Nagios and Plug-ins from yum

```
# yum install nagios -y
# yum install nagios-plugins-all -y
```

Using yum installs Nagios configuration files in /etc/nagios. If you would rather compile Nagios on your own, there are numerous steps that need to be followed. I have outlined some of the basic compiling and installing steps in Listing 7-5. You start off with installing the build dependencies, such as PHP, gcc, and httpd. After that's done, you can download the latest version, which is—as of this writing—4.0.8. After you untar the distribution, you configure it, then run make, followed by make fullinstall. The htpasswd line creates a user that allows us to log in to Nagios using the web user interface.

Listing 7-5. Compiling and Installing Nagios

```
# yum install -y wget httpd php gcc glibc glibc-common gd gd-devel make net-snmp
# wget http://prdownloads.sourceforge.net/sourceforge/nagios/nagios-4.0.8.tar.gz
# tar xvfz nagios-4.0.8.tar.gz
# cd nagios-4.0.8
# ./configure
# make all
# make fullinstall
# htpasswd -c /usr/local/nagios/etc/htpasswd.users nagiosadmin
```

The next step is to install plug-ins manually (if you are not using the yum route), as shown in Listing 7-6.

Listing 7-6. Compiling and Installing Plug-ins

```
# cd /usr/local/
# wget http://nagios-plugins.org/download/nagios-plugins-2.0.3.tar.gz
# tar xvfz nagios-plugins-2.0.3.tar.gz
# cd nagios-plugins-2.0.3
# make
# make install

## You also need the check_nrpe plug-in, which you can download from http://sourceforge.net/
projects/nagios/files/nrpe-2.x/  or you can install using yum as shown here

# yum install nagios-plugins-nrpe -y
```

Additional resources can be found at

- http://nagios.sourceforge.net/docs/3_0/quickstart-fedora.html

- http://assets.nagios.com/downloads/nagioscore/docs/Installing_Nagios_Core_From_Source.pdf

- http://www.nagios.org/download/plugins/

Starting the Nagios Server

After the installation is complete, the next step is to start Apache and Nagios, as shown in Listing 7-7. Before you start Nagios, change the admin contact e-mail address so that you get notifications from Nagios, as shown in Listing 7-7. Also, remember to enable the iptables rule, as shown in the same listing, on port 80. The chkconfig command enables both Apache and Nagios to start on system reboot.

Listing 7-7. Starting Nagios

```
# sed -ie 's/nagios@localhost/yourname@domain.com/'  /usr/local/nagios/etc/objects/contacts.cfg

# iptables -I INPUT -m state --state NEW -m tcp -p tcp --dport 80 -j ACCEPT

## This rule is needed on all clients to allow the Nagios server to connect to them for NRPE
# iptables -A INPUT -s <nagios-server-ip> -p tcp -m tcp --dport 5666 -m state --state
NEW,ESTABLISHED -j ACCEPT

# service httpd  start
# service nagios start
# chkconfig httpd on
# chkconfig nagios on
```

To ensure that Nagios is up and running, view http://<ip-address>/nagios on the Nagios server using your browser. The username and password is nagiosadmin/nagiosadmin based on the htpasswd command you ran during the installation. If you picked another username/password, then use that. A sample Nagios server is shown in Figure 7-1.

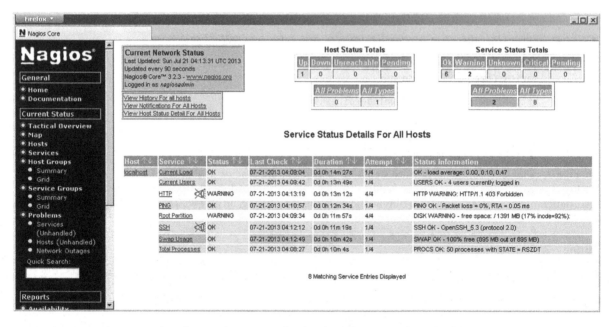

Figure 7-1. *Sample Nagios server (Source: https://upload.wikimedia.org/wikipedia/commons/4/48/ ScalableGridEngineNagios2.png)*

Nagios Check Types

There are at least three types of checks in Nagios, as shown in Figure 7-2.

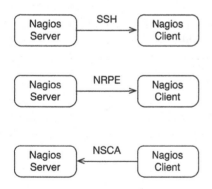

Figure 7-2. *Nagios chtck Types*

The SSH and Nagios Remote Plugin Executor (NRPE) checks are active, and the Nagios Service Check Acceptor (NSCA) check is passive. The server initiates active checks; passive checks are however initiated by the client. In large-scale environments, passive checks might be more suitable because they scale better. If you have thousands of clients, one server opening thousands of SSH or NRPE connections to check client status can result in an overloaded server.

Active Checks

The Nagios server does active checks at regular intervals, as defined by the check_interval option and the retry_interval option in the host and service definition. By default, this period is five minutes in the templates.cfg file for check_interval and one minute for retry_interval. Hosts in HARD state are checked every check_interval seconds; hosts in SOFT state are checked every retry_interval seconds. Active checks can also happen on demand by the server. On-demand checks occur

- When a service associated with the host changes state

- As a result of host reachability

- As part of predictive host dependency checks

Configuring the Nagios Server

Configuring Nagios can get complex because it based on a number of configuration files. Figure 7-3 shows the process work flow in the Nagios configuration.

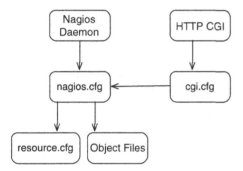

Figure 7-3. *Nagios configuration work flow*

The main configuration file is nagios.cfg and is a good place to start configuration. The file is located in /etc/nagios if you installed using yum. If you compiled Nagios and installed it in the default directory, it will be in /usr/local/nagios/etc/nagios.cfg.

The nagios daemon reads the nagios.cfg file. This file specifies where to look for resources and objects. In addition, it has a number of other settings that control the behavior of Nagios, such as log directory, enabling notifications, which user to run Nagios as, and many other options. Refer to Nagios configuration file documentation at http://nagios.sourceforge.net/docs/3_0/configmain.html to learn more about all the options in this file.

There is also a CGI configuration file called cgi.cfg that is used by HTTPD to determine the CGI configuration for the Nagios front end.

■ **Note**　After making a configuration change, verify your change before restarting Nagios. You can use the -v option to verify changes—for instance, /usr/local/nagios/bin/nagios -v /usr/local/nagios/etc/nagios.cfg.

Object Configuration

Objects are the core components of Nagios. There are different kinds of objects, such as hosts, services, contacts, and time periods. Objects are defined in the objects directory. In `nagios.cfg`, if you look at the `OBJECT CONFIGURATION FILE(S)` section, you will find a listing of some of the object files, as shown in Listing 7-8.

Listing 7-8. Object definitions in `nagios.cfg`

```
cfg_file=/usr/local/nagios/etc/objects/commands.cfg
cfg_file=/usr/local/nagios/etc/objects/contacts.cfg
cfg_file=/usr/local/nagios/etc/objects/timeperiods.cfg
cfg_file=/usr/local/nagios/etc/objects/templates.cfg
```

Hosts are the central component of your monitoring infrastructure. One or more hosts can be in host groups. If you have webserver[1-100], they can all belong to a host group called *web servers*. Hosts can also be routers, switchers, and printers in the world of Nagios.

Services are attributes of hosts. CPU use, load, memory, and uptime are all attributes of hosts. Hosts provide services such as HTTP, FTP, and SMTP. Services can be grouped in service groups. SMTP might be a service group that contains all the mail services being monitored.

Contacts are individuals or e-mail aliases that need to be contacted when hosts or services change state. You might have a contact called *SRE*, for site reliability engineer that needs to be notified if the web server goes down. Contacts can be grouped in contact groups. The network operations center can be grouped with the SRE for notifications regarding downed services.

Time periods are when hosts and services are monitored and notifications occur. You may have an application that is nonmission critical, for which monitoring and alerting should happen only during business hours. By defining a business hours time period, you can apply it to the nonmission-critical servers.

Commands are the names of the plug-ins you want to execute to check hosts and services, and the command line arguments that are passed to them.

Nagios Macros

Macros are an extremely useful way to reference information from checks in commands and plug-ins. Let's review the example in Listing 7-9. There are two snippets from two different files. One is `servers.cfg`, which contains the definitions of hosts and services. First you define a host called `nagios-client`. This host is based on a template called `linux-server`. The host has an IP address of 172.16.127.212.

You also define a service called `PING`, as is seen in the `define service` section of Listing 7-9. Let's do a ping check against a host called `nagios-client`. The command you should use is called `check_ping`. This command should be present in the `/usr/local/nagios/libexec` directory. The command takes four arguments as defined by the `commands.cfg` file. `$HOSTADDRESS$` is a macro that replaces the macro with the `address` field of the host definition. In this case, it is 172.16.127.212. Following this is the first argument, which is the warning threshold, followed by the critical threshold and, last, the number of ping packets to send.

Listing 7-9. Nagios Macros

```
## In /usr/local/nagios/etc/servers.cfg
define host{
        use                     linux-server            ; Name of host template to use
        host_name               nagios-client
        alias                   nagios-client
        address                 172.16.127.212
        }
```

```
define service{
        use                             local-service        ; Name of service template to use
        host_name                       nagios-client
        service_description             PING
        check_command                  check_ping!100.0,20%!500.0,60%
        }

## In /usr/local/nagios/etc/objects/commands.cfg
# 'check_ping' command definition
define command{
        command_name    check_ping
        command_line    $USER1$/check_ping -H $HOSTADDRESS$ -w $ARG1$ -c $ARG2$ -p 5
        }
```

To figure out which macros to use, first run the command with the --help option. This gives you an idea of the number of macros needed. Listing 7-10 shows the arguments that check_ping needs.

Listing 7-10. check_ping Arguments

```
check_ping -H <host_address> -w <wrta>,<wpl>% -c <crta>,<cpl>%
 [-p packets] [-t timeout] [-4|-6]

THRESHOLD is <rta>,<pl>% where <rta> is the round-trip average travel
time (in milliseconds), which triggers a WARNING or CRITICAL state, and <pl> is the
percentage of packet loss to trigger an alarm state.
```

Nagios Server Plug-ins

Checks in Nagios are done with the help of plug-ins. Plug-ins have to be installed after you install Nagios. If you are using yum, then it's as simple as running # yum install nagios-plugins-all –y. Plug-ins are, by default, in the /usr/lib64/nagios/plugins/ directory. If you use the source code and install plug-ins, the file to download is http://nagios-plugins.org/download/nagios-plugins-2.0.3.tar.gz. The default installation from source code is /usr/local/nagios/libexec/ for the plug-ins.

Let's review a simple plug-in to understand how Nagios works. Listing 7-11 shows how to use the check_dig plug-in. Nagios plug-ins return OK if the check succeeds, CRITICAL if the critical threshold is crossed, and WARNING if the warning threshold is crossed. In addition, they return some metrics on the check performed. check_dig queries a specified Domain Name System (DNS) for a certain record. Let's query (-H) a public DNS, 8.8.4.4, that is google-public-dns-b.google.com. The query (-T) is of type A, so given a hostname returns an IP. The warning (-w) time period is five seconds, so if the query exceeds five seconds, then a WARNING value is returned. The critical threshold (-c) is seven seconds, after which the check returns a CRITICAL value and the query record itself is (-l) www.example.com.

Listing 7-11. Using Nagios Plug-ins

```
# /usr/local/nagios/libexec/check_dig -T A -w 5 -c 7 -H 8.8.4.4 -4 -l www.example.com
DNS OK - 0.070 seconds response time (www.example.com. 10885 IN A 93.184.216.119)|
time=0.069719s;5.000000;7.000000;0.000000
```

As can be seen from Listing 7-11, the checks succeed with an OK return value. This proves that, from the host on which the check ran, you we can access a public DNS and are able to get a return value as well. This is a good check to run to verify the health of a DNS.

If the check had failed or not succeeded in the given time frame, then a warning message would have returned, as is shown in Listing 7-12.

Listing 7-12. Nagios Plug-in Warnings

```
# /usr/local/nagios/libexec/check_file_age -w 300 -c 2000 -f /var/log/messages
FILE_AGE WARNING: /var/log/messages is 835 seconds old and 674989 bytes

# /usr/local/nagios/libexec/check_file_age -w 100 -c 200 -f /var/log/messages
FILE_AGE CRITICAL: /var/log/messages is 873 seconds old and 674989 bytes
```

In Listing 7-12, a plug-in called check_file is used that checks the age of a file. In this case, the /var/log/messages file is being checked. In the first case, if the file is older than 300 seconds, a WARNING message is displayed (-w); if it is older than 2000 seconds, then a CRITICAL message is displayed. Because the file is 835 seconds old, which is less than the critical threshold and more than the warning threshold, a WARNING message is displayed.

In the latter case, you want to warn if the file is older than 100 seconds, and raise a CRITICAL message if the file is older than 200 seconds. Because the file is 873 seconds old, which is more than the threshold of 200 seconds, a CRITICAL alert is raised.

Installing the Nagios Client

For the client installation of Nagios, you need the plug-ins that monitor the client, and NSCA and/or NRPE. Listing 7-13 shows how to install the client piece.

Listing 7-13. Installing the Nagios Client

```
# yum install nagios-plugins-all
# yum install nrpe nsca
# service nrpe start
# service nsca start
# chkconfig nrpe on
# chkconfig nsca on
```

By default, the NRPE client allows connections only from localhost, so you have to change the configuration in nrpe.cfg to accept connections from the Nagios server. Listing 7-14 is an example of changing the configuration to accept connections from the Nagios server.

Listing 7-14. NRPE Configuration

```
## By default, only localhost on the client is allowed to connect
client# grep -i 'allowed_hosts=127.0.0.1' /etc/nagios/nrpe.cfg
allowed_hosts=127.0.0.1

## Change the configuration to accept connections from the Nagios server
client# sed -ie 's/allowed_hosts=127.0.0.1/allowed_hosts=172.16.127.210/' /etc/nagios/nrpe.cfg

client# grep -i allowed_hosts /etc/nagios/nrpe.cfg
allowed_hosts=172.16.127.210
```

```
## Restart the NRPE service after making the configuration change
client# service nrpe restart

## From the server, use the check_nrpe plug-in to the client—i.e., to 172.16.127.212
server# /usr/lib64/nagios/plugins/check_nrpe -H 172.16.127.212
NRPE v2.15
```

Adding Clients to Nagios

After you install Nagios plug-ins on a client, and Nagios NRPE/NSCA, you are ready to add that client to the Nagios server. There are various ways of adding clients to the server. One approach is to isolate all client configuration in a directory on the Nagios server, which makes it easy to manage the clients (Listing 7-15).

Listing 7-15. Adding Nagios Clients

```
# grep -i '^cfg_dir' /usr/local/nagios/etc/nagios.cfg
cfg_dir=/usr/local/nagios/etc/servers

# ls /usr/local/nagios/etc/servers/
nagios-client.cfg

# head -15 /usr/local/nagios/etc/servers/nagios-client.cfg
define host{
        use                     linux-server            ; Name of host template to use
        host_name               nagios-client
        alias                   nagios-client
        address                 172.16.127.212
        }

define service{
        use                     local-service           ; Name of service template to use
        host_name               nagios-client
        service_description     PING
        check_command            check_ping!100.0,20%!500.0,60%
        }
```

As seen in Listing 7-15, a new cfg_dir directive is add to Nagios in the nagios.cfg file. This tells Nagios to read all files ending with *.cfg in that directory and process them. In the directory /usr/local/nagios/etc/servers, one file per host is created, which you manage. The file in this case is nagios-client.cfg. As you add more clients, you add more files to this directory, with each file having the name of the client with *.cfg appended to it.

The contents of the file define the host and add services that need to be monitored. In this case, the host is using a template called linux-server, which is discerned by the use directive. The linux-server template is defined in /usr/local/nagios/etc/objects/templates.cfg. It contains the most common settings across the Linux servers being monitored. After this, you specify the hostname with the host_name directive and then the alias. The alias is shown in the graphical user interface and can be different than the actual hostname. Last, there is the IP address of the client; in this case, it's 172.16.127.212. Then you add a service to monitor on the host, and this is the ping check, which uses the template local-service, to define common settings for the ping check.

Nagios Templates

Templates make it easy to define settings across a number of hosts. Instead of specifying common settings numerous times, define them in a template and you can then define hosts and services that use the templates.

Templates, by default, are in the /usr/local/nagios/etc/objects/templates.cfg file, although you can change this file and location by specifying the directive cfg_file=/usr/local/nagios/etc/objects/templates.cfg' in '/usr/local/nagios/etc/nagios.cfg file. Listing 7-16 shows a host and a service template from the default installation of Nagios. You do not have to use the default template; you can create your own if you so desire. Keep in mind, though, that you should understand all the options that are in templates before making changes. You can find out more about the options by reading the configuration documentation at http://nagios.sourceforge.net/docs/3_0/configmain.html.

Listing 7-16 Nagios Templates

```
define host{
name                            generic-host     ; The name of this host template
notifications_enabled           1                ; Host notifications are enabled
event_handler_enabled           1                ; Host event handler is enabled
flap_detection_enabled          1                ; Flap detection is enabled
process_perf_data               1                ; Process performance data
retain_status_information       1                ; Retain status information across program restarts
retain_nonstatus_information    1                ; Retain nonstatus information across program
restarts
notification_period             24x7             ; Send host notifications at any time
register                        0                ; Template only, no registration required
}

define host{
name                            linux-server     ; The name of this host template
use                             generic-host     ; Inherits other values from generic-host
check_period                    24x7             ; Linux hosts are checked around the clock
check_interval                  5                ; Actively check the host every 5 minutes
retry_interval                  1                ; Schedule host check retries at 1 minute
max_check_attempts              10               ; Check each Linux host 10 times (max)
check_command                   check-host-alive ; Default command to check Linux hosts
notification_period             workhours        ; Notify only during work hours
notification_interval           120              ; Resend notifications every 2 hours
notification_options            d,u,r            ; Send notifications for specific host states
contact_groups                  admins           ; Notifications sent to the admins by default
register                        0                ; Template, hence no registration required
}

define service{
name                            generic-service  ; The name of this service template
active_checks_enabled           1                ; Active service checks are enabled
passive_checks_enabled          1                ; Passive service checks are enabled/accepted
parallelize_check               1                ; Active service checks should be parallelized
obsess_over_service             1                ; We should obsess over this service
check_freshness                 0                ; Default is NOT to check service "freshness"
notifications_enabled           1                ; Service notifications are enabled
```

```
event_handler_enabled          1           ; Service event handler is enabled
flap_detection_enabled         1           ; Flap detection is enabled
process_perf_data              1           ; Process performance data
retain_status_information      1           ; Retain status information across restarts
retain_nonstatus_information   1           ; Retain nonstatus information across restarts
is_volatile                    0           ; The service is not volatile
check_period                   24x7        ; Service can be checked at any time of the day
max_check_attempts             3           ; Recheck the service up to 3 times
normal_check_interval          10          ; Check the service every 10 minutes under normal
conditions
retry_check_interval           2           ; Recheck the service every 2 minutes
contact_groups                 admins      ; Notifications get sent out to admins
notification_options           w,u,c,r     ; Notify warning, unknown, critical, recovery
notification_interval          60          ; Renotify about service problems every hour
notification_period            24x7        ; Notifications can be sent out at any time
register                       0           ; Template, hence no registration required
}

define service{
name                           local-service    ; The name of this service template
use                            generic-service  ; Inherit values from generic-service
max_check_attempts             4                ; Recheck the service up to 4 times
normal_check_interval          5                ; Normally check the service every 5 minutes
retry_check_interval           1                ; Recheck the service every minute
register                       0                ; Template, hence no registration required
}
```

Nagios Add-ons

Add-ons are software that can be used to extend the functionality of Nagios. Some of the most common ones include

- *NRPE*: Used extensively to monitor and execute plug-ins on remote hosts. Extremely useful for disk, CPU, memory, and other such monitoring metrics. NRPE enables active checks that initiate from the Nagios server.

- *NSCA*: Enables passive checks to run on the clients and pass information to the server. Very useful for large-scale Nagios implementations.

- *Nagiosgraph*: A graphing tool that uses metrics from Nagios checks to store data in Round Robin Database (RRD) format and graph them. Useful for visual representation of Nagios; checks metrics such as history of CPU load or memory use over time.

You can find a more complete list at http://www.nagios.org/download/addons.

Sample Nagios Checks

Nagios comes with a lot of plug-ins that can help you start monitoring most services in your infrastructure. To start using these plug-ins, you can look at the commands.cfg file. Listing 7-17 shows some of the common checks.

Listing 7-17. Common Nagios Checks

```
# Found in /usr/local/nagios/etc/objects/commands.cfg

# 'check_ssh' command definition
define command{
        command_name    check_ssh
        command_line    $USER1$/check_ssh $ARG1$ $HOSTADDRESS$
        }

# 'check_ping' command definition
define command{
        command_name    check_ping
        command_line    $USER1$/check_ping -H $HOSTADDRESS$ -w $ARG1$ -c $ARG2$ -p 5
        }

# 'check_http' command definition
define command{
        command_name    check_http
        command_line    $USER1$/check_http -I $HOSTADDRESS$ $ARG1$
        }

# 'check_local_load' command definition
define command{
        command_name    check_local_load
        command_line    $USER1$/check_load -w $ARG1$ -c $ARG2$
        }
```

Nagios Front Ends

Nagios comes with a default front end that is used for its web user interface. You can replace this front end with other front ends if you prefer. Some of the more common ones include the following:

- Nagios V-Shell: A lightweight, PHP-based front end (https://github.com/NagiosEnterprises/nagiosvshell)

- Birdseye: Gives a high-level view of Nagios (http://nagiosbirdseye.sourceforge.net/)

- Check_MK Multisite: a very powerful front end that helps manage multiple Nagios servers from one user interface (http://mathias-kettner.com/check_mk.html)

You can view a more complete list at http://www.nagios.org/download/frontends/.

Getting Help

A few resources for getting help with Nagios are found in the following:

- Documentation (http://www.nagios.org/documentation)

- Support forums (http://support.nagios.com/forum/viewforum.php?f=7)

- Nagios Community Exchange (http://www.nagios.org/about/community)

- Mailing lists (https://lists.sourceforge.net/lists/listinfo/nagios-users)

Trend Analysis

Trend analysis with graphing is the ability to view current and historical data related to a given metric of an application or a service. For instance, being able to view CPU load for the past day, week, month, or year on a given system can give you a good idea about how busy the system is. Also, being able to view disk use for a period of a year or more can help an organization plan for storage.

Trend analysis with graphing is a very valuable component of infrastructure management. Some advantages of trend analysis are as follows:

- Proper capacity planning can be done with the right graphs showing system and network use.

- Troubleshooting can be made easier because you can see an increase or decrease in a given metric as an indicator of a cause or a symptom of a problem.

- Pretty graphs are always welcome as a way of reporting on infrastructure usage.

Trend Analysis Software

There is a lot of software in the open source world that can help do trend analysis with graphs, some of them are listed here:

- RRDtool (http://oss.oetiker.ch/rrdtool/)

- Graphite (http://graphite.wikidot.com)

- MRTG (http://oss.oetiker.ch/mrtg/)

- Cacti (http://www.cacti.net)

- Zenoss (http://www.zenoss.com)

- Collectd (https://collectd.org)

- PNP4Nagios (https://docs.pnp4nagios.org/)

- Nagiosgraph (http://nagiosgraph.sourceforge.net/)

All of the software listed here has a dedicated user base. Some of the projects have been around longer than others. RRDtool is the foundation for many graphing software packages.

Installing Cacti

To install Cacti, you can use the RPM packages or download source code and build it. Requirements for installing Cacti v0.8.8.b include the following:

- PHP 5.1+

- MySQL 5.0+

- RRDtool 1.0.49+, 1.4+ recommended

- Net-SNMP 5.2+

- Web server that supports PHP

One big advantage of using yum to install Cacti is that all dependencies are installed automatically. If you build Cacti on your own, then make sure you install the prerequisites before you attempt to build Cacti. Listing 7-18 shows how to download and install Cacti.

Listing 7-18. Installing Cacti

To install Cacti from yum, enable the EPEL yum repository. This assumes CentOS 6.X as your operating system. First, download the RPM and then install it using RPM.

```
# wget http://download.fedoraproject.org/pub/epel/6/x86_64/epel-release-6-8.noarch.rpm
# rpm -ivh epel-release-6-8.noarch.rpm
# yum install cacti
```

If you already have an existing MySQL server that you want to use, then you can skip installing MySQL server; otherwise, install that as well. You can install MySQL server on the same host as Cacti or pick another one.

```
# yum install mysql-server
```

Additional information about downloading Cacti is at http://www.cacti.net/download_cacti.php.

Configuring Cacti

A large amount of Cacti configuration is done via the web user interface. However, you still need to configure the database manually, as seen in Listing 7-19.

Listing 7-19. Configuring Cacti

After installing Cacti, you need to configure it. First, let's start Apache, MySQL, and SNMPD. Apache is needed for the user interface, MySQL for storing data about the values being graphed, and SNMPD is required to query the local host.

```
$ sudo service httpd start
$ sudo service mysqld start
$ sudo service snmpd start
```

You also need to ensure that all three services start when the system is rebooted, and you can do this by using the chkconfig command.

```
$ sudo /sbin/chkconfig --levels 345 httpd on
$ sudo /sbin/chkconfig --levels 345 mysqld on
$ sudo /sbin/chkconfig --levels 345 snmpd on
```

A MySQL database needs to be created for Cacti. You can do this by logging into MySQL and using the create database command. After that, user cacti has to be granted full access to the Cacti database.

```
mysql> create database cacti;
mysql> GRANT ALL ON cacti.* TO cacti@localhost IDENTIFIED BY 'your-password-here';
mysql> FLUSH privileges;
mysql> quit;
```

Now that the database has been created, you have to create the database schema. Cacti includes a file called cacti.sql that includes the schema. By using the rpm -ql command you can locate cacti.sql and load it into MySQL.

```
$ rpm -ql cacti | grep cacti.sql
$ mysql -D cacti -u cacti -p < /usr/share/doc/cacti-0.8.8b/cacti.sql
```

Cacti uses PHP for its web front end, and you have to let PHP know how to access the database you have created, so edit the db.php file and enter the values from the database configuration. Assume, in this case, that the database is running on the same host as Cacti; so, database_hostname is localhost.

```
$ sudo vi /etc/cacti/db.php
/* make sure these values reflect your actual database/host/user/password */
$database_type = "mysql";
$database_default = "cacti";
$database_hostname = "localhost";
$database_username = "cacti";
$database_password = "your-password-here";
$database_port = "3306";
$database_ssl = false;
```

Since Apache is being used, you have to configure Apache to allow access to Cacti. You can do this by creating a file called cacti.conf in the Apache configuration directory of /etc/httpd/conf.d. This file already exists if you installed with yum; just make sure you change the Allow from field for /usr/share/cacti to include your network so that you can browser the user interface.

```
$ sudo vi /etc/httpd/conf.d/cacti.conf
Alias /cacti /usr/share/cacti

<Directory /usr/share/cacti/>
        Order Deny,Allow
        Deny from all
        Allow from <your-network-range>

</Directory>
```

After you add the Cacti configuration to Apache, restart Apache.

```
$ sudo /etc/init.d/httpd restart
```

Cacti uses a cron job to poll clients via SNMP. You have to edit cron for user cacti and "uncomment" the poller to start polling.

```
$ sudo vi /etc/cron.d/cacti

#Uncomment the following line
*/5 * * * *    cacti   /usr/bin/php /usr/share/cacti/poller.php > /dev/null 2>&1
```

Web-Based Configuration

After you finish the command line-based configuration, you have to continue configuration from the web-based user interface. Access the user interface at http://<cacti-server-ip>/cacti. The first screen you should see is the one shown in Figure 7-4. Click Next to move forward.

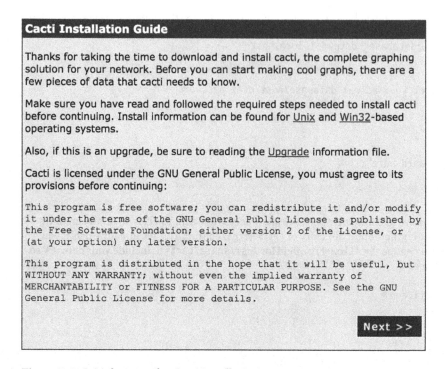

Figure 7-4. Initial screen after Cacti installation

The next screen should look like the one in Figure 7-5. Make sure you select New Install if not already selected and then click Next.

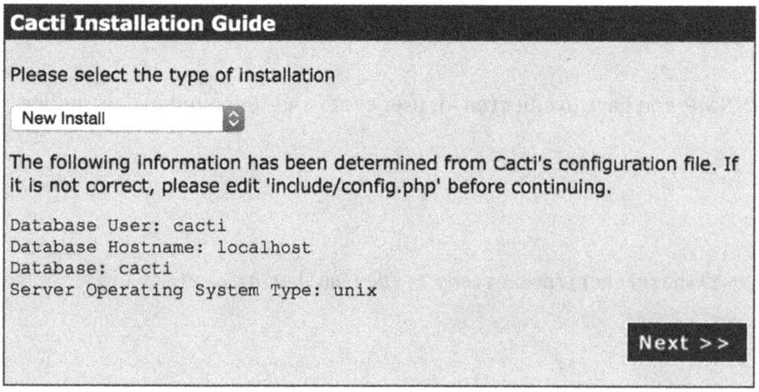

Cacti Installation Guide

Please select the type of installation

New Install

The following information has been determined from Cacti's configuration file. If it is not correct, please edit 'include/config.php' before continuing.

Database User: cacti
Database Hostname: localhost
Database: cacti
Server Operating System Type: unix

Next >>

Figure 7-5. Second screen after installation

The most important setting is in the third screen, as shown in Figure 7-6. Here you should verify the path to all the binaries that are shown. If one or more of the binaries is not found, go back to your system and install the binary using yum, then reload the Cacti page to see if the binary is found. If you miss any of the binaries, you will have problems with Cacti later, so fix it now before moving on.

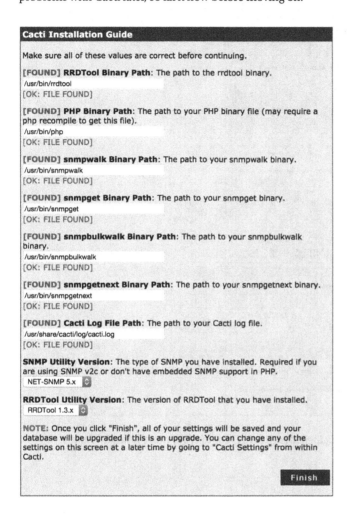

Figure 7-6. *Cacti configuration screen*

As this point, Cacti is pretty much ready to go. You can now start to add hosts to view trend analysis information, as explained in the next section. A sample Cacti server is shown in Figure 7-7.

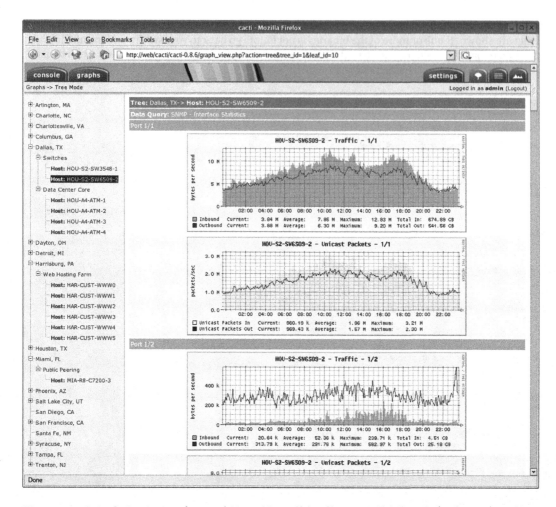

Figure 7-7. *Sample Cacti server (source:* https://en.wikipedia.org/wiki/Cacti_(software)#mediaviewer/
File:Cacti_(software)_screenshot.png)

Cacti Graphs

Cacti uses SNMP to connect to remote hosts and, based on the SNMP query, creates graphs. The basic step for creating graphs is first creating a device, and then a graph for the device. After you log in to Cacti, from the main page click Create Devices, and then click Add at the top right-hand corner. Fill in the device name and click Create. This sequence of steps adds the device and gives you the option to add graphs.

Click the link Create Graphs for this host, and Cacti gives you a choice of various SNMP polled data that can be plotted. Select the graphs you want by clicking on the right-hand side, then click Create, as shown in Figure 7-8.

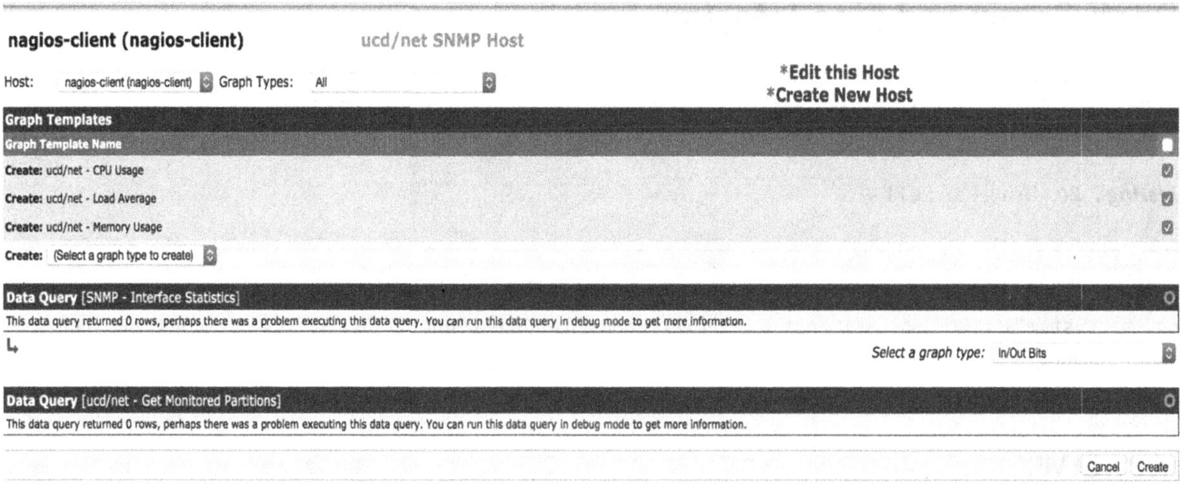

nagios-client (nagios-client)   ucd/net SNMP Host

Host: nagios-client (nagios-client) ◌ Graph Types: All ◌   ***Edit this Host**
***Create New Host**

Graph Templates	
Graph Template Name	☐
Create: ucd/net - CPU Usage	☑
Create: ucd/net - Load Average	☑
Create: ucd/net - Memory Usage	☑
Create: (Select a graph type to create) ◌	

Data Query [SNMP - Interface Statistics]	⊙
This data query returned 0 rows, perhaps there was a problem executing this data query. You can run this data query in debug mode to get more information.	
↳ Select a graph type: In/Out Bits ◌	

Data Query [ucd/net - Get Monitored Partitions]	⊙
This data query returned 0 rows, perhaps there was a problem executing this data query. You can run this data query in debug mode to get more information.	

Cancel Create

Figure 7-8. *Creating Cacti graphs*

At this point, you should have functioning graphs. The next section shows you how to view the graphs in a graph tree.

Graph Trees

Adding a device and then adding graphs to it gets Cacti to start collecting data for the device. The next step is to add the graph to a tree for easy viewing. To do this, click Graph Trees on the left-hand side navigation menu. After this, click Default Tree, then click Add on the right-hand side under Tree Items. In the Tree Item Type select Host, which refreshes the page and you can select the new host you added. Click Create (Figure 7-9).

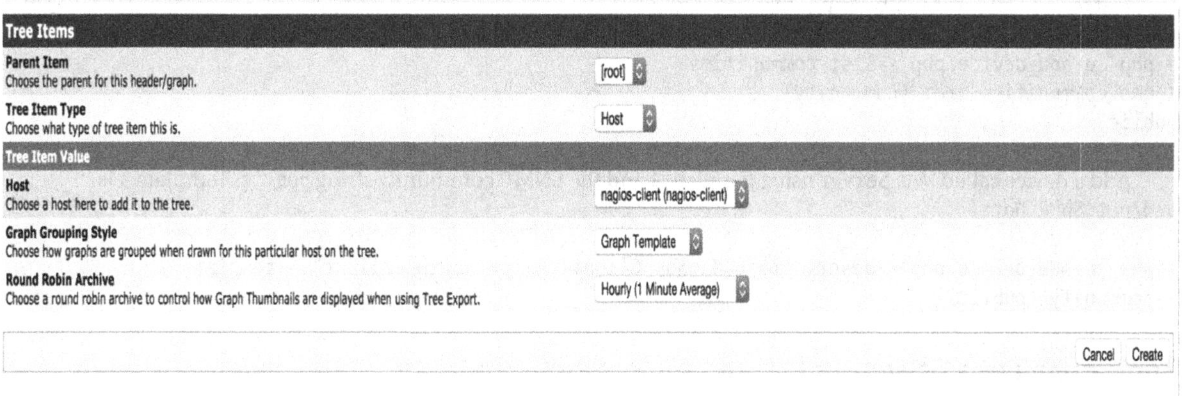

Tree Items	
Parent Item Choose the parent for this header/graph.	[root] ◌
Tree Item Type Choose what type of tree item this is.	Host ◌
Tree Item Value	
Host Choose a host here to add it to the tree.	nagios-client (nagios-client) ◌
Graph Grouping Style Choose how graphs are grouped when drawn for this particular host on the tree.	Graph Template ◌
Round Robin Archive Choose a round robin archive to control how Graph Thumbnails are displayed when using Tree Export.	Hourly (1 Minute Average) ◌

Cancel Create

Figure 7-9. *Adding Cacti graphs to trees*

Cacti Command Line Interface

Adding devices, graphs, and modifying trees can get cumbersome when using the web-based user interface. Cacti has a command line interface (CLI) that lets you add a new device, add a new graph, and do a lot more. You can find the different available commands in the /var/lib/cacti/cli/ directory. Listing 7-20 shows a few examples of using the CLI.

Listing 7-20. Using Cacti CLI

■ **Note** When using the CLI tools, if you see warnings similar to PHP Warning: date(): It is not safe to rely on the system's time zone settings..., edit /etc/php.ini and uncomment the date.timezone line, and fill in your time zone.

ADD A DEVICE

List all the templates available.

```
# cd /var/lib/cacti/cli
# php -q add_device.php --list-host-templates
Valid Host Templates: (id, name)
0       None
1       Generic SNMP-enabled Host
3       ucd/net SNMP Host
4       Karlnet Wireless Bridge
5       Cisco Router
6       Netware 4/5 Server
7       Windows 2000/XP Host
8       Local Linux Machine
```

List the SNMP community strings that you know.

```
# php -q add_device.php --list-communities
Known communities are: (community)
public
```

Add a device called Web Server using template 3 and the SNMP community string public. Template 3 is ucd/net SNMP Host.

```
# php -q add_device.php --description="Nagios Client" --ip="nagios-client" --template=3
--community="public"
```

ADD A GRAPH TO A DEVICE

Next, add a graph for the device you just added. List the devices you know of so far.

```
# php -q add_graphs.php --list-hosts
Known Hosts: (id, hostname,  template,  description)
1           127.0.0.1     8          Localhost
2           nagios-client 3          nagios-client
```

List the graphing templates we know of.

```
# php -q add_graphs.php --list-graph-templates
Known Graph Templates:(id, name)
 2        Interface - Traffic (bits/sec)
 3        ucd/net - Available Disk Space
 4        ucd/net - CPU Usage
 5        Karlnet - Wireless Levels
 6        Karlnet - Wireless Transmissions
 7        Unix - Ping Latency
 8        Unix - Processes
 9        Unix - Load Average
10        Unix - Logged in Users
11        ucd/net - Load Average
12        Linux - Memory Usage
13        ucd/net - Memory Usage
14        Netware - File System Cache
15        Netware - CPU Utilization
16        Netware - File System Activity
17        Netware - Logged In Users
18        Cisco - CPU Usage
19        Netware - Volume Information
20        Netware - Directory Information
21        Unix - Available Disk Space
22        Interface - Errors/Discards
23        Interface - Unicast Packets
24        Interface - Non-Unicast Packets
25        Interface - Traffic (bytes/sec)
26        Host MIB - Available Disk Space
27        Host MIB - CPU Utilization
28        Host MIB - Logged in Users
29        Host MIB - Processes
30        Netware - Open Files
31        Interface - Traffic (bits/sec, 95th Percentile)
32        Interface - Traffic (bits/sec, Total Bandwidth)
33        Interface - Traffic (bytes/sec, Total Bandwidth)
34        SNMP - Generic OID Template
```

Because the returned list is fairly long and you want to add Linux hosts only, you can reduce the listing size by viewing the graphs you can generate for host template 3, which is ucd/net SNMP Host.

```
# php -q add_graphs.php --list-graph-templates --host-template-id=3
Known Graph Templates:(id, name)
4         ucd/net - CPU Usage
11        ucd/net - Load Average
13        ucd/net - Memory Usage
```

Let's add a CPU graph to the host called nagios-client. The host ID is 2, based on your --list-hosts query. For CPU, the graph type is cg and the graph template is 4, based on the earlier --list-graph-templates query.

```
# php -q add_graphs.php --host-id=2 --graph-type=cg --graph-template-id=4
```

ADD A NODE TO A GRAPH TREE

First, list all the hosts that you have in Cacti. In this case, there are two hosts: one is the local host, on which Cacti is running, and the other is a host called nagios-client.

```
# php -q add_tree.php --list-hosts
Known Hosts: (id, hostname,  template,  description)
1               127.0.0.1     8           Localhost
2               nagios-client 3           nagios-client
```

Next, list the graph trees you know of. By default, Cacti comes with a tree called *Default Tree*; the ID of this tree is 1.

```
# php -q add_tree.php --list-trees
Known Trees:
id        sort method                       name
1         Manual Ordering (No Sorting)      Default Tree
```

Let's review all the nodes that are part of the Default Tree. You can see that you have two nodes: the Cacti host itself and nagios-client added earlier.

```
# php -q add_tree.php --list-nodes --tree-id=1
Known Tree Nodes:
type        id       parentid    title          attribs
Host        7        N/A         127.0.0.1      Graph Template
Host        8        N/A         nagios-client  Graph Template
```

Review the graphs that our Cacti node has.

```
# php -q add_tree.php --list-graphs --host-id=1
Known Host Graphs: (id, name, template)
1          Localhost - Memory Usage      Linux - Memory Usage
2          Localhost - Load Average      Unix  - Load Average
3          Localhost - Logged in Users   Unix  - Logged in Users
4          Localhost - Processes         Unix  - Processes
```

Add a new tree called 'Linux Servers'

```
# php -q add_tree.php --type=tree --name="Linux Servers" --sort-method=alpha
Tree Created - tree-id: (2)
```

Add the Cacti node to the graph tree called 'Linux Servers'

```
# php -q add_tree.php --type=node --node-type=host --tree-id=2 --host-id=1
```

Cacti Support

Cacti support is available from the following sources:

- Support forums (`http://forums.cacti.net`)

- Documentation (`http://docs.cacti.net http://www.cacti.net/downloads/docs/html/`)

- Mailing lists (`http://www.cacti.net/mailing_lists.php`)

RRDtool

The round robin database tool, or RRDtool, is extremely powerful software for logging and graphing data. Cacti, Munin, and Collectd use RRDtool to store data. RRDtool can store any numerical values, such as those returned from SNMP. Some uses of RRDtool include storing CPU load, memory usage, disk usage, and network use.

Some of the commands included with RRDtool are as follows:

- rrdcreate: Used to set up a new round-robin database (`http://oss.oetiker.ch/rrdtool/doc/rrdcreate.en.html`)

- rrdupate: Used to update an existing database (`http://oss.oetiker.ch/rrdtool/doc/rrdupdate.en.html`)

- rrdgraph: Used to create a graph from a database (`http://oss.oetiker.ch/rrdtool/doc/rrdgraph.en.html`)

Conclusion

This chapter has provided insight into the world of monitoring and graphing. We looked at what to monitor and how to monitor it using tools such as Nagios and SNMP for monitoring, as well as cloud-based monitoring solutions, and we examined Cacti for graphing. We also briefly examined RRDtool, which is used extensively for data collection and graphing. Although there are lot of options in the open source world for both monitoring and trend analysis, a few of the software projects mentioned in this chapter have a wider audience than the other, or have been around longer. I picked Nagios and Cacti because I have found them to have a wider audience during my career. You should evaluate a couple of them and pick the ones that suit your environment the most.

■ ■ ■

## CHAPTER 8

DNS Using BIND and DHCP

Domain Name System (DNS) is the backbone of the Internet. Without DNS we would be lost in navigating websites. For many enterprises, choosing a robust DNS solution—one that is easy to manage and able to meet to the needs of the enterprise—can be a challenging task. This chapter focuses on how to design an enterprise-friendly DNS solution using BIND. BIND is an open source DNS implementation that has become the de facto reference implementation (https://www.isc.org/downloads/bind/). BIND stands for Berkeley Internet Name Domain, because the software was developed at the University of California at Berkeley during the early 1980s. Currently, the Internet Systems Consortium (ISC) maintains BIND.

There are two branches of BIND: one is 9.x and, as of the writing of this chapter, 9.10.0-P2 is the current stable release in this branch. The other branch is BIND10, release 1.2. BIND10 has, however, been renamed to Bundy (http://bundy-dns.de/) because the ISC has concluded its work on BIND10 and is no longer updating the source pool. Because BIND 9 is much more widely used, the ISC has decided to focus on BIND 9 and not on BIND10 anymore.

In this chapter we look at BIND 9.x, which is the more popular version of BIND. For an enterprise, the choice of which solution to use (BIND 9.x or BIND10) depends on whether the enterprise wants ISC support with the software. Because the ISC is focusing on BIND 9.x, and not on BIND10, 9.x might be a more suitable option if you want ISC's support.

Dynamic Host Configuration Protocol (DHCP) is tied closely to DNS because DHCP provides network devices with an IP address, which often needs to be updated in a DNS namespace. Many enterprises use DHCP and often struggle to update DHCP-assigned IP addresses in DNS. Using ISC DHCP (https://www.isc.org/downloads/dhcp/), I explain how to set up an enterprise-friendly DHCP infrastructure.

In both cases, of DNS and DHCP, I assume you have a good understanding of how the protocol works. Although I do cover some protocol details, my focus is on an enterprise implementation.

Role of DNS in an Enterprise

What role should DNS play in an enterprise? DNS is crucial to an enterprise's name brand. If your enterprise is called Example Enterprise and you do not own Example.com, you may end up losing business because Internet users are most likely to type in Example.com when trying to view your web site. In addition, the material hosted on Example.com may misrepresent your company's message to its customers if your company does not own the domain. Hence, it's crucial to protect their brand identity on the Internet.

There are laws against cybersquatting, that prevent nontrademark holders from holding domain names that represent trademark names, and then try to sell the domain names to trademark owners. The Anticybersquatting Consumer Protection Act was enacted in 1999 by the U.S. Congress to help preserve trademarks on the Internet. Additional information about the law can be found at http://cyber.law.harvard.edu/property00/domain/legislation.html.

There is also the Uniform Domain Name Dispute-Resolution Policy, which is an Internet corporation for assigned names and numbers (ICANN) rule that can help enterprises with their trademark name preservation on the Internet. The URL https://www.icann.org/resources/pages/udrp-2012-02-25-en has more information about the Uniform Domain Name Dispute-Resolution Policy.

Unfortunately, these safeguards are not global. For instance, the Anticybersquatting Consumer Protection Act is a law in the United States only, and an enterprise may find itself fighting foreign entities that do not respect the law. ICANN, on the other hand, has global authority and can help if your trademark is infringed on the Internet by anyone in the world. Things can get complicated when two different companies have the same name in different countries, with the same registered trademark in their respective countries.

In an enterprise, DNS plays an enabling role for corporate applications. For instance, if `Example.com` is your domain, all development servers can be in a DNS zone called `dev.example.com`, quality assurance (QA) servers can be in `qa.example.com`, and production servers can be in `prod.example.com`. Furthermore, applications can use a naming scheme to identify servers uniquely. A production web server that serves a company's web front end can potentially be called `web001-fe.prod.example.com`, where `web001` stands for the number one web server and `fe` stands for front end. A database server could be called `db001-fe.prod.example.com` if it is serving the front-end application services.

In an enterprise, DNS can make it easy to find web portals. One such instance can be with URL redirection. Let's say you want to make it easy to find the human resources page. One way is to make an internal web site such as `http://hr.example.com`, which is easy to remember.

Another way is to use DNS shortcuts, such as `http://example.com/payroll`, that goes to `http://hr.example.com/hr/payroll`. The `/payroll` at the end can be replaced with other useful shortcuts, such as `http://example.com/holidays`, which can point to a human resources page that lists holidays for the company.

URL shorteners are another way an enterprise can make use of DNS so that it's easy to locate information. For long URLs such as `http://hr.example.com/holidays/2014`, using a URL shortener service can reduce it to, say, `http://example.com/xylt`. Although these are not easy to remember, they are easier to embed in documents that need to refer to the long URLs. You can download and install open source URL shorteners in your enterprise. A few open source shorteners that are available are

- `http://yourls.org/`

- `http://www.tighturl.com/project/p/tighturl/`

- `https://code.google.com/p/phurl/`

DNS Solutions

Should an enterprise outsource DNS to a cloud provider such as Google Cloud or should it host it in-house? If the enterprise does decide to host it in-house, should a commercial solution be picked or an open source version? The answer to this question depends on the following:

- The installed operating system base in the enterprise

- The availability of engineering resources

- The corporate preference for open source or commercial tools

If an enterprise has a Windows installed base, it may prefer a Windows-based solution, such as Microsoft DNS. On the other hand, if there is a Linux base in the company, and a preference toward open source tools, then BIND may be a good option. Regardless of the installed base operating system, some companies may prefer commercially supported closed source tools, and as such may pick providers such as Nominum or Cisco.

A few commercial DNS solutions include the following:

- Nominum Vantio (`http://nominum.com`)

- Cisco Prime IP Express (`http://www.cisco.com/c/en/us/products/cloud-systems-management/prime-ip-express/index.html`)

- Simple DNS Plus (`http://www.simpledns.com/`)

A few open source DNS solutions are as follows:

- BIND (https://www.isc.org/downloads/bind/)

- PowerDNS (https://www.powerdns.com/)

- TinyDNS (http://tinydns.org/)

- NSD (https://www.nlnetlabs.nl/projects/nsd/)

In this chapter I assume an installed operating system base of Linux—specifically, CentOS or RedHat 6.x—and explain how to install and use ISC BIND, which is an open source DNS solution.

Domain Registrars

To register a domain such as Example.com, you have to pick a domain registrar. My recommendation is to go with ICANN-accredited registrars, because an accredited registrar provides protection for registrants and accountability for registrars. An updated list of registrars can be found at https://www.icann.org/registrar-reports/accredited-list.html. The choice of registrars is bewildering. I can't recommend any one in particular, because your decision on which one to pick should be your own; however, one approach is to follow the lead of major Internet presence companies such as Google, Yahoo, and Facebook and use the same registrar they use, which is MarkMonitor.com. To determine the domain registrar of a particular domain, use the whois command or http://www.internic.net/whois.html. The whois command uses the whois protocol as defined in RFC 3912 (http://tools.ietf.org/html/rfc3912). It is the de facto way of querying domain information. There are also web interfaces that provide an interface to the registration information. Listing 8-1 shows the output of the whois command.

Listing 8-1. whois Command

```
#view registration information about EXAMPLE.ORG using the 'whois' command
$ whois example.org
Domain Name:EXAMPLE.ORG
Domain ID: D2328855-LROR
Creation Date: 1995-08-31T04:00:00Z
Updated Date: 2010-07-27T20:57:51Z
Registry Expiry Date: 2010-08-30T04:00:00Z
Sponsoring Registrar:Internet Assigned Numbers Authority (IANA) (R193-LROR)
Sponsoring Registrar IANA ID: 376
WHOIS Server:
Referral URL:
Domain Status: serverDeleteProhibited
Domain Status: serverRenewProhibited
Domain Status: serverTransferProhibited
Domain Status: serverUpdateProhibited
Registrant ID:IANA
Registrant Name:Internet Assigned Numbers Authority
Registrant Organization:Internet Assigned Numbers Authority (IANA)
Registrant Street: 4676 Admiralty Way
Registrant City:Marina del Rey
Registrant State/Province:CA
Registrant Postal Code:92092
Registrant Country:US
Registrant Phone:+1.3108239358
```

```
Registrant Phone Ext:
Registrant Fax: +1.3108238649
Registrant Fax Ext:
Registrant Email:res-dom@iana.org
Admin ID:IANA
Admin Name:Internet Assigned Numbers Authority
Admin Organization:Internet Assigned Numbers Authority (IANA)
Admin Street: 4676 Admiralty Way
Admin City:Marina del Rey
Admin State/Province:CA
Admin Postal Code:92092
Admin Country:US
Admin Phone:+1.3108239358
Admin Phone Ext:
Admin Fax: +1.3108238649
Admin Fax Ext:
Admin Email:res-dom@iana.org
Tech ID:IANA
Tech Name:Internet Assigned Numbers Authority
Tech Organization:Internet Assigned Numbers Authority (IANA)
Tech Street: 4676 Admiralty Way
Tech City:Marina del Rey
Tech State/Province:CA
Tech Postal Code:92092
Tech Country:US
Tech Phone:+1.3108239358
Tech Phone Ext:
Tech Fax: +1.3108238649
Tech Fax Ext:
Tech Email:res-dom@iana.org
Name Server:A.IANA-SERVERS.NET
Name Server:B.IANA-SERVERS.NET
...[SNIP]...
DNSSEC:signedDelegation
DS Created 1:2010-07-27T20:57:22Z
DS Key Tag 1:31589
Algorithm 1:8
Digest Type 1:1
Digest 1:7b8370002875dda781390a8e586c31493847d9bc
DS Maximum Signature Life 1:1814400 seconds
DS Created 2:2010-07-27T20:57:36Z
DS Key Tag 2:31589
Algorithm 2:8
Digest Type 2:2
Digest 2:3fdc4c11fa3ad3535ea8c1ce3eaf7bfa5ca9ae8a834d98fee10085cfaeb625aa
DS Maximum Signature Life 2:1814400 seconds
...[SNIP]...
```

The registrant is the entity to whom the domain is registered. The `Admin` contact is the administrative contact for the domain, for billing purposes. The `Tech` contact is the technical contact for technical issues relating to the domain.

Not all domain names are available for registration. The Internet Assigned Numbers Authority (IANA) maintains a list of reserved domain names at `https://www.iana.org/domains/reserved`.

ICAAN has an excellent document on picking domain names and registrars. You can view the article at `https://www.icann.org/en/system/files/files/domain-names-beginners-guide-06dec10-en.pdf`.

Top-Level Domains

There are different kinds of top-level domains (TLDs) available for registering a domain. In short, they can be classified into the following:

- Two-letter country code TLDs, such as `.us` for the United States and `.mx` for Mexico. A full list can be found at `http://www.iso.org/iso/country_codes.htm`.

- Special TLDs. Currently only one, called `.arpa`, which is administered by ICANN, is also known as an infrastructure TLD and is not available for registration (`http://icannwiki.com/index.php/.arpa`).

- Generic TLDs (gTLDs), which are—at the most—three or more characters, such as `.com`. More than 300 gTLDs have been delegated, a list of which can be found at `http://newgtlds.icann.org/en/`. gTLDs can be divided further.

- The three gTLDs, `.com`, `.net`, and `.org`, which are unrestricted and anyone can use them

- `.edu`, `.gov`, `.int`, and `.mil`, which are for limited purposes, and you have to qualify in the specified category to register

- Sponsored gTLDs, such as `.aero`, `.coop`, and `.museum`, which have to be requested by an organization and have additional requirements

- Unsponsored gTLDs, which are everything else, such as `.biz`, `.info`, `.name`, and `.pro`

- Internationalized domain names, which include non-Latin TLDs, such as those in Hindi, Arabic, and other languages. A list can be found at `https://www.icann.org/resources/pages/idn-2012-02-25-en`.

The decision to pick certain TLDs for business domain registration is an important one. The most common top-level domains are a good way to start registering your business and include `.com`, `.net`, and `.org`. It can get very expensive for a business to try to register its name in every TLD available. There are also restrictions on who can pick certain TLDs. IANA maintains a list of top-level domains at `https://data.iana.org/TLD/tlds-alpha-by-domain.txt`.

After a TLD has been picked, the name of the domain is the next decision-making point. There are limitations on the length of a domain. Latin characters can be no more than 63 characters, not including the `.`, and the TLD. Additional rules are found at `https://www.register.com/policy/domain-extension-rules.rcmx`.

Enterprises generally pick their company name as the domain name for their external Internet-facing presence. For an intranet, it is also a common practice to have a different domain than the external-facing one. Example Inc. might pick `Example.com` for its external-facing site, and `example.int` for its intranet site.

A limited representation of the DNS hierarchy is shown in Figure 8-1.

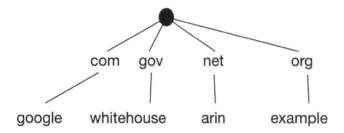

Figure 8-1. *Limited representation of DNS hierarchy*

Protecting Your Domain Registration

Your domain is part of your brand identity. Loss of your Internet presence can result in loss of business.

The most important entry you should keep track of is the registry expiry date when registering a domain. This field is viewable when you use the whois command. This is the date that the registry of the domain name expires and, unless renewed, you can potentially lose the domain name to someone else who will register it.

The other important field to keep track of is Domain Status. You can request that the registrar enable the following security features on your domain registration:

- clientTransferProhibited: Prevents your domain from getting transferred to someone else; a safeguard against hijacking

- clientDeleteProhibited: Prevents your domain from getting deleted accidentally; a safeguard against your own self and against hackers

- clientUpdateProhibited: Prevents any updates to the domain; for instance, a hacker can change the administrative contact information for the domain and then delete it if this feature is not enabled

A list of different domain statuses can be found at https://www.icann.org/en/system/files/files/ epp-status-codes-30jun11-en.pdf. There are additional status codes, such as

- Active: This is the normal status of a domain.

- RedemptionPeriod: When a deletion is requested, the domain goes into a five-day redemption period, during which a domain restore can be requested.

- PendingRestore: If, during the redemption period, the domain is requested to be restored, it goes into the pending restore phase.

Another way to project your domain is to use private registration. The advantage of using private registration is that no one knows the end user who owns the domain. Under the administrative and technical contacts for the domain are listed the registrar's contact information. This may prevent you from getting spammed by marketing entities, because they do not know who owns the domain. Additional details about this topic can be found at https://www.icann.org/resources/pages/privacy-proxy-registration-2013-03-22-en.

An additional offsite name server for your external-facing domain provides safety when your enterprise connectivity to the Internet is down. For instance, if your enterprise wide area network covers California, Texas, and Virginia, then host a DNS server in a public cloud outside of these sites. In case your wide area network goes off the Internet, your company's external-facing DNS still resolves, based on the off-site DNS server located in a public cloud. A public cloud could be Google Cloud Platform, which offers a hosted DNS service.

DNS Record Types

There are numerous DNS record types. Which record an enterprise uses is entirely up to the enterprise; but, for a functional DNS solution, you need a few basic records:

- A maps the hostname to an IP address.

- PTR maps an IP to a hostname.

- MX is used for mail records—in other words, where to send mail.

- NS is for the authoritative name server.

- SOA, which means start of authority, includes a serial number and other timers relating to the domain.

- TXT stores information about a server, such as operating system or location.

Listing 8-2 shows a few resource record types of DNS.

Listing 8-2. A Few DNS Resource Records

```
#TTL is time to live. Because we are specifying one for the zone, all records inherit this default
value. TTL is how long the record is valid for before it is considered stale.
$TTL 1d

#the zone is dev.example.org and the contact e-mail address in case of a problem with the zone is
admin@example.org. The serial number and other time-related values are discussed after the example
listing.
@ IN SOA dev.example.org. admin.example.org. (
        2014082601      ;serial
        1h              ;refresh->slave refresh from master
        15m             ;retry->how long will slave try
        5d              ;expiry->expire slave data after
        5m)             ;nx->negative cache

        #two name servers
        IN NS ns01.example.org.
        IN NS ns02.example.org.
        #two mail records, the lower value one will be attempted first
        #in our case the lower value of '10' is mail01
        IN MX 10 mail01.example.org.
        IN MX 20 mail02.example.org.

#one web server with IP 10.1.1.100
#the web server has an alias calling it 'www'
#it also has a TXT record that specifies the operating system of the web server
web     IN      A       10.1.1.100
www     IN      CNAME   web
web     IN      TXT     "CentOS 6.4"
```

Comments in a BIND file start with a semicolon. I use a hash symbol in the preceding code to explain what the values are.

The serial number is a random sequential number that lets the slave servers know if they need to pull updates from the master. For instance, you can start at serial number 100, and each time you make a zone change, increase it by one. The slave servers check their serial number against the master's and will know they need to update their zone data. The maximum value of the serial number is $2^{32} - 1$, which is 4,294,967,295.

The next value is the slave refresh value, which is how often the slave reaches out to the master to update its data. RFC 1912 recommends 1200 (20 minutes) to 43,200 (12 hours) seconds. If you are using NOTIFY, then this value can be set to a high number, because the master will notify the slave if there are any updates. This is a signed 32-bit value.

The retry value is how long the slave waits before retrying if it is unable to reach the master when it tries to refresh its data. Typical values can be between 3 minutes and 15 minutes. This is a signed 32-bit value.

The expiry value is how long a slave keeps its data and responds to queries before stopping. The timer for expiry and refresh is reset each time a slave contacts the master and the contact is successful. This value is a signed 32-bit value.

nx is negative cache. It is signed 32 bit. This is basically the time a NAME ERROR = NXDOMAIN value is retained. The maximum value for this should be less than three hours.

CNAME stands for canonical name, and is used for an alias. For instance, if the server name is web and you want to refer to it as www as well, then use a CNAME record.

The TXT record can store any value you want. Be careful what you put in this record. If the zone is public facing and you put confidential information in the TXT field, it can be used to attempt to hack the server. For instance, if you put the operating system name in the TXT field, it allows hackers to attempt attacks against your host for the specified operating system.

We have three resource records related to the hostname web. One of type A, which converts the hostname to an IP address; the other is type CNAME, which provides an alias called www for the host web; and the last is a TXT record, which lists the operating system of the server.

The values an enterprise picks for time to live (TTL), serial, refresh, retry, expire, and nx are dependent on the setup of the DNS infrastructure of the enterprise as well as the technical needs of the company. The TTL, for instance, will be a low value for a company for which the refresh and retries (RRs) change frequently. An online hosting provider, such as Google Compute Engine, will probably have low TTLs because instances or virtual machines are created and deleted often during a given day, and they have to be updated in DNS quickly. On the other hand, an enterprise for which new RRs are added infrequently can afford a longer TTL.

The value for RR can be based on how often edits to the master's zone occur. DNS supports a NOTIFY wherein the master sends a notice to the slave saying there are updates to be pulled, and the slave pulls the updates. This allows you to set a higher threshold for refresh—say, a day, if the zone file is really large.

The value for retry can also be based on how stable your network environment is. If the network connection between the master and the slave is stable, and the master rarely crashes, then the value of retry can be set to a higher number, such as a couple of hours.

Last, the value of expiry should be set very carefully, because if the slave is unable to reach the master and the expiry value is reached, the slave stops responding to queries, which can cause production-related outages. Set this value as high as possible. In the example I included I used five days, but you can go even higher.

A full list of DNS record types can be found at https://www.iana.org/assignments/dns-parameters/dns-parameters.xhtml#dns-parameters-4.

DNS Reverse Mapping

DNS has a resource record called PTR, which maps an IP address to a hostname, and is called *reverse mapping*. This is one area of DNS that is often overlooked and can cause problems with certain applications. Reverse mapping is similar to forward lookup zones, except that with reverse mapping you are restricted to a special root zone called .arpa. Listing 8-3 shows a reverse zone specified in named.conf.

Listing 8-3. Reverse Zone in named.conf

```
#in named.conf, you can specify a reverse zone as follows
#the special .arpa root domain lets BIND know that this is a reverse zone
zone "1.1.10.in-addr.arpa" {
    type master;
    file "maps/reverse/10.1.1.rev";
};
```

When we write a hostname with domain name, the root of the domain is on the right. For instance, with www.example.org, the root is ., followed by the child .org, followed by the child .example. With IP addresses, this is reversed. For instance, with the IP address 10.1.1.5, the root after .arpa and .in-addr is 10 instead of 5.

In Figure 8-2, you can see the reverse zone tree for 10 and also the 192 networks. The 10 network is 10.0.0.0/8 and the 192 network is 192.0.0.0/8.

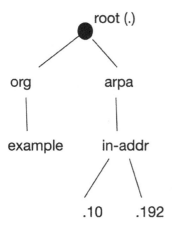

Figure 8-2. *arpa root zone*

Listing 8-4 shows a zone file with reverse address mapping. The zone file is reference in the BIND named.conf. For instance, it could be called 10.1.1.rev, where rev indicates it is a reverse zone file.

Listing 8-4. Reverse Zone File

```
$ORIGIN 1.1.10.in-addr.arpa.
$TTL 1d
@ IN SOA example.org. admin.example.org. (
        100                 ;serial
        1h                  ;slave refresh from master
        15m                 ;how long will slave try
        5d                  ;expire slave data after
        5m)                 ;negative cache

        IN NS ns01.example.org.
        IN NS ns02.example.org.
```

```
1        IN      PTR     gw01.example.org.
2        IN      PTR     time1.example.org.
6   .    IN      PTR     www.example.org.
```

```
#testing the zone file
$ dig +short -x time1.example.org
10.1.1.2
```

In the sample reverse lookup zone file, there is a reverse zone for the network 10.1.1.0/24. The $ORIGIN directive is optional; however, it makes it easy to read the zone file. It basically completes any RRs that are not fully qualified. In this case, the IP addresses 10.1.1.[1,2,6] are being used, so the $ORIGIN directive prepends the 1,2 and 6 with 10.1.1, to get the complete IP address.

The TTL value is one day, and the other values were explained earlier. Notice that for the hostname, fully qualified domain name (FQDN) is used with a . at the end. Without this, the reply will be gw01.example.org.example.org, which is not accurate.

Root Servers

Root servers are used to bootstrap DNS. The root of a domain name is the ., which is at top of the tree. There are 13 named authorities, [a-m].root-servers.net, with hundreds of root servers throughout the world. A list is located at https://www.iana.org/domains/root/servers.

For BIND, you need to download the root hints file located at http://www.internic.net/domain/named.root. In /etc/named.conf, you can refer to the hints file, as shown in Listing 8-5.

Listing 8-5. Root Hints Reference in named.conf

```
#ROOT SERVERS
zone "." {
    type hint;
    file "root.hints";
};
```

Instead of attempting to create your own root hints file, it might be safer to download the one that the Internet's Network Information Center (InterNIC) provides. Because the file contains the A, NS, and AAAA records of the named authorities, you have to be extra careful to ensure their values are correct; otherwise, DNS does not work. Listing 8-6 shows the partial contents of the root hints file.

Listing 8-6. Sample Partial Root Hints File

```
;       This file holds the information on root name servers needed to
;       initialize the cache of Internet domain name servers
;       (e.g., reference this file in the "cache . <file>"
;       configuration file of BIND domain name servers).
;
;       This file is made available by InterNIC
;       under anonymous FTP as
;           file                /domain/named.cache
;           on server           FTP.INTERNIC.NET
;       -OR-                     RS.INTERNIC.NET
;
```

```
;       last update:    June 2, 2014
;       related version of root zone: 2014060201
;
; formerly NS.INTERNIC.NET
;
.                       3600000  IN  NS   A.ROOT-SERVERS.NET.
A.ROOT-SERVERS.NET.     3600000      A    198.41.0.4
A.ROOT-SERVERS.NET.     3600000      AAAA 2001:503:BA3E::2:30
;
; FORMERLY NS1.ISI.EDU
;
.                       3600000      NS   B.ROOT-SERVERS.NET.
B.ROOT-SERVERS.NET.     3600000      A    192.228.79.201
B.ROOT-SERVERS.NET.     3600000      AAAA 2001:500:84::B
...[SNIP]...
; OPERATED BY WIDE
;
.                       3600000      NS   M.ROOT-SERVERS.NET.
M.ROOT-SERVERS.NET.     3600000      A    202.12.27.33
M.ROOT-SERVERS.NET.     3600000      AAAA 2001:DC3::35
; End of File
```

Installing BIND

BIND is available with most if not all Linux distributions. For instance, if you are using CentOS, you can install BIND using the yum repos, as shown in Listing 8-7.

Listing 8-7. Installing BIND Using yum

```
#install BIND using yum on CentOS
# yum install bind
...[SNIP]...
Setting up Install Process
Resolving Dependencies
--> Running transaction check
---> Package bind.x86_64 32:9.8.2-0.23.rc1.el6_5.1 will be installed
--> Finished Dependency Resolution
...[SNIP]...
Total download size: 4.0 M
Installed size: 7.3 M
Is this ok [y/N]: y
Downloading Packages:
bind-9.8.2-0.23.rc1.el6_5.1.x86_64.rpm
...[SNIP]...
Running rpm_check_debug
Running Transaction Test
Transaction Test Succeeded
...[SNIP]...
Installed:
  bind.x86_64 32:9.8.2-0.23.rc1.el6_5.1
Complete!
```

That's about all you need to do to install BIND. The steps after installing are all configuration based and are covered in different sections of this chapter. I recommend starting with the "Named Config File" section next.

BIND has different branches that have different support models. Using yum, you get the version in the yum repository. In this case, it is version 9.8.2. The statuses of the different branches include the following:

- Current stable: This is the most recent version of BIND that is stable and suitable for production use.

- Current stable, extended support version (ESV): This is also recommended for production use, because it is stable, with the added advantage that it is guaranteed extended support, compared with a current stable version, which may have a shorter support life.

- Approaching EOL: Bug and security patches only are provided for these releases, and no new features are added.

- Development: Do not use this version for production. It is only meant for testing and evaluation.

- EOL: Do not use this software; there is no support for it.

- Deprecated: This is definitely not recommended, because it is beyond EOL.

Downloading and compiling BIND is another way of getting the current, stable ESV. First, download BIND from https://www.isc.org/downloads/bind/. Then, compile it using the instructions shown in Listing 8-8.

Listing 8-8. Compiling BIND

```
#install development tools yum group on CentOS or RedHat
$ sudo yum groupinstall "Development Tools" -y

#after untarring the distribution, run configure #in this case we want BIND installed in
/opt/bind-9.9.5 so we use -prefix option
#to get a detailed explanation of configure options run ./configure --help
$ ./configure --prefix=/opt/bind-9.9.5 --enable-newstats --with-libxml2
$ make
# make install
```

Tracking Changes

BIND configuration files should be maintained with configuration management so you can restore easily to a previous version in case of an error. One way of doing this is to use Git. To do this, you will have two Git repositories for the master: one is called etc and the other is called maps. In etc, you place all BIND config files; in maps, you place all zone files.

```
#On a git server, in /gitrepos/dns/master directory
$ git -bare init etc
Initialized empty Git repository in /gitrepos/dns/master/etc/

$git -bare init maps
Initialized empty Git repository in /gitrepos/dns/master/maps/

#On the BIND master server if BIND is installed in, say, /opt/bind
$ cd /opt/bind
$ git clone git@gitserver.example.com:/gitrepos/dns/master/etc
$ git clone git@gitserver.example.com:/gitrepos/dns/master/maps
```

For the slave servers, maintain a separate repo for etc and maps. All slaves can share the same etc Git repo.

```
#On a git server, in /gitrepos/dns/slave directory
$ git -bare init etc
Initialized empty Git repository in /gitrepos/dns/slave/etc/

$ git -bare init maps
Initialized empty Git repository in /gitrepos/dns/slave/maps/

#On the BIND server in if BIND is installed in, say, /opt/bind
$ cd /opt/bind
$ git clone git@gitserver.example.com:/gitrepos/dns/slave/etc
$ git clone git@gitserver.example.com:/gitrepos/dns/slave/maps
```

To make changes to zone files, clone the Git repo on your desktop, make changes, test, and then do Git push. After that test do a Git pull on the BIND master server.. Repeat this process for any slave DNS servers.

Avoid making any changes directly in the production master or the slaves. Always make the changes in your local Git repository, test it, push to a test server, test again, and then push to production hosts.

Named Config File

The BIND configuration file, called named.conf, is the starting point for BIND's work flow. This file controls the behavior and the functionality of BIND. The location of this file is normally in the /etc directory. This file consists of clauses, which are grouped together in statements. You can also have comments in this file, which can begin with either #, /*, or //. If you use C-style comments with /*, you must also end them C style with */. BIND is very picky about the contents of named.conf, so be extra careful when editing this file. Even small syntax errors cause the loading of BIND to fail. Exercise 8-1 displays a sample named.conf configuration.

EXERCISE 8-1. SAMPLE NAMED.CONF

The logging statement specifies where the logs go and what is being logged. In this case, we are logging to a file called named.log in the log directory. There are numerous severities, such as critical, error, warning, notice, info, debug, and dynamic. Let's pick the info level, which logs info and everything above info, which includes info, notice, warning, critical, and error. I recommend monitoring logging to ensure you have sufficient space on disk. In this case, we are keeping five versions of the log file, with each file being, at most, 10MB.

```
#logging-specific statements
logging {
    channel default_log {
        file "log/named.log" versions 5 size 10m;
        severity info;
        print-time yes;
        print-severity yes;
        print-category yes;
    };
    category default {
        default_log;
    };
};
```

The next clause controls general server options, such as in which directory BIND is going to run. In this case, we are using a chroot environment for security, so we need to specify /. The query cache and query control seem similar; however, the difference is that allow-query is for any query, including nonauthoritative data, whereas query-cache allows access to the entries in cache. The cache entries are usually the ones learned through recursion by the server. You only need to specify both if the networks to which they grant access are different; otherwise, specifying one is sufficient, because the other will behave the same way with access control lists (ACLs). You can read more about it at https://kb.isc.org/article/AA-00503/0/Whats-the-difference-between-allow-query-cache-and-allow-recursion.html.

The my-networks statement defines a group of networks that are later defined in the ACL clause. The allow-transfer statement is used for the authoritative transfer (AXFR) query type, which we are restricting to our secondary servers only.

notify tells BIND to notify slave/secondary servers when a change is made on the master server. statistics-file logs statistics about the performance of BIND and, of course, pid-file logs the process id (PID) of the running process.

```
#general server options
options {
    directory "/";
    allow-query-cache { my-networks; };
    allow-query { my-networks; };
    allow-recursion { my-networks; };
    allow-transfer { 10.1.1.100; 10.1.2.100; };
    notify yes;
    statistics-file "log/named.stats";
    pid-file "log/named.pid";
};
```

ACLs are how you control access to data in BIND. In this case, in the general server options clause, we allow recursion only from my-networks, which are now defined. They contain the local host and a /16 network of 10.1.0.0/16.

```
#acl-related statements
acl "my-networks" {
    127.0.0.1;
    localhost;
    localnets;
    10.1.0.0/16;
};
```

■ **Caution**   **Access Control Lists** (ACLs) are key to protecting who can access your DNS zone information. Make sure you always use ACLs, and specify only the networks that need access to DNS zone data.

For some zones, you may want to redirect queries to a proxy DNS server. In this case, for incoming queries on example.org, let's forward them to the DNS servers of example.org, which are listed in the forwarded pragma. You do not need a forwarders zone for every zone you think your DNS server will be queried about. You can read about the additional advantages of forwarding at http://www.zytrax.com/books/dns/ch4/#forwarding.

```
# a forwarding sample
zone "example.org" {
                type forward;
                forwarders { 199.43.132.53; 199.43.133.53; };
};
```

BIND allows for the administration of BIND using a tool called rndc. This tool is key based, so we need a clause for specifying the key name, key file location, and the port on which to listen.

```
#rndc statements
include "etc/rndc.key";
controls {
    inet 127.0.0.1 port 953
    allow {127.0.0.1;} keys { "rndc-key"; };
};
```

Bootstrapping of BIND is done through root hint servers. You can download root.hints from http://www.internic.net/domain/named.root.

```
#dns bootstrapping statements
zone "." {
    type hint;
    file "etc/root.hints";
};
```

The next clause is for a zone we are hosting, which is example.com. The file example.com.zone contains all the non-PTR-related records, such as NS, SOA, A, CNAME, MX, TXT, and others.

```
#example.com zone
zone "example.com" {
    type master;
    file "maps/example.com.zone";
    allow-transfer {
        10.1.0.0/16;
    };
};
```

Last but not the least is the location of the reverse lookup, or PTR zone file. In this case, we are specifying one for the 10.1.1.0/24 network.

```
zone "1.1.10.in-addr.arpa" {
    type master;
    file "maps/reverse/1.1.10.rev";
};
```

Types of DNS Servers

There are four kinds of DNS servers: primary, secondary, forwarding, and caching. Primary servers are where all edits are made, secondaries are read-only copies that store a complete configuration, and caching and forwarding DNS servers are similar in responding from their cache, with the important difference that a caching DNS server does recursive queries but a forwarder does not. The push/pull relationship is shown in Figure 8-3.

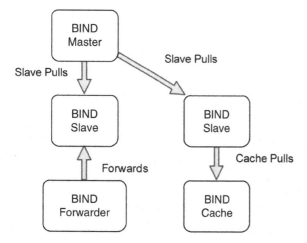

Figure 8-3. *DNS server types*

The order of setting up DNS servers should be primary first, then secondary, then caching. To set up a primary DNS server, in the named.conf file you specify the type to be master.

```
#example.com zone
zone "example.com" {
    type master;
    file "maps/example.com.zone";
    allow-transfer {
        10.1.0.0/16;
    };
};
```

The secondary has a similar setup, except that instead of master, the type is slave.

```
#example.com zone
zone "example.com" {
    type slave;
    masters { 10.1.1.10; }
    file "maps/example.com.zone";
    allow-transfer {
        10.1.0.0/16;
    };
};
```

Caching DNS server configuration is even simpler.

```
options {
        ...[SNIP]...
        recursion yes;
        allow-query { my-networks };
        dnssec-validation auto;
        ..[SNIP]..
}
```

For forwarding a DNS server, you should have a configuration similar to the caching server. Add a few additional statements that indicate it should forward all queries to a given set of DNS servers. A forwarding server generally forwards to caching or to secondary DNS servers.

```
#a forwarding server, with queries being forwarded to Google
options {
        ...[SNIP]...
        recursion yes;
        allow-query { my-networks };
        forwarders {
                8.8.8.8;
                8.8.4.4;
        }
        forward only;
        dnssec-enable yes;
        dnssec-validation yes;
        ..[SNIP]..
}
```

For an enterprise setup, there can be a combination of each type of server. For instance, if an enterprise has remote small offices, caching servers are ideal because most queries can be answered locally. For the larger data centers, have at least one master and as many secondaries as needed based on the load of the clients. Forwarding servers are also useful for stub DNS zones.

Sender Policy Framework

Sender policy framework (SPF) is a way of preventing sender address forgery using DNS. SPF protects the envelope sender address. E-mail addresses have two kinds of addresses: one is called *envelope sender address* and the other is called *header sender address*. The envelope sender address, also known as the return path, is usually not displayed by most e-mail programs and is used for mail delivery from server to server. The header sender address is the From and To fields of an e-mail message, as shown by most e-mail clients.

Let's take example.com—to use SPF for example.com—as the DNS administrator and create a text record with SPF in it.

```
$ dig example.com txt
"v=spf1 mx -all"
```

The item of interest is v=spf -all, which means that if any e-mail originates from the MX record of the domain, then it should be considered valid; otherwise, it can be ignored. To look up the MX record, you then run another query.

```
$ dig example.com mx
10 mx10.example.com.
20 mx20.example.com.
```

If you want to say that you do not send any e-mail from example.com, then you set up your TXT.

```
$ dig example.com txt
"v=spf1 -all"
```

If you want to allow only certain networks to be considered valid senders of e-mail for example.com, then the entry should contain the network numbers.

```
$ dig example.com txt
"v=spf1 ip4: 93.184.216.0/24"
```

You can find our more information about SPF at http://www.openspf.org/.

DNS Security Extensions

To address vulnerabilities in the domain delegation mechanism, DNS security extensions (DNSSEC) was introduced (RFC 4033; http://www.ietf.org/rfc/rfc4033.txt). DNSSEC works by signing zone data digitally using a public key infrastructure. The zone signing starts at the root zone, which is ., and continues down the TLDs, such as com and org. Enterprises can also sign their zone data. In the case of example.com, there we would three places where the zone is signed: ., com, and example.

There are two types of signatures: zone signing key (ZSK) and key signing key (KSK). The process for setting up DNSSEC is a bit complicated. However, it is worth the effort, because it provides an extra layer of confidence about the validity of the DNS zone data for your enterprise. Exercise 8-2 shows how to set up DNSSEC using BIND.

EXERCISE 8-2. DNSSEC SETUP USING BIND

The first step is to enable DNSSEC in /etc/named.conf.

```
options {
    dnssec-enable yes;
    dnssec-validation yes;
    dnssec-lookaside auto;
}
```

The next step is to create the KSK and ZSK keys.

```
# mkdir /etc/pki/dnssec-keys/
# cd dnssec-keys/
# dnssec-keygen -a RSASHA1 -b 1024 -n ZONE example.com
Generating key pair..........++++++ .....++++++
Kexample.com.+005+20898
```

```
# dnssec-keygen -a RSASHA1 -b 4096 -n ZONE -f KSK example.com
Generating key pair....................++ ...................++
Kexample.com.+005+28642
# ls
Kexample.com.+005+20898.key Kexample.com.+005+20898.private Kexample.com.+005+28642.key
Kexample.com.+005+28642.private
```

Now that we have the keys, include them in each of the zone files we need to sign.

```
$INCLUDE /etc/pki/dnssec-keys/Kexample.com.+005+20898.key
$INCLUDE /etc/pki/dnssec-keys/Kexample.com.+005+28642.key
```

We are ready to sign the zone because we have created the keys and included the path in the zone file.

```
cd /var/named
dnssec-signzone -S -K /etc/pki/dnssec-keys -e +3024000 -o example.com -N INCREMENT
example.com.hosts
```

For the zone file in /etc/named.conf, replace the zone information with the signed zone.

```
#in /etc/named.conf
zone "example.com" {
    file "example.com.signed";
};
```

Restart named after completing the previous steps.

```
# service named reload
```

By default, zone signatures expire 30 days after creation, so create a script to sign the zone automatically and stick it in cron.monthly.

```
#!/bin/bash
SIGNZONE="/usr/sbin/dnssec-signzone"
DNSSEC_KEYS="/etc/pki/dnssec-keys"
ZONEFILES="/var/named"
cd $ZONEFILES
for zones in *.signed; do
ZONE=`echo $zones | /bin/cut -d. -f1-2`
$SIGNZONE -S -K $DNSSEC_KEYS -e +3024000 -o $ZONE -N INCREMENT \
$ZONE.hosts
done
/sbin/service named reload
```

BIND Zone Delegation

One way of reducing the load on a BIND master server is to delegate zones to other servers. The other servers then become masters for the concerned zones that have been delegated to them. For instance, with example.com, va.example.com may be delegated to a server in Virginia and tx.example.com may be delegated to a master server in Texas. Exercise 8-3 shows how to set up BIND zone delegation.

EXERCISE 8-3. BIND ZONE DELEGATION EXAMPLE

On the master BIND server for example.com, we have one zone configured: example.com in named.conf. For the subdomain tx.example.com, we are acting as secondary. Being secondary is optional and not required.

```
#named.conf file on the master for example.com
zone "example.com" {
  type master;
  file "master/master.example.com";
};

zone "tx.example.com"  {
  type slave;
  file "slave/slave.tx.example.com";
  masters {10.1.2.53;};
};
```

In the zone file for example.com, we specify the SOA, and NS record for example.com. After that, we have the A record for ns1 and ns2, which are the two name servers for example.com. Zone delegation of tx.example.com is done right after that to the name server ns3.tx.example.com.

```
----------------------------------
#example.com zone file on master
$TTL 1d ; default TTL is 1 day
$ORIGIN example.com.
@              IN      SOA   ns1.example.com. admin.example.com. (
               100           ; serial number
               2h            ; refresh =  2 hours
               15M           ; update retry = 15 minutes
               3W12h         ; expiry = 3 weeks + 12 hours
               2h20M         ; minimum = 2 hours + 20 minutes
               )
; main domain name servers
               IN      NS    ns1.example.com.
               IN      NS    ns2.example.com.
; A records for name servers above
ns1            IN      A     10.1.1.53
ns2            IN      A     10.1.1.54
```

```
# zone delegation being done in this section
#master is ns3.tx.example.com and slave is ns1.example.com
$ORIGIN us.example.com.
tx.example.com.          IN      NS      ns3.tx.example.com.
                         IN      NS      ns1.example.com.
ns3.tx.example.com.              A       10.1.2.53
```

On ns3.tx.example.com, in /etc/named.conf, we specify the tx.example.com master to be ns3.tx.example.com. We also allow transfer to ns1.example.com because ns1.example.com is our secondary.

```
#on ns3.tx.example.com, our named.conf
options {
    allow-transfer {"none";};
};
zone "tx.example.com" {
        type master;
        file "master/master.us.example.com";
        allow-transfer {10.1.1.53;};
};
```

The zone file for tx.example.com has $ORIGIN set to tx.example.com and it contains the SOA and the NS record for ns3.example.com.

```
#on ns3.tx.example.com, our zone file
$TTL 1d ; default TTL = 1 days
$ORIGIN tx.example.com.
@           IN      SOA     ns3.tx.example.com. hostmaster.tx.example.com. (
            100         ; serial number
            2h          ; refresh =  2 hours
            15M         ; update retry = 15 minutes
            3W12h       ; expiry = 3 weeks + 12 hours
            2h20M       ; minimum = 2 hours + 20 minutes
            )
            IN      NS      ns3.tx.example.com.
            IN      NS      ns1.example.com.

ns3         IN      A       10.1.2.53
```

Where to Get BIND Help

There are numerous mailing lists that are helpful with BIND. You can find a complete list of them at https://lists.isc.org/mailman/listinfo. A few that I recommend include the following.

- bind-announce: helps you keep up to date with new releases of BIND

- bind-users: contains general questions about BIND

- dhcp-announce: contains announcements about DHCPD

- dhcp-users: helps with DHCPD

In addition, there are some very good books on DNS and BIND that I recommend you read. One of them is *DNS and Bind*, 5th edition, by Cricket Liu and Paul Albitz; the other is *DNS & Bind Cookbook* by Cricket Liu.

The ISC also offers professional support for BIND at `http://www.dns-co.com/solutions/bind-subscription/`. The most basic support starts at an annual rate of $10,000 as of this writing.

BIND Enterprise Architecture

After deciding on a TLD, registrar, domain name, and DNS software, the next step is to decide how to place DNS servers in an enterprise. Because this chapter covers installing BIND, let's use BIND setup examples. As mentioned, BIND supports primary, secondary, and caching servers. Edits to zones are made on the primary server, and secondary and caching pull the edits from the primary. The number of zones and the number of records affect the performance of BIND.

Dividing your domain namespace into zones is a crucial component of the architecture. One approach is to have a zone per region. Let's say `example.com` has offices in California, Texas, Virginia, and Singapore. The subdomains that can be created are

- `ca.example.com`
- `tx.example.com`
- `va.example.com`
- `sg.example.com`

There can be a further division of these zones based on the type of application. For instance,

- Production servers can be in `prd.<site>.example.com`
- QA servers can be in `qa.<site>.example.com`
- Development servers can be in `dev.<site>.example.com`

For the servers themselves, the hostname can be the type of server and the application, such as the following:

- `web001-fe.prd.va.example.com`, for an Apache production server that is part of the `fe` or front-end application out of Virginia
- `db002-erp.qa.tx.example.com`, for a MySQL QA database server in the `erp`, or enterprise resource planning, application out of the Texas location

Regarding the type of servers, BIND supports only a single primary, where edits are made, so you will have one primary. This primary can be clustered with Linux HA, such as `http://www.linux-ha.org/wiki/Main_Page`. Or you can avoid the complexity of an HA solution and rely on a single master. The location of the master should be at a site that has the most redundant and fast network links. In this case, let's say Texas has the most bandwidth, so you would place the master in Texas.

If there are a large number of subdomains, then instead of having one single master, delegate the subdomains to other DNS servers. This strategy offloads the responsibility of a single master. Offloading of DNS subdomains is done through zone delegation, which is different than forwarding. Zone delegation means that another child server is responsible for the zone data, and any queries should be sent to the child DNS zone server.

Each site should have a minimum of two secondary servers. One possibility is to have at least two name servers per subnet so that you avoid an issues dealing with router failures. However, this may be excessive for some organizations; instead, they may prefer to go with couple of name servers for every *x* number of subnets. The number of actual secondaries is based on the number of queries expected and the type of hardware. For instance, if you pick ten core processors, and a secondary has at least two ten-core processors, with a large amount of physical memory—say, 512GB—a couple of secondaries might be sufficient to handle many thousands of queries per second.

Both servers should be listed in clients' /etc/resolv.conf; however, the order is different in one half of the clients. One half of the clients should have one secondary listed first; the other half should have the other secondary listed first. In this way, load is split up between the two.

For storing zone information, let's use Git (http://git-scm.com/). The advantage of using Git is that you can have revision control along with the decentralized model of Git, which makes it easy to make edits in the zone files.

Understanding DHCP

DHCP is a quick-and-easy way to provide network devices with IP addresses. DNS and DHCP are closely related—one provides IP addresses and the other provides mapping of IP addresses to hostnames and vice versa. DHCP can be integrated with DNS so that when a DHCP IP address is handed to a network device, DNS is then updated to reflect the name of the device. Alternatively, DHCP IP addresses can be given predetermined names so there is no need to update DNS dynamically. DHCP is used in enterprises for numerous reasons, such as providing the following:

- An IP address during host provisioning using Kickstart

- IP addresses for wireless clients in a corporate network, such as for laptops and smartphones

- Voice over Internet Protocol (VoIP) client IP addresses, such as for VoIP phones

- Desktop IP addresses

- Laptop IP addresses for employees, guests, and contractors

Servers are generally not given DHCP IP addresses; instead, they are given static IP addresses.

DHCP Enterprise Architecture

Security engineers at enterprises may frown on DHCP because it is difficult to track down DHCP-assigned IP addresses. For instance, if an attack is happening from a given IP address, in the case of static IP address assignment, one can look up to which device the IP belongs in an IP address management database, and then track it down. With DHCP, unless DHCP reservations are made, the IP address could belong to any DHCP-enabled node on the network. For wired DHCP clients, you would have to look at router/switch media access control (MAC) address tables to figure out to which port the device is connected, and also the vendor ID of the MAC address, and go from there. If the DHCP IP address is from a wireless device, then it becomes more difficult to track the IP, unless some sort of extensible authentication protocol (EAP) is being used.

DHCP can still play a role in enterprise architecture. Using reserved DHCP IP addresses, you can assign an IP to a given MAC address, which helps you keep track of devices on the network. MAC addresses can be spoofed, however; they are one more layer of complexity an attacker has to penetrate.

The question then arises: Which devices should use DHCP in an enterprise? For certain, do not use DHCP IP addresses for servers. Give servers static IP addresses; it's a lot easier to manage them with static IP addresses. Use DHCP for wireless clients and for guests that use your network. If you use EAP, with Radius authentication, you can track DHCP-assigned IP address to usernames, thereby making accounting easier.

For kick-starting Linux hosts, use DHCP with static reservation based on the MAC address of the server. This enables you to use PXE boot, while ensuring that DHCP IP addresses are not assigned to rogue devices.

How many DHCP servers are needed for an enterprise is a question that should be answered before you start deploying DHCP servers. The location of each of the servers also matters. One approach is that, on each server network, set up the router with an IP helper to forward all DHCP requests to a pair of DHCP servers. Because DHCP will be used sparingly (only during the PXE boot installation process), you do not need a large number of DHCP servers. A robust DHCP server can handle thousands of requests at a time, so a couple of DHCP servers for, say, 1000 clients should be sufficient. If a given site has, say, 5000 servers, then five pairs of DHCP servers—one pair per 1000 clients—should be sufficient. The actual number of DHCP clients your DHCP server can serve at a given time is based on the hardware used and the number of simultaneous requests.

Primary DHCP Server

To set up the first DHCP server, you can either download ISC DHCP or use the one that comes with your Linux distribution. Similar to BIND, DHCP is available as an ESV, current, or current stable. Current stable is recommended for production and so is ESV. As of this writing, version 4.1-ESV-R10 is the latest ESV. For enterprises that prefer the latest stable version, select current-stable, for enterprises that prefer infrequent updates, but more stability, pick ESV. After you download DHCP from `https://www.isc.org/downloads`, next step is to compile it.

```
### Configure will automatically select the most suitable otions
### make will build DHCP and make install will install it in /usr/local
$ ./configure
# make
# make install
```

Most Linux distributions come with DHCP. For example, with CentOS you can install DHCPD using yum repositories.

```
$ yum search dhcp | egrep -i '^dhc'
dhcping.x86_64 : DHCP daemon ping program
dhcp-common.x86_64 : Common files used by ISC dhcp client and server
dhcp-devel.i686 : Development headers and libraries for interfacing to the DHCP
dhcp-devel.x86_64 : Development headers and libraries for interfacing to the
dhclient.x86_64 : Provides the dhclient ISC DHCP client daemon and
dhcp.x86_64 : Dynamic host configuration protocol software
```

The packages you need are dhclient, dhcp-common, and dhcp. Installing the package using the distribution yum repositories might save you the trouble of compiling your own.

DHCP consist of two different components: one is the client and the other is the server. You do not need the client on the server. The server configuration file is /etc/dhcp/dhcpd.conf. If you want the server itself to use DHCP to get an IP address, that should be specified in /etc/sysconfig/network-scripts/ifcfg-eth0, in which you would set BOOTPROTO=dhcp.

■ **Note**   DHCPD does not start if /var/lib/dhcpd/dhcpd.leases is missing on CentOS/RedHat default installation. You can touch this file to start DHCPD.

The server's main configuration file has numerous statements, which are grouped in clauses. DHCP is very particular about syntax, so make sure you double-check your syntax after making a change; otherwise, DHCP does not start. A sample DHCPD.conf file is show in Exercise 8-4.

EXERCISE 8-4. DHCPD.CONF FILE

Global settings are those that apply to all clients. Normally, they are listed at the top of the file. Within global settings, there are parameters that start with the option keyword, which is DHCP option. Other parameters that do not start with the option keyword are specifically for DHCPD. DHCPD can be authoritative for a given network, which means that it responds to all DHCP requests even if it is not aware of the IP address. The unknown-clients parameter allows DHCP to respond to requests from clients that are not specifically defined in the DHCPD file. For enterprises, it is common to have numerous authoritative DHCPD servers. Either a DHCPD server has multiple physical networks attached to it or one physical network that is trunked, and virtual local area networks (vlans) are configured on the DHCPD server.

```
#global settings
authoritative;
allow unknown-clients;
allow bootp;

option domain-name   "example.com";
option domain-name-servers  10.1.1.2,10.1.1.3;
option ntp-servers 10.1.1.4,10.1.1.5;
```

Lease time is a crucial component of DHCP configuration. If you configure a short lease time, clients come back repeatedly for an IP address, which may overload the DHCP sever. On the other hand, if you configure a long DHCP lease time, then it may result in clients holding on to IP addresses. The ideal time is dependent on the use of the DHCP clients. For instance, if DHCP is primarily being used for imaging of servers, a short lease time makes sense, because the client only needs a DHCP IP addresses during the installation of the operating system, after which it can be assigned a static IP address. If the DHCP server is used for virtual private network (VPN) clients and for wireless clients, then a longer lease time may be helpful to reduce the load on the DHCP server. The time is specified in seconds, and in this case it is set to be one hour for default and two hours for max lease. The difference between default and max is that when a client does not request a specific lease time, the default value is assigned. On the other hand, if a client requests a specific lease time, it can be no longer than the max lease time.

```
default-lease-time 3600;
max-lease-time 7200;
```

For each subnet that requires DHCP service and is attached to the DHCPD server, a subnet declaration is required. The DHCP range option specifies the range of IP addresses that a DHCPD server hands out to clients. This range is dependent on the available IP addresses in the subnet. In our case, with a subnet mask of /24, we picked 200 IP addresses from 10.1.1.50 to 10.1.1.250 for the DHCP range. The other IP addresses have been left for administrative purposes, such as routers, DNS servers, the DHCP server itself, and other services.

```
#subnet declaration
subnet 10.1.1.0 netmask 255.255.255.0 {
    option routers                10.1.1.254;
    option subnet-mask            255.255.255.0;
    option broadcast-address      10.1.1.255;

    option domain-name            "dev.example.com";

      range 10.1.1.50 10.1.1.250;
}
```

Groups are a way of having common settings for a set of DHCP clients. For instance, let's say we have to ensure that two specific laptops are in a certain time zone. We can use `option time-offset` to specify this using DHCP. In addition, we want to ensure the two specific clients come back online with the same IP as before, so we use the `host` statement as part of the group.

```
#groups
group {
   # Specific TZ for database servers
   option time-offset              -21000;

   host myclient1 {
      option host-name "db001.example.com";
      hardware ethernet XX:XX:XX:XX:XX:XX;
      fixed-address 10.1.1.20;
      allow booting;
   }

   host myclient2 {
      option host-name "db002.example.com";
      hardware ethernet XX:XX:XX:XX:XX:XX;
      fixed-address 10.1.1.21;
      allow booting;
   }
```

For an enterprise, the settings in a DHCPD configuration file are dependent on the underlying network infrastructure and the number of DHCP clients. As a general rule, though, have only as many DHCP servers as needed—not more—because giving out IP addresses to network devices can turn into a potential security risk if rogue devices show up on the network.

Some enterprises go as far as giving out DHCP IP addresses only to known MAC addresses. Although this strategy is not fail-proof, because MAC addresses can be spoofed, it does offer one more layer of protection.

DHCP Failover

As part of any reliable enterprise infrastructure, there needs to be a failover DHCP server. Fortunately, ISC DHCP supports primary and secondary mode—meaning, if one DHCP server dies, the other one can take over the DHCP IP address provisioning.

It is crucial that both the primary and the secondary DHCP servers are running the same version of DHCPD. Both DHCP servers should also have their time synchronized using NTP. They should both be on the same networks as well, and have access to all the networks for which they are servicing DHCP IP addresses.

After you have decided how many DHCP servers are needed, and the location of each of these servers, create a pair of DHCP servers for each location. The pair serves the same networks and shares the same configuration. A sample DHCP failover configuration is explained in Exercise 8-5.

EXERCISE 8-5. DHCP FAILOVER EXAMPLE CONFIGURATION

We can run DHCPD in a load-balancing mode with failover, or just failover without load balancing. With load balancing, as is seen in this example, the split value is defined at 128, which means that 50% of requests go to the primary server and 50% of requests go to the secondary server, which helps split the load between the servers. If the primary goes down, the secondary starts answering for the primary as well.

The mclt value is the maximum client lead time value, or the number of seconds a recovering primary must wait after it has received its peer lease database, and before it can start assuming the primary role. Both the split and mclt values are defined only on the primary, not on the secondary. The max response delay value is set to 45 seconds, and it is the time a primary waits before considering a peer connection down.

max-unacked-updates allows up to ten unacknowledged binding updates, which means the server has to wait for an acknowledgment of outstanding packets prior to sending out additional messages.

```
failover peer "failover-partner" {
    primary;
    address dhcp-primary.example.com;
    port 519;
    peer address dhcp-secondary.example.com;
    peer port 520;
    max response delay 45;
    max unacked updates 10;
    mclt 3600;
    split 128;
    load balance max seconds 3;
}
```

The secondary DHCP server has a heartbeat port of 520 and the primary has one of 519. Both these port numbers are arbitrary; you can set them to whatever you want.

```
failover peer "failover-partner" {
    secondary;
    address dhcp-secondary.example.com;
    port 520;
    peer address dhcp-primary.example.com;
    peer port 519;
    max response delay 45;
    max unacked updates 10;
    load balance max seconds 3;
}
```

The subnet statement refers to `failover-partner`, which we defined earlier in the configuration file.

```
subnet 10.1.1.0 netmask 255.255.255.0 {
    option domain-name-servers 10.1.1.10;
    option routers 10.1.1.1;
    pool {
        failover peer "failover-partner";
        range 10.1.1.50 10.1.1.254;
        }
}
```

For the primary and secondary to communicate securely, we need a key. We can use `dnssec-keygen` to generate that key. Make sure you enter the key in both the primary and the secondary configuration files.

```
#replace the secret key with your own key
#you can generate a key as follows
#  $dnssec keygen  a HMAC MD5  b 512  n USER DHCP_OMAPI

omapi-port 7911;
omapi-key omapi_key;

key omapi_key {
    algorithm hmac-md5;
    secret yoursecretkey;
}
```

Conclusion

ISC BIND DNS and ISC DHCPD are robust, enterprise-friendly applications that together can provide your enterprise with DNS and DHCP services. As part of a larger infrastructure design strategy for your enterprise, both of these solutions should be included.

CHAPTER 9

■ ■ ■

Log Collection, OpenVPN, and iptables

This chapter covers three topics related to security: log collection, virtual private networks (VPNs), and firewalls. Log collection and analysis is an integral part of an effective infrastructure support strategy. OpenVPN enables secure VPNs and iptables is a fast and powerful firewall built into Linux.

Why Collect Logs?

Log management is a crucial component of infrastructure engineering. Logs are generated from numerous sources, such as applications, operating systems, networks, system devices, and services. Logs can be useful for the following:

- *Troubleshooting applications*: Log files are the first place to look when trying to figure out what is wrong with applications. By supporting various debug levels, you can leave a breadcrumb trail for where to look for problems.

- *Security review*: Log files provide useful information about security-related issues. For instance, the /var/log/secure file lets us know about who ran sudo commands and who logged in to the system.

- *Forensic analysis*: In the case of a system breakin, log files offer clues on how the attack occurred. Of course, it is possible that the attacker manipulated the log files as well.

- *Monitoring and alerting*: Although it is not the most ideal approach, you can use tools such as Logwatch to monitor log files for events and then to send out alerts based on that.

- *Trend analysis*: If metrics are output to log files, they can be collected and displayed using graphs. For instance, the Apache status page shows metrics about Apache performance.

As a developer and a site reliability engineer, you have to be proficient at writing to log files while developing applications, and reading from log files while debugging applications. Syslog protocol as, defined in RFC 5424 (https://tools.ietf.org/html/rfc5424), is widely used by network devices to send logs to a centralized logging server.

Logging Solutions

There are a wide variety of logging solutions:

- rsyslog (http://www.rsyslog.com/)

- systemd-journald (https://wiki.archlinux.org/index.php/systemd#Journal)

- syslog-ng (http://www.balabit.com/network-security/syslog-ng)

- Splunk (http://www.splunk.com/)

- fluentd (http://www.fluentd.org/)

- logstash (http://logstash.net)

- Graylog2 (http://www.graylog2.org)

- Apache Flume (http://flume.apache.org)

- logwatch (http://sourceforge.net/projects/logwatch/files/)

Application logging can use Syslog or logging solutions designed specifically for applications, including

- Logback (http://logback.qos.ch/)

- Log4j (https://logging.apache.org/log4j/2.x/)

The choice of a logging solution can be complex. They all support logs in the Syslog format. Some of them have commercial versions as well, such syslog-ng and Splunk. For simplicity's sake, rsyslog might be the easiest options because it comes installed by default with CentOS/RedHat. All the other tools you have to install and configure.

Splunk has gained a lot of popularity because it has a good graphical representation of logs. However, the free version of Splunk supports up to 500MB of indexing per day, whereas the enterprise version has no limit. You can read more about the differences between the free and enterprise versions at http://www.splunk.com/view/SP-CAAAE8W. logstash and Graylog2 are popular alternatives to Splunk. Both are open source and free. logstash uses ElasticSearch (http://www.elasticsearch.org) for indexing and Kibana for visual graphing (http://www.elasticsearch.org/overview/kibana/). Log4j is a very popular Java-based logging mechanism that can be used to send logs to Syslog or to other logging back ends from within applications. Apache Flume is very popular in the Hadoop world, where it is used to collect logs and send to Hadoop for processing. logwatch is a customizable solution that lets you send alerts based on events in log files. An enterprise might have numerous logging solutions installed. As an IT standard, though, you might find it easier if you pick one or two solutions and use them throughout the organization.

rsyslog

rsyslog is the default logging mechanism in many Linux distributions, such as CentOS and RedHat. The configuration of rsyslog is handled through the /etc/rsyslog.conf file. Because rsyslog is included with most Linux distributions, you do not have to install it manually, unless you want to download a different version. You can visit the rsyslog web site at http://www.rsyslog.com, then download and install the latest version if you wish.

A large number of Linux services use rsyslog by default. Looking at /var/log/messages on CentOS, you can see the different services using rsyslog:

```
# awk '{print $5}' /var/log/messages | awk -F'[' '{print $1}' | sort -u  | head -5
abrtd:
acpid:
audispd:
auditd
bluetoothd
```

The configuration file of rsyslog can be fairly complex. The file is divided into three sections:

1. Modules

2. Global directives

3. Rules

Modules allow rsyslog to communicate with external sources and to divide up the work of rsyslog into different components. Some of the types of modules are as follows:

- Input

- Output

- Parser

- Message modification

- String generator

- Library

The input module, for instance, is used to gather input from various sources, such as imfile for text files, imtcp for TCP syslog, and imklog for kernel logging. There are many more input modules, and you can read about them in file:///usr/share/doc/rsyslog-<version>/rsyslog_conf_modules.html on your CentOS/RedHat distribution system.

Global directives apply to all modules. An example of a global directive is $IncludeConfig /etc/rsyslog.d/*.conf, which indicates to rsyslog that configuration files in the /etc/rsyslog.d/ directory should be read. Another global directive of interest is $ActionResumeInterval <seconds>, which is used to specify how long rsyslog should wait before reattempting an action that did not succeed the first time. For instance, if a connection with a host is lost, rsyslog waits the specified number of seconds in this directive before attempting to reconnect. You can read more about these directives in file:///usr/share/doc/rsyslog-<version>/rsyslog_conf_global.html on your CentOS/RedHat system.

Rules specify where to send log files and are composed of a selector and an action. An example of a mail rule that sends all mail logs to /var/log/maillog is

```
mail.*    /var/log/maillog
```

Additional information about modules, directives, and rules is in section "rsyslog Configuration" later in the chapter.

Logging Architecture

The simplest design for a log architecture is to have one rsyslog server per data center, assuming the log server is powerful enough to handle all the logs from the systems in the data center (Figure 9-1).

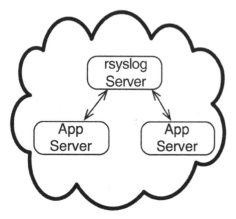

Figure 9-1. *One log server per data center*

This design is not a scalable and is also not fault tolerant. It can be made scalable and fault tolerant by adding a load balancer and increasing the number of rsyslog servers. The problem with load balancers is that not all of them support UDP, and, by default, log messages are in UDP format. You can change log messages to be sent via TCP; however, there is protocol overhead associated with TCP that should be kept in mind.

Another approach is to use near-term and long-term logging storage. As shown in Figure 9-2, you can send data to rsyslog, and from there you can then move logs that are not needed to, say, Amazon S3 or something similar.

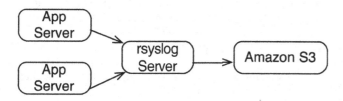

Figure 9-2. *Using near-term and long-term log storage*

You can also add log analysis to this scenario, as shown in Figure 9-3.

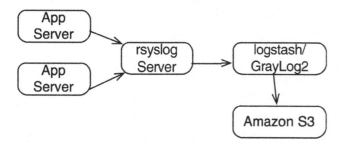

Figure 9-3. *Using rsyslog with logstash/Graylog2 and Amazon S3*

Figure 9-4 shows a TCP-based load balancer example with rsyslog. Some of the more popular load balancers that can be used include the following:

- HAProxy (`http://www.haproxy.org`)

- Linux Virtual Server (`http://www.linuxvirtualserver.org`)

- nginx (`http://nginx.org`)

- Apache mod_proxy (`http://httpd.apache.org/docs/2.2/mod/mod_proxy.html`)

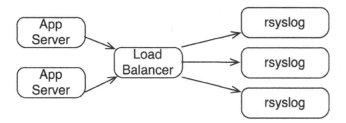

Figure 9-4. *Using a load balancer with rsyslog*

rsyslog Configuration

The configuration file for rsyslog is, by default, `/etc/rsyslog.conf`. Any additional configurations can be stored in the `/etc/rsyslog.d` directory. Listing 9-1 explains the format of the `rsyslog.conf` file.

LISTING 9-1. RSYSLOG CONFIGURATION FILE

The first section is the modules section. Let's load three modules: one is for Unix sockets (`imuxsock`) and the other is for kernel logging (`imklog`). Then, we need to tell the UDP module to accept incoming UDP connections on port 514.

```
$ModLoad imuxsock
$ModLoad imklog
$ModLoad imudp
$UDPServerRun 514
```

In the next section we need to specify the global directives. Let's list two directives, the first of which specifies the log file format. In our case, it is a traditional syslog format. For greater precision timestamps, remove the traditional file format and rsyslog defaults to the RFC 3339 timestamp format (`https://www.ietf.org/rfc/rfc3339.txt`). Let's also ask rsyslog to include any configuration settings in the `/etc/rsyslog.d` directory.

```
$ActionFileDefaultTemplate RSYSLOG_TraditionalFileFormat
$IncludeConfig /etc/rsyslog.d/*.conf
```

The last section specifies rules. Each line here has two parts: an initial selector and an action. The selector itself is divided into two parts: a facility and a priority. `mail`, for instance is a facility, and the priority is `*`, which means any priority. The action for `mail.*` is to send to a file called `/var/log/messages`. You can view a list of all facilities at `http://wiki.gentoo.org/wiki/Rsyslog#Facility`; a list of priorities are in the syslog(3) main page.

We now have four rules being listed: one is to send all `info` messages from any source, except for `mail`, `authpriv` and `cron` to go to `/var/log/messages`. This is because we have other files for those messages.

All mail messages go to `/var/log/maillog`. Any emergency messages go to all destinations, and all `uucp` as well as `news.crit` go to `/var/log/spooler`. Last, any `local7` messages go to `/var/log/boot.log`.

```
*.info;mail.none;authpriv.none;cron.none          /var/log/messages
mail.*                                            -/var/log/maillog
*.emerg                                           *
uucp,news.crit                                    /var/log/spooler
local7.*                                          /var/log/boot.log
```

The actions available for the rules sections are the following:

- *Regular file*: Specify the full path of the file.

- *Named pipe*: Specify using the pipe (|) symbol. Create the pipe first using `mkfifo`. This action is useful for debugging.

- *Terminal and console*: Specify using `-tty` or `/dev/console`.

- *Remote machine*: Use `@@remote-host-name` to send to the remote host, using UDP on port 514.

- *List of users*: Specify the logged-in users, in the format :omusrmsg:root,user1

- *Everyone logged in*: Use the same format as list of users, replacing the username with a wildcard: `:omusrmsg:*`

- *Database table*: Use to send output to a database, such as MariaDB

- *Discard*: Use to discard messages you do not want.

- *Output channel*: Use to indicate the output channel, defined via the `$outchannel` directive. The syntax is `$outchannel name,file-name,max-size,action-on-max-size`

- *Shell execute*: Use to execute a program in a subshell—for example, `^program-to-execute;template`. The program receives the messages as a single string: `argv[1]`.

Which action to pick is dependent on how many logs you are collecting and the type of storage available. For instance, using files may work out just fine if you are using network-attached storage (NAS) that can be grown dynamically. If you have a small disk size on the rsyslog server, definitely do not store log files locally. Some possible strategies for log storing include

- Storing files locally, then log rotating them onto a NAS device every hour

- Not storing files locally at all, and having all of them on the NAS device

- Uploading file to an online cloud such as Amazon S3

Log Retention

How long are logs kept is a question that should be answered based on numerous factors, including the following:

- Regulatory requirements of industry
- Security needs of the organization
- Cost of storing logs
- Management complexity

Regulatory requirements might apply to companies in the finance, insurance, or other such industries. In the United States, the Securities & Exchange Commission might have rules on how long application logs from trading applications be kept, and government offices might have certain requirements on how long logs should be kept as well. Figure 9-5 illustrates one possibility of storing logs with different retention periods.

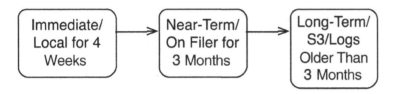

Figure 9-5. *Log retention policies*

Log Rotation

Log rotation is the process of moving current logs into older log files. For instance, because Linux system messages are stored in /var/log/messages, using log rotation they can be moved to /var/log/messages.<date>, representing each day of the week. The command used to rotate logs is logrotate. By default, CentOS/RedHat have a logrotate script that runs daily, as specified in /etc/cron.daily (Listing 9-2).

Listing 9-2. logrorate Script in /etc/cron.daily

```sh
#!/bin/sh

/usr/sbin/logrotate /etc/logrotate.conf >/dev/null 2>&1
EXITVALUE=$?
if [ $EXITVALUE != 0 ]; then
    /usr/bin/logger -t logrotate "ALERT exited abnormally with [$EXITVALUE]"
fi
exit 0
```

logrotate configuration is stored in /etc/logrotate.conf. Additional configuration settings are stored in the /etc/logrotate.d directory. Listing 9-3 shows an example of a logrotate.conf file.

LISTING 9-3. LOGROTATE.CONF

The keyword `weekly` indicates that log files should be rotated on a weekly basis. Other options include `daily` and `monthly`, or are based on size.

```
# rotate log files weekly
weekly
```

They keyword `rotate` indicates how many instances of the log should be kept. In our case, we want to keep—at most—four instances, after which the oldest one is overwritten.

```
# keep 4 weeks worth of backlogs
rotate 4
```

Considering that a process may have a log file open, renaming it may cause file handle issues with the log file. Therefore, we need to create a new log file after rotating the older one.

```
# create new (empty) log files after rotating old ones
create
```

A self-explanatory statement needs to be added about using the date to append to the log file indicating the date it was rotated. An example is `/var/log/messages-20141012`, indicating October 12, 2014, as the log rotation date.

```
# use date as a suffix of the rotated file
dateext
```

Compress logs after rotation. You can use the keyword `nocompress` if you want to avoid compression.

```
# compress log files
compress
```

Let `logrotate` know that it should also read the `/etc/logrotate.d` directory for additional configuration options.

```
# additional configuration directory
include /etc/logrotate.d
...[SNIP]...
```

Although in Listing 9-3 we specified some general options for `logrotate` in `logrotate.conf`, we did not specify which files it needs to rotate. This can be done in the `/etc/logrotate.d` directory. For instance, there exists a file called `/etc/logrotate.d/syslog` on CentOS that specifies a number of files to be included in the log rotation (Listing 9-4). In the syslog file, let's specify five different log files to be rotated.

After the file names are the directives for those files. The global directives are inherited from `/etc/logrotate.conf`, and then the file-specific ones are applied. For all these five files, there is one set of directives, indicated by the opening { and ending by the }. The keyword `sharedscripts` indicates to `logrotate` that the `postrotate` script should be run only once after all five files are rotated, not once per file rotation. The `postrotate` script is specified as sending the HUP signal to syslog so that it rereads the log files. The keyword `endscript` indicates the end of the postscript section.

Listing 9-4. /etc/logrotate.d/syslog

```
# cat syslog
/var/log/cron
/var/log/maillog
/var/log/messages
/var/log/secure
/var/log/spooler
{
    sharedscripts
    postrotate
        /bin/kill -HUP `cat /var/run/syslogd.pid 2> /dev/null` 2> /dev/null || true
    endscript
}
```

You can read more about the format of logrotate.conf in its man page.

Log Rotation Strategy

There are numerous log rotation scripts provided by default in Linux. They cover a large number of system log files. For application log files, you have two choices: one is to add application-specific log rotation in the /etc/logrotate.d directory and the other is to use log4j or other in-application methods for log rotation. An advantage of using logrotate is that a lot of maturity is built in to it and you can centralize the handling of logs.

Role of VPNs in an Enterprise

VPNs play at least two important roles in an organization. First, they provide remote connectivity for users; second, they enable site-to-site connectivity between the organization's remote networks. Remote connectivity for users might enable access from home, on the road, or any other location that is not the corporate office. Site-to-site connectivity might be between two data centers or between headquarters and another office site.

Distance is generally not a factor in VPN consideration; rather, transit medium must be considered. As soon as an organization's traffic leaves it network, using a VPN becomes a necessity. A VPN is very useful for authorization, authentication, and accounting of remote end points. Edward Snowden revealed that the National Security Agency (NSA) has been snooping in corporate offices, especially unencrypted links between different data centers belonging to the same company, such as Google and Yahoo!. Using a VPN ensures encryption that protects your data from the snooping eyes of even the government. (http://www.theguardian.com/us-news/the-nsa-files.)

With employees working remotely, a VPN can help in securing corporate electronic assets through the use of authorization, authentication, and accounting. A large corporation banned remote workers when they found out, using auditing of VPNs, that work-from-home employees were barely connecting to the VPN.

Even within a corporate network, using encryption whenever possible is a more secure way of doing business. The cost of adding encryption to an application is generally not high and is worth the effort.

Picking a VPN Technology

Two of the popular VPN technologies available are:

1. Secure socket layer (SSL)

2. Internet Protocol Security (IPSec)

IPSec operates at layer 3, or the network layer; SSL operates at layer 6, or the presentation layer. SSL VPNs are easier to deploy than IPSec VPNs, primarily because of this difference between them. Also, when it comes to crossing network address translation (NAT) boundaries, you do not need any additional configuration with SSL, but you might need it with IPSec. SSL VPNs work on any port you want them to run on—generally 1194 for OpenVPN and 443 for other SSL VPNs. IPSec requires the following ports:

- *Internet key exchange*: UDP port 500

- *Encapsulating security payload*: IP protocol number 50

- *Authentication header*: IP protocol number 51

- *IPSec NAT traversal*: UDP port 4500, when NAT traversal is in use

IPSec VPN limitations stem from the fact that they are at layer 3 of the Open Systems Interconnection (OSI) layer, the network layer. This means that polices that get applied have to be at layer 3. On the other hand, with SSL-based VPNs you have more options with respect to policies and protection.

Implementations of IPSec may vary across vendors; therefore, it is important to pick the same vendor for both end points of a VPN tunnel. However, SSL is more forgiving, and you will find it easier to integrate different software providers with SSL than you would with IPSec.

How Does SSL Work?

As noted earlier, SSL stands for secure socket layer. Transport layer security (TLS) is the replacement of SSL. SSL works based on certificates, which can be issued by a public key infrastructure system. The steps involved in setting up and using SSL are:

1. Generate a certificate signing request and submit it to the certificate authority (CA).

2. Receive from the CA a certificate based on the submitted certificate signing request and install the certificate.

3. The client initiates an SSL hello to server, in which the client provides the SSL version number, cipher settings, session-specific data, and other relevant information to the server.

4. The server responds with its own hello to client, including the SSL version number, cipher settings, and its certificate.

5. The client then validates the certificate by using the CAs it trusts.

6. So far, all the communication has been unencrypted. The next step is for the client to create a premaster secret for the session, encrypt it with the server's public key (provided in step 5), and send it to the server. This is the first encrypted packet.

7. The server then uses the premaster secret to generate a session key, which is symmetric. The client does the same on its end.

8. The client then sends a message to the server, indicating that all future communication is to be encrypted with the session key, and it also sends another message, indicating the client portion of the handshake is over.

9. The server sends a message to the client, indicating that future messages are to be encrypted with the session key, and it also lets the client know the server portion of the handshake is over.

A sample SSL handshake between a client and www.google.com is showing in Listing 9-5.

Listing 9-5. SSL Handshake between a Client and www.google.com

```
$ OpenSSL s_client -connect www.google.com:443 -state -ssl3
CONNECTED(00000003)
SSL_connect:before/connect initialization
SSL_connect:SSLv3 write client hello A
SSL_connect:SSLv3 read server hello A
depth=2 /C=US/O=GeoTrust Inc./CN=GeoTrust Global CA
verify error:num=20:unable to get local issuer certificate
verify return:0
SSL_connect:SSLv3 read server certificate A
SSL_connect:SSLv3 read server done A
SSL_connect:SSLv3 write client key exchange A
SSL_connect:SSLv3 write change cipher spec A
SSL_connect:SSLv3 write finished A
SSL_connect:SSLv3 flush data
SSL_connect:SSLv3 read finished A
---
Certificate chain
 0 s:/C=US/ST=California/L=Mountain View/O=Google Inc/CN=www.google.com
   i:/C=US/O=Google Inc/CN=Google Internet Authority G2
 1 s:/C=US/O=Google Inc/CN=Google Internet Authority G2
   i:/C=US/O=GeoTrust Inc./CN=GeoTrust Global CA
 2 s:/C=US/O=GeoTrust Inc./CN=GeoTrust Global CA
   i:/C=US/O=Equifax/OU=Equifax Secure Certificate Authority
---
Server certificate
-----BEGIN CERTIFICATE-----
...[SNIP]...-----END CERTIFICATE-----
subject=/C=US/ST=California/L=Mountain View/O=Google Inc/CN=www.google.com
issuer=/C=US/O=Google Inc/CN=Google Internet Authority G2
---
No client certificate CA names sent
---
SSL handshake has read 3242 bytes and written 430 bytes
---
New, TLSv1/SSLv3, Cipher is RC4-SHA
Server public key is 2048 bit
Secure Renegotiation IS supported
Compression: NONE
Expansion: NONE
SSL-Session:
    Protocol  : SSLv3
    Cipher    : RC4-SHA
    Session-ID: 53D6430533F752C4C5790A849B8C25613B45A8C03CFCD4BC51CF07F458698798
    Session-ID-ctx:
    Master-Key:
```

377EEC39AB7BA705836F1C47794DD307E16889F401C8E2C897687869A2B2A75BD9423B8B1CD6CD2FD383B140DD172041
```
    Key-Arg    : None
    Start Time: 1413660093
    Timeout    : 7200 (sec)
    Verify return code: 0 (ok)
---
```

The way OpenVPN uses SSL is by issuing a certificate to both the server and the client. For simplicity's sake, let's assume we have a CA in the organization. The CA issues a certificate to the OpenVPN sever and to each of the users who wish to connect.

Initially, when the client and server talk to each other, they exchange SSL encryption information; this includes the cipher type and strength. After a secure connection has been established using their certificates, both ends exchange a symmetric key for encryption.

VPN Software

The choice of open source VPN server software will be dictated by the choice of VPN technology. The most common open source VPN servers are the following:

- OpenVPN: Uses SSL (`https://openvpn.net/`)

- strongSwan: Uses IPSec (`https://www.strongswan.org/`)

- SoftEther: Uses SSL (`https://www.softether.org/`)

There are also many commercial VPN providers, in addition to open source VPN software. VPN appliances have gained popularity as well, because they have dedicated hardware for speeding up encryption.

VPN Design

A simple VPN design consists of a single VPN server used for remote user connectivity and for site-to-site connectivity between different office locations (Figure 9-6). This is not an ideal design because it is not fault tolerant. In addition, it is not as secure as it could be because both end users and remote offices are using the same appliance.

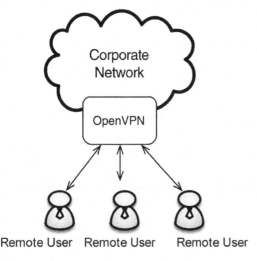

Figure 9-6. *Remote user VPN*

The VPN server is, ideally, placed in a demilitarized zone (DMZ), and only specific protocols are allowed from the DMZ to the internal network. There is a firewall that guards the VPN server from the Internet, allowing only port 1194 TCP for OpenVPN. Also, there is firewall that guards the internal network from the OpenVPN server. In the case of a break-in on the VPN server, the internal network is not compromised. For extra security, you can have a jump host that allows access to the VPN server from the internal network for management. This strategy prevents direct access to the VPN server from the internal network.

Another approach is to have a site-to-site VPN dedicated to intraoffice connectivity. This can be a different server than the one to which remote users connect (Figure 9-7).

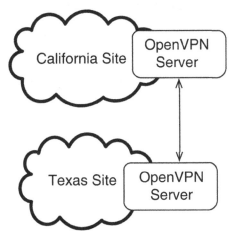

Figure 9-7. *Site-to-site VPN*

For fault-tolerance, you can use Keepalived, as shown in Figure 9-8. Two VPN servers share a single virtual IP and have Keepalived installed on both of them. In case one VPN server fails, the instance of Keepalived on the second VPN server takes over the IP.

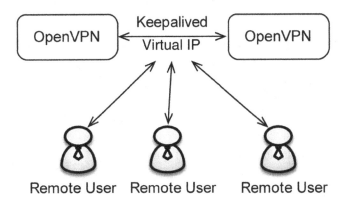

Figure 9-8. *OpenVPN with Keepalived*

A simpler approach to fault tolerance is to have multiple OpenVPN servers and configure the clients to use them individually. The OpenVPN servers can share the same configuration, perhaps through Git. One OpenVPN server is not aware of the other OpenVPN server.

Split Tunnel

By default, OpenVPN client software routes all traffic going to the Internet directly from the client, and only sends VPN-directed traffic to the VPN. This is known as "*split tunnel*" and is shown in Figure 9-9. An advantage of this method is that you avoid any end user traffic coming into your network that is not intended for your network.

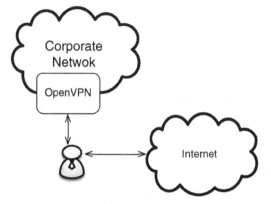

Figure 9-9. *Split tunnel*

Advantages of split tunnel include the following:

- Reduced bandwidth cost
- Increased security because your network does not see traffic not destined for it
- Protection of the privacy of the end user as well

Another alternative is to route all traffic through the VPN server, as shown in Figure 9-10. The disadvantages of routing all traffic through the VPN are as follows:

- Remote clients may not be able to renew their DHCP lease if the DHCP server is local to their network, because OpenVPN tries to route that traffic over the VPN
- Web browsing for remote users might be slow because all traffic is now routed through the corporate network
- Windows clients have some issues receiving Domain Name System (DNS) updates

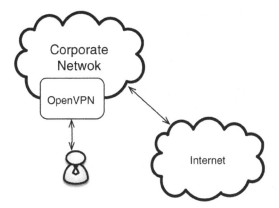

Figure 9-10. *Enabling gateway redirect*

To enable gateway redirect, add the following lines to the `server.conf` file of OpenVPN:

```
push "redirect-gateway def1"
push "dhcp-option DNS <ip-of-corp-dns-server>"
```

If your VPN is over a wireless network, for which the wireless clients and the server are on the same wireless subnet, then add the following to your `server.conf` file:

```
push "redirect-gateway local def1"
push "dhcp-option DNS <ip-of-corp-dns-server>"
```

OpenVPN Configuration File

OpenVPN uses a configuration file to specify its settings. Be careful what you place in this file, because a misconfiguration can turn into a security risk. The default location of this file is /etc/openvpn. You can call the file whatever you want, but the norm is to call it `server.conf`. Listing 9-6 shows a sample file and explains the different options available in the file.

LISTING 9-6. OPENVPN CONFIGURATION FILE

The interfaces that OpenVPN listens on are defined by the `local` keyword. A typical OpenVPN server has two interfaces—one external and one internal. The external interface is what you want OpenVPN to listen on.

```
local 100.94.1.2
```

The port is the standard OpenVPN port of 1194. You can specify an alternative port if you wish, just remember to let the clients know about the alternative port as well.

```
port 1194
```

To improve the performance of OpenVPN, let's use shared memory as a temporary directory. We can use any file system mounted as `tmp`, if you like, for OpenVPN.

```
tmp-dir /dev/shm
```

TCP and UDP are both supported by OpenVPN for connections. TCP is more reliable but a bit slower than UDP. You can try either one and pick one that suits your network needs.

```
proto tcp
```

OpenVPN supports bridging and routing modes, and each of these is explained in the following section. By specifying `dev tun`, we are configuring our server to use routing mode.

```
dev tun
```

Here we specify the keys for the server. The section "OpenVPN Certificates" in this chapter explains how to generate these keys.

```
ca /etc/openvpn/keys/ca.crt
cert /etc/openvpn/keys/server.crt
key /etc/openvpn/keys/server.key  # This file should be kept secret
dh /etc/openvpn/keys/dh1024.pem
```

The certificate revocation list is crucial for security, and is specified using the `crl-verify` parameter.

```
crl-verify  /etc/openvpn/keys/crl.pem
```

The `server` directive is used to specify the network and netmask range from which OpenVPN gives out IP addresses to clients that connect.

```
server 10.1.1.0 255.255.255.0
```

Any DHCP-related options can be pushed out using the `push dhcp-option` directive. This includes DNS, Windows Internet Name Service (WINS), or any of the other options in DHCP.

```
push "dhcp-option DNS 10.1.2.10"
push "dhcp-option DNS 10.1.3.10"
```

VPN clients need routes into the internal network. The `push route` configuration directive takes care of pushing routes to the clients. Let's set up two routes here:

```
push "route 192.168.0.0 255.255.0.0"
push "route 10.0.0.0  255.0.0.0"
```

Normally, OpenVPN does not allow client-to-client communication, but the following option enables this.

```
client-to-client
```

We'll send keepalive pings every 10 seconds. If no answer is received in 120 seconds, then we assume the link is down. You can adjust these values based on the reliability of client connectivity to the OpenVPN server.

```
keepalive 10 120
```

We then need to enable compression between the server and the client. Also, we must remember to enable this setting on the client side.

```
comp-lzo
```

It is a security risk to run OpenVPN as root user, so let's use the nobody user. The persist-key and persist-tun commands are part of being able to switch to an underprivileged mode when running OpenVPN.

```
user nobody
group nobody
persist-key
persist-tun
```

The status file lists current client connections, once per minute. The log-append directive is for not sending logs to syslog; instead, it is used for logging to the file specified. The status version specifies the log format version and the verb directive is for how verbose you want OpenVPN to be. You can increase this number for more verbose logging. Values can range from zero to nine.

```
status /etc/openvpn/status/tcp-1194.log
log-append /etc/openvpn/status/openvpn.log
status-version 2
verb 5
```

You can "telnet" to a given port of OpenVPN—in our case, it is port 7505—and issue management commands, which is bound only on localhost.

```
management localhost 7505
```

Routing or Bridging

OpenVPN can run in routed mode or bridge mode. Use bridging if you need any of the following:

- The VPN needs to handle non-IP traffic, such as IPX.
- Network broadcasts need to be enabled over the VPN, such as for local area network games.
- Windows file share browsing needs to work across the VPN without using a Windows Internet Name Service (WINS) server.

Routing uses tunnel interfaces. On the OpenVPN server, when you run an ip addr show command, you will see an interface called tun0, which means tunneling is being used. The advantages of using routing are as follows:

- No broadcast traffic crosses over the VPN tunnel.
- Only layer 3 packets are transported.

To use the routing mode, ensure that routing is enabled on the OpenVPN server:

```
## enable routing on OpenVPN server
# sysctl -w net.ipv4.ip_forward=1
```

Next, in the /etc/openvpn/server.conf file, enter the line dev tun. This causes OpenVPN to use routing mode.

If you want to use bridging mode, then replace the dev tun line with dev tap0. In addition, to use bridging, replace the line that says server <ip> <netmask> with server-bridge <ip> <netmask>.

Bridging requires that the IP address of the bridge be configured outside of OpenVPN, because OpenVPN cannot set the IP of the bridge automatically. To see sample scripts to set up a bridge and its IP, go to https://openvpn.net/index.php/open-source/documentation/miscellaneous/76-ethernet-bridging.html.

OpenVPN Certificates

There are two choices when going with certificate-based authentication: one is to create your own certificate authority and self-sign certificates, and the other is to use a third-party CA. Some examples of third-party CAs include

- Thawte (https://www.thawte.com/)

- Verisign (https://www.verisign.com/)

- GeoTrust (https://www.geotrust.com/)

Using a self-signed certificate saves money. If you are not connecting the enterprise to another vendor's network through a VPN, then self-signed might be the way to go. If you already have an existing public key infrastructure in the enterprise, then you can use that as well to issue certificates to the OpenVPN server and individual users that need to connect.

For self-signed certificates, some tools that can be used to manage certificates include the following:

- OpenSSL (https://www.openssl.org/)

- gnoMint (http://gnomint.sourceforge.net/)

- EJBCA (http://www.ejbca.org/)

Creating Your Own Certificates

Using the easy-rsa package on CentOS/RedHat, you can install your own CA and create certificates for end users as well as OpenVPN server. Listing 9-7 shows you how to install easy-rsa and how to create your own certificates.

LISTING 9-7. GENERATING YOUR OWN CERTIFICATES

First off, we install the easy-rsa package.

```
# yum install easy-rsa -y
```

Next, we run clean-all to remove any keys from a past install. Do not remove the index.txt and serial number files; they are needed for building certificates.

```
# cd /usr/share/easy-rsa/2.0
# . ./vars
# ./clean-all
# ls keys
index.txt  serial
```

We can now build the CA itself, which creates two files: one is the certificate of the CA (ca.crt) and the other is its private key (ca.key).

```
# ./build-ca
# ls keys
ca.crt  ca.key index.txt serial
```

We are ready to issue a certificate to our OpenVPN server using the CA we created earlier. The output of this command includes the server certificate request file (server.csr), the server certificate (server.crt), and the private key of the server (server.key).

```
# ./build-key-server server
# ls keys
01.pem ca.crt  ca.key  index.txt  index.txt.attr  index.txt.old  serial  serial.old  server.
crt server.csr  server.key
```

Clients can now be issued certificates using the build-key command. In place of user1-client, type in the username that is being issued the certificate. This generates the user certificate (user1-client.crt) and the private key (user1-client.key). Repeat this process for as many users to whom you want to issue a certificate.

```
# ./build-key user1-client
# ls keys
01.pem  ca.crt   index.txt index.txt.attr.old  serial server.crt  server.key  user1-client.csr
02.pem  ca.key   index.txt.attr  index.txt.old serial.old  server.csr  user1-client.crt
user1-client.key
```

The previous steps complete the process of creating your first certificates for the CA, server, and user. You can copy the certificates into the OpenVPN /etc/openvpn/keys directory. The private keys of the CA and the server should be kept private and should not be given to anyone. For end users, you can give out three files: ca.crt, user1-client.crt, and user1-client.key. Users then install these files in their OpenVPN client, and they can connect to the server.

OpenVPN Security

OpenVPN server is a gateway into your network, it is important to harden the server and protect it from attacks. A few steps you can take to harden the server, including the following:

- Install the minimal server version of the operating system. Do not install any software that is not needed.

- Disable any services that are not needed.

- Have only those users on the system that need to be on the system.

- Revoke certificates of users that no longer need access (Listing 9-8).

- Use two-factor authentication for additional security.

Listing 9-8. Revoking a client certificate

```
## in /etc/openvpn/server.conf enable the revocation list
crl-verify crl.pem

## use the easy-rsa tools to revoke the certificate
# cd /usr/share/easy-rsa/2.0
# . ./vars
# ./revoke-full client-name
# cp keys/crl.pem /etc/openvpn/keys/
```

The OpenVPN server reads the `crl.pem` file in the following instances:

- Each time the server is started

- Whenever a client connects

- On SSL/TLS renegotiation by existing connected clients, which is generally done once per hour

OpenVPN with Dual Authentication

Using certificates alone for authentication is not a good idea for remote user connectivity. If users misplace their laptop, then anyone who has access to their certificate can access your network. One option is to enable username/password authentication along with certificates. Also, you can use a two-factor authentication system such as RSA SecureID so that end users need a token to access the network. Different plug-ins are available for the type of authentication you want to use. Listing 9-9 shows how to enable username and password authentication in addition to client certificates.

Listing 9-9. OpenVPN Dual Authentication

```
# grep auth-pam /etc/openvpn/server.conf
plugin /usr/lib64/openvpn/plugin/lib/openvpn-auth-pam.so login
```

OpenVPN Management Interface

The management interface is enabled using the following in /etc/openvpn/server.conf:

```
# grep -i management /etc/openvpn/server.conf
management localhost 7505
```

To run management commands, telnet to the local host on port 7505 from the OpenVPN server as, shown Listing 9-10. The port only accepts connections from the OpenVPN server itself and not from other hosts.

Listing 9-10. Managing OpenVPN

```
# telnet localhost 7505
Trying 127.0.0.1...
Connected to localhost.
Escape character is '^]'.
>INFO:OpenVPN Management Interface Version 1 -- type 'help' for more info
status
TITLE,OpenVPN 2.3.2 x86_64-redhat-linux-gnu [SSL (OpenSSL)] [LZO] [EPOLL] [PKCS11] [eurephia] [MH]
[IPv6] built on Sep 12 2013
TIME,Sat Sep 27 00:06:00 2014,1411776360
HEADER,CLIENT_LIST,Common Name,Real Address,Virtual Address,Bytes Received,Bytes Sent,Connected
Since,Connected Since (time_t),Username
CLIENT_LIST,<username>,<client-remote-public-ip>:33662,<client-remote-dhcp-ip>,367083,77966,Fri Sep
26 23:56:11 2014,1411775771,UNDEF
HEADER,ROUTING_TABLE,Virtual Address,Common Name,Real Address,Last Ref,Last Ref (time_t)
ROUTING_TABLE,<client-remote-dhcp-ip>,<username>,<client-remote-public-ip>:33662,Sat Sep 27 00:06:00
2014,1411776360
GLOBAL_STATS,Max bcast/mcast queue length,0
END
```

Additional information about the management interface can be found at https://openvpn.net/index.php/open-source/documentation/miscellaneous/79-management-interface.html.

Graphical User Interface Management Interface

OpenVPN does not come with management of the graphical user interface (GUI). One option is to try an open source-version GUI available at http://openvpn-web-gui.sourceforge.net/. If you purchase the commercial version, also known as OpenVPN Access Server, an extremely useful user interface is available.

OpenVPN Access Server Versus Community Edition

OpenVPN has two versions: one is free and the other is commercial. The commercial version is called OpenVPN Access Server. The version you get should be based on one or more of the differences listed in Table 9-1.

Table 9-1. *OpenVPN Community Server Versus OpenVPN Access Server*

Feature	Open Source	Enterprise
Secured VPN tunnel	Yes	Yes
Web-based GUI	No	Yes
GUI Windows client	Yes	Yes
Preconfigured client	No	Yes
Automated certificate creation	No	Yes
Bridging	Yes	Yes
Failover solution	No	Yes

You can find a more detailed comparison at http://openvpn.net/index.php/access-server/section-faq-openvpn-as/32-general/225-compare-openvpn-community-and-enterprise-editions-.html.

OpenVPN Access Server

You can download OpenVPN Access Server at https://openvpn.net/index.php/access-server/download-openvpn-as-sw.html. To install OpenVPN Access Server, use the RPMs provided by OpenVPN:

```
# rpm -Uvh http://swupdate.openvpn.org/as/openvpn-as-2.0.10-CentOS6.x86_64.rpm
Retrieving http://swupdate.openvpn.org/as/openvpn-as-2.0.10-CentOS6.x86_64.rpm
Preparing...              ########################################### [100%]
   1:openvpn-as           ########################################### [100%]
The Access Server has been successfully installed in /usr/local/openvpn_as
Configuration log file has been written to /usr/local/openvpn_as/init.log
Please enter "passwd openvpn" to set the initial
administrative password, then login as "openvpn" to continue
configuration here: https://X.X.X.X:943/admin
To reconfigure manually, use the /usr/local/openvpn_as/bin/ovpn-init tool.

Access Server web UIs are available here:
Admin  UI: https://X.X.X.X:943/admin
Client UI: https://X.X.X.X:943/
```

When installed, you can access the user interface at https://<ip-of-server>:943/admin.

iptables

iptables is a free, built-in firewall available in Linux. Protecting your system with iptables provides an additional layer of security. iptables consists of two parts. The first part is the user-space module; it lets the user modify firewall rules. The other is netfilter (http://www.netfilter.org/), which is a kernel module that does the actual filtering of packets. Development is underway to replace iptables in the future with nftables (http://netfilter.org/projects/nftables/).

iptables consists of tables, which in turn consists of chains, and chains contain rules, as seen in Figure 9-11.

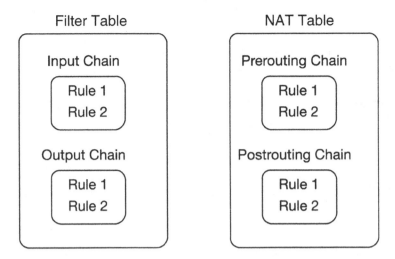

Figure 9-11. *iptables showing a sample of two tables*

The five different kinds of tables available are as follows:

1. *Filter*: The filter table is the default table, which contains chains for input, forward, and output packets. Input packets are packets destined for local sockets, output packets are generated locally, and forward packets are routed through the box.

2. *NAT*: The NAT table is consulted when a packet that creates a new connection is encountered. It consists of prerouting, postrouting, and output chains. Prerouting is for packets as soon as they come in, postrouting is for packets before they are about to leave the system, and output chains are for locally generated packets before routing.

3. *Mangle*: Mangle is a special table that can be used for packet alterations. It consists of prerouting, postrouting, input, output, and forward chains. Prerouting is for altering packets before routing, postrouting is for altering packets as they are about to go out, input is for packets coming into the box itself, output is for packets leaving the box, and forward chains are for packets that are being routed through the box.

4. *Raw*: The raw table is the table with the highest priority, because it is called before any other table. It is used primarily for exemptions in connection tracking. This table provides two chains: prerouting and output. Prerouting is for packets arriving via any network interface; output is for packets generated by local processes.

5. *Security*: The security table is used for mandatory access control networking rules, such as those enabled by SECMARK and CONNSECMARK targets. It is used for SELinux and other security modules. It consists of input, output, and forward chains.

For more information on iptables filter rules, and for NAT, mangle, and the other tables, refer to the online documentation at http://www.netfilter.org/documentation/index.html.

iptables in a Network

The most basic design of iptables in a network is to use it as a gateway firewall between the Internet and your corporate network, as seen in Figure 9-12.

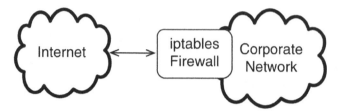

Figure 9-12. *Basic iptables gateway design*

This design is simple and easy to use; however, it lacks failover capabilities. In addition, when the iptables server is compromised, each network device within the network is vulnerable to an attack from the Internet. Another more secure design is to have iptables running on each Linux server within the network, in addition to having an Internet gateway running iptables, as seen in Figure 9-13.

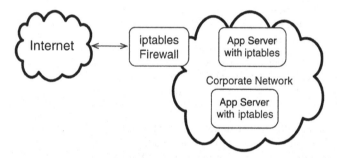

Figure 9-13. *iptables gateway and internal hosts*

The advantage of running iptables on each server in your network is that you get the added protection from attacks from internal and external networks. If an attacker has somehow managed to penetrate the external gateway, your internal servers each have their own firewall the attacker has to penetrate. One potential disadvantage of this approach is the complexity of managing rules on each of the servers in the network. In addition, there is a small penalty for having iptables inspect each packet before it is allowed in the system.

A third and yet more secure approach might be to have another leg on the iptables gateway, and place all Internet-facing hosts in what is known as the DMZ, as seen in Figure 9-14. This design separates from the Internet those network devices that need inbound connectivity to their own network zone called the DMZ. If there is a potential security flaw in them, it does not compromise the internal corporate network devices that do not need inbound Internet connectivity.

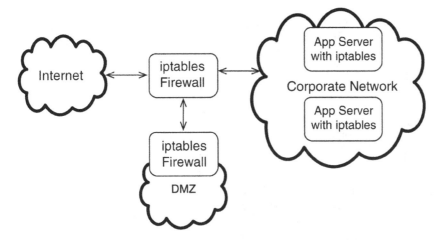

Figure 9-14. *iptables with DMZ*

Another approach is to include an additional layer of security by adding a protected network that is used to store finance, human resources, and other personnel-related data in the network, as seen in Figure 9-15.

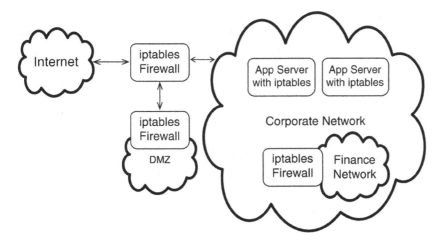

Figure 9-15. *Using iptables to secure financial data*

One more layer of security can be added to protect end user personal and financial data in the corporate network (Figure 9-16). This design is different from the corporate financial data. End user personal and financial data might include credit card numbers of customers, personal address information, and other private information relating to the customers of the enterprise.

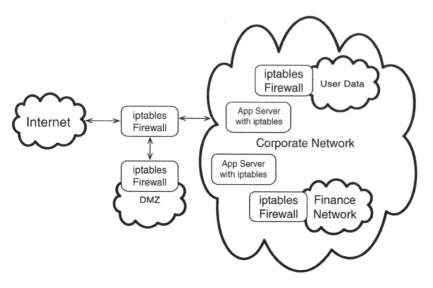

Figure 9-16. *Protecting customer data with iptables*

Filter Table

The most common use of iptables is as a firewall. Having the filter table as the default table is helpful because the filter table does packet filtering. Let's view a working example of the filter table in Listing 9-11 and start with no rules on a system, to which we then add rules. If you find using iptables commands difficult, consider using a wrapper around iptables such as Shorewall (http://shorewall.net).

LISTING 9-11. USING THE FILTER TABLE

First we need to check to make sure we have no rules installed on the system.

```
# iptables -L
Chain INPUT (policy ACCEPT)
target     prot opt source              destination

Chain FORWARD (policy ACCEPT)
target     prot opt source              destination

Chain OUTPUT (policy ACCEPT)
target     prot opt source              destination
```

Next, we add a rule to deny all traffic. Using the -t option, we specify the table. The -A appends to the specified chain—in our case, it is the input chain—and the -j jumps to an action. The action in this case is to drop all packets. Running this command kills our SSH connection to the host, so we need to make sure we perform this action from a console connection.

```
# iptables -t filter -A INPUT  -j DROP
```

Let's check to make sure the rule got accepted. The –v option is for verbose and the –L option is to list the chain. In our case, it is the input chain. We can see that 22 packets were dropped, which equals 1792 bytes.

```
# iptables -t filter -vL INPUT
Chain INPUT (policy ACCEPT 0 packets, 0 bytes)
 pkts bytes target     prot opt in     out     source               destination
   22  1792 DROP       all  -- any    any     anywhere             anywhere
```

We have to allow SSH traffic to the host, so let's set up a rule for that. Because SSH uses TCP, we can specify the protocol using the –p option, and the destination port as port 22. Instead of using the –A option to append, we use the –I option, which inserts at the top, because we want to allow SSH before we block all traffic.

```
# iptables -t filter -I INPUT -p tcp --destination-port 22 -j ACCEPT
```

Next, we should allow all outbound traffic for outbound DNS and other services to work.

```
# iptables -I OUTPUT -d 0.0.0.0/0 -j ACCEPT
# iptables -I INPUT -m state --state ESTABLISHED,RELATED -j ACCEPT
```

We can verify that SSH traffic is being accepted to the host by trying to "SSH" to it, then checking the INPUT chain. We can see that 237 packets have been accepted for the SSH rule.

```
# iptables -vL INPUT -t filter
Chain INPUT (policy ACCEPT 0 packets, 0 bytes)
pkts bytes target     prot opt in     out     source        destination
2787   11M ACCEPT     all  -- any    any     anywhere      anywhere      state RELATED,ESTABLISHED
1777  151K ACCEPT     tcp  -- any    any     anywhere      anywhere      tcp dpt:ssh
10612 656K DROP       all  -- any    any     anywhere                    anywhere
```

You can view line numbers of the rule by the following:

```
# iptables -vL INPUT --line-number
 pkts bytes target     prot opt in     out     source        destination
1 2787   11M ACCEPT    all  -- any    any     anywhere      anywhere      state
RELATED,ESTABLISHED
2 1777  151K ACCEPT    tcp  -- any    any     anywhere      anywhere      tcp dpt:ssh
3 10612  656K DROP     all  -- any    any     anywhere                    anywhere
```

Popular iptables Rules

Listed here are some popular rules for iptables.

On a SaltStack master (http://www.saltstack.com), set these two rules to allow the client to connect to the master:

```
# iptables -I INPUT -m state --state new -m tcp -p tcp --dport 4505 -j ACCEPT
# iptables -I INPUT -m state --state new -m tcp -p tcp --dport 4506 -j ACCEPT
```

Port 80 and 443 for the web server:

```
# iptables -I INPUT -m state --state new -m tcp -p tcp --dport 80 -j ACCEPT
# iptables -I INPUT -m state --state new -m tcp -p tcp --dport 443 -j ACCEPT
```

Port 25 for the mail server:

```
# iptables -I INPUT -m state --state new -m tcp -p tcp --dport 25 -j ACCEPT
```

DNS server:

```
# iptables -I INPUT -m state --state new -m udp -p udp --dport 53 -j ACCEPT
# iptables -I INPUT -m state --state new -m tcp -p tcp --dport 53 -j ACCEPT
```

OpenVPN server:

```
# iptables -I INPUT -m state --state new -m udp -p udp --dport 1194 -j ACCEPT
# iptables -I INPUT -m state --state new -m tcp -p tcp --dport 1194 -j ACCEPT
```

Deleting iptables Rules

iptables can be deleted using the iptables -F command, which deletes all the rules in all the chains for the specified table. Use this with care, because your system will be vulnerable if you delete all rules. For deleting individual rules, you have two options, as shown in Listing 9-12.

Listing 9-12. Deleting iptables Rules

```
# show the rules in the INPUT chain with line numbers prepended
# iptables -L INPUT --line-numbers
1   ACCEPT    tcp  --  anywhere           anywhere           state NEW tcp dpt:http
2   ACCEPT    tcp  --  anywhere           anywhere           state NEW tcp dpt:https

# Option 1 is to use the rule number to delete rule 2
# iptables -D INPUT 2

# verify that the rule has been deleted
# iptables -L INPUT --line-numbers
1   ACCEPT    tcp  --  anywhere           anywhere           state NEW tcp dpt:http

# Option 2 is to specify the rule itself instead of the rule number
# iptables -D INPUT -m state --state new -m tcp  -p tcp -s 0/0  --dport 443 -j DROP
```

Saving iptables

Any rules that are created with iptables using the `iptables` command can be lost at system reboot or when the rules are flushed. To save the rules, run `iptables-save`. By default, `iptables-save` outputs the rules to STDOUT, which can redirect to a file so that the rules persist on the next reboot, as seen in Listing 9-13.

Listing 9-13. Save iptables Rules to Persist across Reboots

```
# iptables-save > /etc/sysconfig/iptables
# chkconfig iptables on
```

Conclusion

Logging, remote access with VPNs, and firewalls with iptables are all integral to an organization's security. VPNs and firewalls are perimeter-based security tools, and logging helps audit the success and failure of both of them. By making choices suitable for your organization, you can build a practical Linux infrastructure that is stable and secure.

CHAPTER 10

■ ■ ■

Troubleshooting Tools

Troubleshooting is an art as well as a science. To be effective at troubleshooting, you have to understand how something works, and where to look for issues. Knowledge helps to provide an understanding about how something works; experience helps to figure out where to look. Troubleshooting is an art because everyone has a unique way of approaching problems; it is a science because there is a methodology that, if followed, can help solve a large subset of the most common errors.

This chapter is about troubleshooting the various applications explained in this book. It is also about general troubleshooting of Linux systems needed for someone who manages a Linux infrastructure.

TCP/IP

Networking fundamentals start with the Open Systems Interconnection (OSI) layer (https://en.wikipedia.org/wiki/OSI_model). Effective troubleshooting means being extremely comfortable with this layer and its components. A brief summary of the OSI layer is shown in Table 10-1. The protocol acronym expansion is in Table 10-2.

Table 10-1. *OSI Layer*

OSI layer	Protocol example
Application	HTTP, FTP, DHCP, IRC
Presentation	TLS, IPSec, ASCII
Session	NFS, RPC, SMB, SOCKS
Transport	TCP, UDP, AH, DCCP
Network	IP, IPX, AppleTalk
Data link	LLDP, PPP, CDP, VLAN, IEEE 802.11
Physical	Ethernet, USB, DSL, ISDN, IEEE 1394

Table 10-2. *Protocol Acronym Expansion*

Acronym	Expansion	Acronym	Expansion
HTTP	Hypertext Transfer Protocol	FTP	File Transfer Protocol
DHCP	Dynamic Host Configuration Protocol	IRC	Internet Relay Chat
TLS	Transport Layer Security	IPSec	Internet Protocol Security
ASCII	American Standard Code for Information Interchange	NFS	Network File System
RPC	Remote Procedure Call	SMB	Server Message Block
SOCKS	Abbreviations for sockets	TCP	Transmission Control Protocol
UDP	User Datagram Protocol	AH	Authentication Header
DCCP	Datagram Congestion Control Protocol	IP	Internet Protocol
IPX	Internetwork Packet Exchange	LLDP	Link Layer Discover Protocol
PPP	Point-to-Point Protocol	CDP	Cisco Discovery Protocol
VLAN	Virtual Local Area Network	USB	Universal Serial Bus
DSL	Digital Subscriber Line	ISDN	Integrated Services Digital Network
IEEE	Institute of Electrical and Electronics Engineers		

Effective network troubleshooting entails working your way up or down the OSI layers. Given a source and destination network device that are not communicating with each other, a typical workflow that may start the troubleshooting process includes the following:

1. In the application layer, check that the application itself is up by reviewing log files. Use commands such as `strace` and `ltrace` to analyze application behavior after you have exhausted the basics (`ps`, `top`).

2. Move to the presentation layer. If the application is using a public key infrastructure (PKI), look at the certificate status and the key exchange.

3. The session layer can be debugged using protocol-specific commands. Network File System (NFS) statistics can be obtained with `nfsstat`; remote procedure call (RPC) can be debugged using `rpcinfo`.

4. The transport and network layers can be debugged using `tcpdump`, `ifconfig`, `traceroute`, `ping`, `ip`, `netstat/ss`, and `lsof`.

5. The data link layer should be looked at next. Sometimes virtual local area networks are misconfigured or there can be wireless configuration issues.

6. Last, troubleshooting the Ethernet can be done with `ethtool` and `arp`, and by looking at the physical defects in cables as well as connectors.

In a large organization, troubleshooting often involves more than one team. Network engineering may own layers one through four, whereas site reliability engineering might own layers five through seven.

tcpdump

tcpdump is used to dump network traffic. By analyzing network traffic, you can get a lot of information about a particular problem. tcpdump is one of the most useful network debugging utilities on Linux. Wireshark (https://www.wireshark.org) is a graphical user interface application for capturing network traffic as well.

When trying to debug a connection problem between two network end points, you can use tcpdump to analyze the conversation between them. Listing 10-1 shows a three-way TCP handshake as captured by tcpdump.

Listing 10-1. Three-Way TCP Handshake

```
## SYN PACKET (1st packet in conversation)
10.1.1.1.58632 > 10.1.1.2.domain: Flags [S], cksum 0xfff6 (correct), seq 2475756890, win 14600,
options [mss 1460,sackOK,TS val 2829551529 ecr 0,nop,wscale 7], length 0

## SYN WITH ACK (2nd packet in conversation)
10.1.1.2.domain > 10.1.1.1.58632: Flags [S.], cksum 0xa5f3 (correct), seq 1846955773, ack
2475756891, win 14480, options [mss 1460,sackOK,TS val 2888298798 ecr 2829551529,nop,wscale 7], length 0

#ACK (3rd packet in conversation)
10.1.1.1.58632 > 10.1.1.2.domain: Flags [.], cksum 0x0cdd (correct), ack 1, win 115, options
[nop,nop,TS val 2829551529 ecr 2888298798], length 0
```

The source initiating connection is 10.1.1.1. The destination is 10.1.1.2. In the first step, the source sends a SYN packet. You can tell it is a SYN packet because the SYN flag is set: (Flags [S]). In a TCP packet, there are 9 bits for a flag. If the SYN bit is set, then the packet is a SYN packet (https://en.wikipedia.org/wiki/Transmission_Control_Protocol).

The second packet is from the destination 10.1.1.2 to the source 10.1.1.1. This is also a SYN packet, as is visible from the Flags [S.] field. In addition, it has the ACK bit set, as specified by the period next to the S. The destination is acknowledging the first SYN packet from the source.

The third packet, which completes the handshake, is the ACK packet from 10.1.1.1 to 10.1.1.2, as is visible with Flags [.].

To troubleshoot connection closing, tcpdump can be very helpful as well, as shown in Listing 10-2. Connection 10.1.1.1 sends a FIN packet; because the packet was sent by 10.1.1.1, it is considered to be in the ACTIVE CLOSE state. The reason the packet includes an ACK is because it is acknowledging the previous packet from 10.1.1.2. The second packet is sent by the destination 10.1.1.2; it consists of a FIN packet and includes an ACK for the FIN sent by 10.1.1.1. At the destination, the port is considered to be in the PASSIVE CLOSE state. Host 10.1.1.1 then acknowledges the FIN packet sent by 10.1.1.2 and the connection is closed.

Listing 10-2. Closing a TCP Connection

```
#FIN WITH ACK
10.1.1.1.58632 > 10.1.1.2.domain: Flags [F.], cksum 0x0cdc (correct), seq 1, ack 1, win 115, options
[nop,nop,TS val 2829551529 ecr 2888298798], length 0

#FIN WITH ACK
10.1.1.2.domain > 10.1.1.1.58632: Flags [F.], cksum 0x0cdb (correct), seq 1, ack 2, win 114, options
[nop,nop,TS val 2888298799 ecr 2829551529], length 0

#ACK
10.1.1.1.58632 > 10.1.1.2.domain: Flags [.], cksum 0x0cd9 (correct), ack 2, win 115, options
[nop,nop,TS val 2829551530 ecr 2888298799], length 0
```

Ethernet Frame

An Ethernet frame is the most basic building block of a wired network. A media access control (MAC) address is a unique identifier assigned to devices using Ethernet.

MAC addresses are 48 bits; 24 bits are the organizationally unique identifier assigned by the Institute of Electrical and Electronics Engineers. The other 24 bits can be assigned by the organization itself, as long as uniqueness is maintained. You can search for an assigned organizationally unique identifier at http://standards.ieee.org/develop/regauth/oui/public.html. For instance, Apple owns 28:cf:e9.

Besides the obvious field of source and destination MAC address, an Ethernet frame contains another important field that can be useful in troubleshooting network issues: the EtherType field. This field describes the protocol of the packet encapsulated in the payload of the Ethernet frame. The most common type is 0x800 for IP packets. You can find out more about the different types of protocols that can be encapsulated at https://en.wikipedia.org/wiki/EtherType. Figure 10-1 shows an Ethernet Type II Frame (https://en.wikipedia.org/wiki/Ethernet_frame#mediaviewer/File:Ethernet_Type_II_Frame_format.svg).

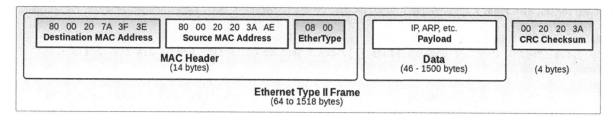

Figure 10-1. *An Ethernet frame*

Network devices use the Address Resolution Protocol (ARP) to figure out the MAC address of another device with which they need to communicate. Listing 10-3 shows an ARP broadcast on the network. In the listing, 10.1.1.50 is the IP address of the host looking for 10.1.1.40, it therefore sends a broadcast ARP packet. After the packet is received by destination 10.1.1.40, the destination responds with its MAC address.

Listing 10-3. ARP Broadcast

```
# tcpdump -c 1 broadcast
22:10:52.140086 ARP, Request who-has 10.1.1.50 tell 10.1.1.40, length 46

# arp -a
www.example.com (10.1.1.40) at 00:12:f2:9a:17:00 [ether] on eth0
```

You can find out more about Ethernet at

- https://standards.ieee.org/develop/regauth/tut/eui.pdf
- https://en.wikipedia.org/wiki/Address_Resolution_Protocol

IP Packets

To troubleshoot networks effectively, you first have to understand the building blocks of the network. Figure 10-2 shows an IPv4 packet (http://courses.oreillyschool.com/sysadmin5/Tcpdump_Intro.html).

Byte		0				1				2				3	
	Bit	0 1 2 3	4 5 6 7	8 9 10 11 12 13	14 15	16 17 18 19 20 21 22 23	24 25 26 27 28 29 30 31
0	0	Version	IHL	DSCP	ECN	Total Length	
4	32	Identification				Flags	Fragment Offset
8	64	Time to Live		Protocol		Header Checksum	
12	96	Source IP Address					
16	128	Destination IP Address					
20	160	Options (Could be non-existant or longer than 4 bytes)					

Figure 10-2. *IPv4 packet (IPv6 packets are significantly different)*

IP packets are the foundation of the Internet, and of pretty much all other networks. Besides the obvious source and destination IP address, another important field to keep track of is the time-to-live (TTL) field. When the TTL of a packet expires, it is discarded. Troubleshooting IP packets should involve keeping track of the TTL field.

The protocol field specifies the next-level protocol. You can view a list of all protocols at https://www.iana.org/assignments/protocol-numbers/protocol-numbers.xhtml. For a TCP packet, the protocol field has a value of 6.

The flags field specifies whether the packet is fragmented. Bit 1 means do not fragment; bit 2 means there are more fragmented packets that follow this packet.

TCP Packets

Becoming familiar with the format of a TCP packet makes troubleshooting a lot easier. TCP packets are the foundation of protocols such as HTTP and SSH. Figure 10-3 shows a TCP packet with an IP header. When using tools such as tcpdump, you can view TCP packets going across the wire. Some of the important fields in the packet are as follows:

- Source and destination port

- Sequence and acknowledgement number

- TCP flags, such as ACK, SYN, and FIN

One way of using TCP packet information to analyze network traffic is to ensure that a three-way TCP handshake has completed successfully when a new connection is established, which is demonstrated earlier in this chapter.

The different TCP flags give you an idea of where a network conversation is when you capture the output. By looking at the sequence and acknowledgment numbers, you can determine the latency and bandwidth issues across the wire. TCP window size also plays an important role in figuring out latency and bandwidth issues. TCP window size is adjusted dynamically based on the send and receive window. The port numbers associated with TCP give you an idea of which protocol is being used. For instance, secure shell (SSH) uses port 22; HTTP uses port 80 and HTTPS uses port 443. Using the source and destination port numbers, you can figure out if there are any connection problems between two network devices communicating over the wire.

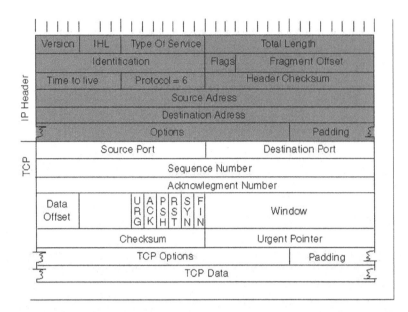

Figure 10-3. TCP Packet with IP header (https://upload.wikimedia.org/wikipedia/commons/5/50/Ntwk_tcp_header.jpg)

Network Services

Network services are applications listening on specific ports. Secure shell daemon (SSHD) is a network service that provides SSH login capabilities. Site reliability engineers encounter issues relating to network services, and should know how to resolve them. Listing 10-4 provides an example of troubleshooting SSHD service. The steps in the listing are explained as well.

Step 1: Figure out on which port the service is listening. To find out the port number of a service, look in the /etc/services file. Because you are troubleshooting SSH, you can "grep ssh" in /etc/services. This action shows that SSH is listening on port 22.

Step 2: Use the netstat command to figure out whether SSHD is actually listening on the port to which it is supposed to be attached. In Listing 10-4, you can see that SSHD is listening on 0.0.0.0:22, which implies all interfaces. The -n asks netstat to show the numerical IP only, -l shows listening sockets only, and -p shows the process ID (PID) attached to the socket. You can also use the ss command to show similar output.

Step 3: Use pgrep to confirm the PID, as shown by the netstat command. The netstat command in the last column shows that process 2106 is running SSHD. The other PIDs belonging to SSH are spawned SSH processes for different SSH connections.

Step 4: Use lsof to view which sockets are open by PID 2106, and it's confirmed that IPv4 and IPv6 sockets are open and listening on port 22.

Step 6: From another host, use nc to connect via TCP to port 22. Based on the output of the nc command, you can conclude that you are able to connect successfully. The reason to try this is, when a firewall is blocking the service, it is still listening, but incoming connections are not allowed.

Because all six steps have worked, you can conclude that the service is running and listening, and that no firewall is blocking connections. The next step is to use the ssh command and determine whether the connection works or whether you get an error.

Listing 10-4. Troubleshooting SSHD

```
#STEP 1
# egrep -i '^ssh ' /etc/services
ssh            22/tcp                          # The Secure Shell (SSH) Protocol
ssh            22/udp                          # The Secure Shell (SSH) Protocol
ssh            22/sctp                         # SSH

#STEP 2
# netstat -nlp | grep -i ssh
tcp       0       0 0.0.0.0:22                 0.0.0.0:*          LISTEN      2106/sshd
tcp       0       0 :::22                      :::*               LISTEN      2106/sshd

# ss -nlp | grep -i ssh
LISTEN    0      128            *:22                       *:*      users:(("sshd",2106,5))

#STEP 3
# pgrep -l ssh
2106 sshd
13048 sshd
13050 sshd
17947 sshd
17949 sshd

#STEP 4
# lsof -p 2106 | grep LISTEN
sshd    2106 root    3u   IPv4  13932      0t0    TCP *:ssh (LISTEN)
sshd    2106 root    4u   IPv6  13934      0t0    TCP *:ssh (LISTEN)

#STEP 5
$ nc -z www.example.com 22
```

Connection to www.example.com port 22 [tcp/ssh] succeeded!

CPU

CPU bottlenecks can cause a major headache for applications. In the past, symmetric multiprocessing (SMP) was very popular. It implied equal access to memory for processors. Because there were not many processor sockets per system, SMP worked fine. Modern systems have numerous processors, so SMP can become a bottleneck. Instead of using SMP, modern systems use nonuniform memory access (NUMA). The NUMA architecture has a bank of memory for each processor, which allows for faster memory access and less contention. The access is faster because the bank of memory is closer to the CPU. There is less contention because you can try to reduce the CPU's need to access memory outside of its own bank. Figure 10-4 shows NUMA versus SMP.

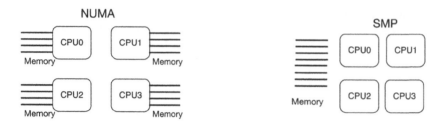

Figure 10-4. *.NUMA versus SMP*

On RedHat/CentOS systems there is a user level daemon called numad that tries to allocate memory for CPU usage efficiently. To view per-node hit and miss numbers, there is an extremely useful command called numastat. numa_hit is the number of times the processor node is able to find what it needs in its own memory bank. The larger this number, the better it is. numa_miss is the number of times the node's local memory did not contain the data needed. For each numa_miss, there is a corresponding numa_foreign on another node. As seen in Listing 10-5, for node0, the numa_miss value and the node1 numa_foreign values are the same, as expected. If you see large number of numa_miss values, then numad may not be running.

Listing 10-5. numastat

```
# numastat -s
                         node0            node1
numa_hit            1372185763        967156789
numa_miss             41539199         18158406
numa_foreign          18158406         41539199
interleave_hit           74145            66562
local_node          1370279665        959977346
other_node            43445297         25337849

## Ensure that numad is configured to run on start
# chkconfig numad --list
numad               0:off     1:off     2:on     3:on     4:on     5:on     6:off
```

To use NUMA effectively, you have three options:

1. Enable numad and let it manage your NUMA architecture.

2. Use the taskset command to assign affinity to processes.

3. Use numalib when writing your program to take advantage of NUMA.

Processes

A process in Unix consists of the following components:

- *Stack*: a single region of contiguous memory address space

- *Text*: program source code

- *Data*: all inputs to the program

- *Heap*: memory that stores files, locks, and sockets

Threads are lightweight processes; they have their own unique stack, but share text, data, and heap between the other threads. The /proc pseudo-file system has a wealth of information about a running process. Listing 10-6 shows some of the useful things that can be found in /proc. In the listing you view two processes: one has process id (PID) 1 and the other is PID 1766. PID 1 is init, which is the first process in Linux. In Listing 10-6, PID 1766 is rsyslog. Each process has a unique PID in Linux. There is a directory for each PID under /proc. systemd (http://en.wikipedia.org/wiki/Systemd) is replacing init as PID 1 in newer versions of Linux.

Processes in Linux are started with an environment. Being able to view the environment that a process is using can help in troubleshooting. For instance, the PATH variable can let us know where the process looks for commands that it needs. Viewing the init processes environment, we see three variables: one is HOME, the other is TERM, and the last is PATH. tr formats the output for easy reading.

Listing 10-6. Using the /proc File System

```
# (cat /proc/1/environ; echo) | tr '\000' '\n'
HOME=/
TERM=linux
PATH=/sbin:/bin:/usr/sbin:/usr/bin
```

Each time a file is open, there is a file descriptor associated with it. By viewing the file descriptors a process has open, we can figure out file and file system issues. PID 1766 is rsyslog, and we can see it has various log files open.

```
# ls -l 1766/fd
total 0
lrwx------ 1 root root 64 Oct  3 12:24 0 -> socket:[12975]
l-wx------ 1 root root 64 Oct  3 12:24 1 -> /var/log/messages
l-wx------ 1 root root 64 Oct  3 12:24 2 -> /var/log/cron
lr-x------ 1 root root 64 Oct  3 12:24 3 -> /proc/kmsg
l-wx------ 1 root root 64 Oct  3 12:24 4 -> /var/log/secure
l-wx------ 1 root root 64 Oct  3 12:24 5 -> /var/log/maillog
```

Users and processes in Linux have limits on the resources they can consume. Sometimes, processes can hit these limits and stop functioning. It is important to be able to view the limits and figure out what they are. Most of these limits can be fixed by editing the /etc/security/limits.conf file. The limits in bold type are often encountered more than the other limits.

```
# cat 1766/limits
```

Limit	Soft Limit	Hard Limit	Units
Max cpu time	unlimited	unlimited	seconds
Max file size	unlimited	unlimited	bytes
Max data size	unlimited	unlimited	bytes
Max stack size	10485760	unlimited	bytes
Max core file size	**0**	**unlimited**	**bytes**
Max resident set	unlimited	unlimited	bytes
Max processes	**127199**	**127199**	**processes**
Max open files	**1024**	**4096**	**files**
Max locked memory	65536	65536	bytes
Max address space	unlimited	unlimited	bytes
Max file locks	unlimited	unlimited	locks
Max pending signals	127199	127199	signals

Max msgqueue size	**819200**	**819200**	**bytes**
Max nice priority	0	0	
Max realtime priority	0	0	
Max realtime timeout	unlimited	unlimited	us

Max core file size relates to the size of a memory dump when a program crashes. It is extremely useful to keep this limited, because a very large program that core dumps can cause your file system to fill up.

Max processes is especially useful for a multiuser system. It restricts the number of processes a user can create, thereby safeguarding the system from, say, a fork bomb that might be created accidentally by a user on a multiuser system.

Max open files restricts the number of files a process can open, or the number of files a user can open. Setting this value can prevent a process or user from filling up a file system with files.

Max msgqueue size is useful for systems that use message queues, such as databases. This number often has to be tweaked per database vendor recommendations.

The command line, which includes the process and the command-line arguments, can also be viewed from the /proc file system. This helps us figure out what options were given to the process when it was starting.

```
# cat 1766/cmdline
/sbin/rsyslogd-i/var/run/syslogd.pid-c5
```

Another useful piece of information in /proc is the link to the executable of the process. If the full path is not visible when you use the ps command, check the soft link in /proc/<pid>/exec.

```
# ls -l 1/exe
lrwxrwxrwx 1 root root 0 Sep 30 14:03 1/exe -> /sbin/init
```

statm lists memory usage statistics. At first glance they are cryptic; however, they are for specific metrics. The sizes are measured in pages. The page size itself should be taken into account to calculate the correct size of the total program and other numbers.

```
# cat 1766/statm
62385 1326 209 89 0 57069 0

# Explanation of the numbers as seen by statm
total program size -> 62385
resident -> 1326
share -> 209
text -> 89
lib -> 0 (unused)
data -> 57069
dirty pages -> 0 (unused)
```

The status file is also very useful when troubleshooting applications. In our rsyslogd example, we can see the process is sleeping, as shown by the State row. In addition, we can get an idea of peak virtual memory usage, which includes physical and swap as being 314MB. We also get useful information on the different signals the process has received. One more important field to keep track of is nonvoluntary_ctxt_switches. This field specifies how many times the CPU had to divert its cycles away from the process. A large number here may require further investigation.

```
# cat /proc/1766/status
Name:       rsyslogd
State:       S (sleeping)
Tgid:       1766
```

```
Pid:            1766
PPid:           1
TracerPid:      0
Uid:        0   0       0       0
Gid:        0   0       0       0
Utrace:         0
FDSize:         64
Groups:
VmPeak:             314688 kB
VmSize:             249540 kB
VmLck:          0 kB
VmHWM:      5320 kB
VmRSS:      5304 kB
VmData:  228120 kB
VmStk:       156 kB
VmExe:       356 kB
VmLib:      2360 kB
VmPTE:        88 kB
VmSwap:             0 kB
Threads:        4
SigQ:       2/127199
SigPnd:         0000000000000000
ShdPnd:         0000000000000000
SigBlk:         0000000000000000
SigIgn:         0000000001001206
SigCgt:         0000000180114c21
CapInh:         0000000000000000
CapPrm:         ffffffffffffffff
CapEff:         ffffffffffffffff
CapBnd:         ffffffffffffffff
Cpus_allowed: ff
Cpus_allowed_list:      0-7
Mems_allowed:           00000000,00000000,00000000,00000000,00000000,00000000,00000000,00000000,0000000
0,00000000,00000000,00000000,00000000,00000000,00000000,00000001
Mems_allowed_list:      0
voluntary_ctxt_switches:        64
nonvoluntary_ctxt_switches:         0
```

Another use of the /proc file system, besides getting per-process information, is getting general system information. To figure out all the mounts of the system, we can use `cat /proc/mounts`, which shows the options the different mount points have on them.

```
# cat /proc/mounts | head -5
rootfs / rootfs rw 0 0
proc /proc proc rw,relatime 0 0
sysfs /sys sysfs rw,relatime 0 0
devtmpfs /dev devtmpfs rw,relatime,size=8140740k,nr_inodes=2035185,mode=755 0 0
devpts /dev/pts devpts rw,relatime,gid=5,mode=620,ptmxmode=000 0 0
```

For an additional reference, see http://www.tldp.org/LDP/Linux-Filesystem-Hierarchy/html/proc.html.

Understanding ps

To troubleshoot processes, the ps commands are very handy. Listing 10-7 shows a few useful ps options. Figuring out how long a process has been running can help in resolving memory exhaustion issues. Sorting based on PID can be used to figure out which process started first, if you have multiple instances of a process running. You can also sort by start time to figure this out.

Listing 10-7. Using ps to Troubleshoot a Process

```
# Figure out how long a process has been running. In this case, it's init and rsyslog
$ ps -eo pid,cmd,etime | egrep -E 'init|rsyslog'
    1 /sbin/init                 45-13:00:59
 1766 /sbin/rsyslogd -i /var/run/ 45-12:52:42
10419 egrep -E init|rsyslog          00:01


# Sort based on process id
$ ps kpid -ef | head -5
UID        PID  PPID  C STIME TTY      STAT  TIME CMD
root         1     0  0 Aug18 ?        Ss    0:08 /sbin/init
root         2     0  0 Aug18 ?        S     0:00 [kthreadd]
root         3     2  0 Aug18 ?        S     0:01 [migration/0]
root         4     2  0 Aug18 ?        S     0:40 [ksoftirqd/0]


# Sort based on start time of process
$ ps kstart_time -ef | head -5
UID        PID  PPID  C STIME TTY      STAT  TIME CMD
root         1     0  0 Aug18 ?        Ss    0:08 /sbin/init
root         2     0  0 Aug18 ?        S     0:00 [kthreadd]
root         3     2  0 Aug18 ?        S     0:01 [migration/0]
root         4     2  0 Aug18 ?        S     0:40 [ksoftirqd/0]
```

Disk

When an application or Linux server is having trouble with input/output (I/O), a few places to start looking for include the following:

- Disk performance
- File system tuning
- Redundant array of inexpensive disks (RAID) type
- Caching

The type of disk has an effect on disk I/O. A couple of commands that are very useful in figuring out disk bottlenecks include iostat and iotop.

iostat shows values since the last boot when you first run it. After that, each next value is since the last run. To figure out which device is busy, look at the transfers per second, or tsp, value. After that, look at the Blk_read and Blk_wrtn values, which indicate the amount of data read or written, respectively, in blocks per second. Each block is 512 bytes.

In the output of iostat, one of the more important values to look at is iowait. This is the time the CPU was waiting on a block device, such as a disk. If this number is large, then processes on the system are waiting on disk I/O, and you should consider getting a faster disk subsystem.

Another value to keep an eye on is the "steal" percentage. This indicates the time a hypervisor stole CPU cycles from a virtual machine to give to another virtual machine. If this number is large, then you have too many virtual machines running on a hypervisor and you need to move some of the virtual machines to another hypervisor. Listing 10-8 shows a sample of iostat output.

Listing 10-8. iostat

```
# iostat
avg-cpu:  %user   %nice %system %iowait  %steal   %idle
           0.88    0.01    0.19    0.01    0.00   98.92

Device:            tps   Blk_read/s   Blk_wrtn/s   Blk_read   Blk_wrtn
sda               0.29         1.16         5.52     570626    2704192
dm-0              0.09         0.68         0.32     333948     158440
dm-1              0.00         0.01         0.00       2576          0
dm-2              0.65         0.40         5.19     197626    2544776
dm-3              0.00         0.02         0.00      11834        912

avg-cpu:  %user   %nice %system %iowait  %steal   %idle
          22.55    0.00   76.47    0.98    0.00    0.00

Device:            tps   Blk_read/s   Blk_wrtn/s   Blk_read   Blk_wrtn
sda               7.84         0.00      5498.04          0       5608
dm-0            687.25         0.00      5498.04          0       5608
dm-1              0.00         0.00         0.00          0          0
dm-2              0.00         0.00         0.00          0          0
dm-3              0.00         0.00         0.00          0          0

avg-cpu:  %user   %nice %system %iowait  %steal   %idle
           6.86    0.00   93.14    0.00    0.00    0.00

Device:            tps   Blk_read/s   Blk_wrtn/s   Blk_read   Blk_wrtn
sda            1210.78         0.00    928674.51          0     947248
dm-0         120155.88         0.00    961247.06          0     980472
dm-1              0.00         0.00         0.00          0          0
dm-2              0.00         0.00         0.00          0          0
dm-3              0.00         0.00         0.00          0          0
```

When troubleshooting disks on a system, you have to map the partition universally unique identifier (UUID) to a partition name. The blkid command shows the relationship between the UUID and the partition, as seen in Listing 10-9. Also shown is the lsblk command, which gives a nice tree structure of disk partitions, thereby, helping you troubleshoot disk-related issues.

Listing 10-9. Linux Partition UUID

```
# blkid
/dev/loop0: LABEL="CentOS_6.4_Final" TYPE="iso9660"
/dev/sda1: SEC_TYPE="msdos" UUID="0D0B-EDD2" TYPE="vfat"
/dev/sda2: UUID="2494e765-1e20-47e2-a068-d2165e9d6863" TYPE="ext4"
/dev/sda3: UUID="qkXEix-y7nX-KfTD-zGQz-QBgE-f9Uu-0xYO2K" TYPE="LVM2_member"
/dev/sda4: UUID="18PFqD-P7kz-lnzG-4kUe-gL6C-dIer-ShYeVa" TYPE="LVM2_member"
/dev/mapper/vg_hv1-lv_swap: UUID="32a60536-ae0d-4d5b-ac04-2b721e9abee5" TYPE="swap"
```

```
/dev/mapper/vg_hv1-lv_root: UUID="7b51a9fa-2514-4c76-b91c-ddb91c336315" TYPE="ext4"
/dev/mapper/vg_hv1-lv_var: UUID="19750d8a-ccf0-4196-a6c2-be7678985cf0" TYPE="ext4"
/dev/mapper/vg_hv1-lv_home: UUID="20e57eef-1be8-4be2-b9a7-aac90ed979c9" TYPE="ext4"
/dev/mapper/vg_hv1-lv_tmp: UUID="0dd34d7a-8749-4c7e-9163-ea78c278cf1d" TYPE="ext4"
```

```
# lsblk
NAME                       MAJ:MIN   RM    SIZE  RO  TYPE MOUNTPOINT
loop0                          7:0    0    4.1G   0  loop /mnt/CentOS6.4
sda                            8:0    0    931G   0  disk
├─sda1                         8:1    0    200M   0  part /boot/efi
├─sda2                         8:2    0    600M   0  part /boot
├─sda3                         8:3    0  195.3G   0  part
│ ├─vg_hv1-lv_swap (dm-0)    253:0    0    7.8G   0  lvm  [SWAP]
│ ├─vg_hv1-lv_root (dm-1)    253:1    0   39.1G   0  lvm  /
│ ├─vg_hv1-lv_var (dm-4)     253:4    0    9.8G   0  lvm  /var
│ ├─vg_hv1-lv_home (dm-7)    253:7    0   19.5G   0  lvm  /home
│ └─vg_hv1-lv_tmp (dm-8)     253:8    0    9.8G   0  lvm  /tmp
└─sda4                         8:4    0  362.7G   0  part
  ├─vg_ic-lv_cdrive (dm-2)   253:2    0     80G   0  lvm
sr0                           11:0    1   1024M   0  rom
```

File System

To troubleshoot file system issues, you first need to understand disk geometry and how a file system is created on the disk. Disks have platters, which are double-sided. On each platter are concentric circles called *tracks*. Tracks are divided into sectors. Each sector is usually 512 bytes. A cylinder is a corresponding set of tracks on all surfaces of the platter. Listing 10-10 shows an example of a disk.

Listing 10-10. Disk Partition

```
# parted
GNU Parted 2.1
Using /dev/sda
Welcome to GNU Parted! Type 'help' to view a list of commands.
(parted) unit mb print
Model: Dell Virtual Disk (scsi)
Disk /dev/sda: 999654MB
Sector size (logical/physical): 512B/512B
Partition Table: gpt
```

Number	Start	End	Size	File system	Name	Flags
1	1.05MB	211MB	210MB	fat16		boot
2	211MB	840MB	629MB	ext4		
3	840MB	210555MB	209715MB			lvm
4	210555MB	600000MB	389445MB		bigdisk	

For additional information, see http://kias.dyndns.org/comath/42.html.

Read Ahead

Changing the read-ahead value can help speed up reads on a file system. Read ahead speeds up file access by prefetching data and loading it into the page cache. The default size is 1024 and you can increase this to speed up file reading, as seen in Listing 10-11.

Listing 10-11. Enabling Read-Ahead

```
# blockdev --getra  /dev/sda
1024

# blockdev --setra 2048 /dev/sda

# blockdev --getra  /dev/sda
2048
```

Benchmarking

To prevent problems with application disk I/O, one possible approach is to figure out the disk I/O needs of the application and then test various storage subsystems using benchmarking tools. This strategy enables proper application deployment. Some of the tools that can be used to benchmark storage subsystems include:

- Iozone (http://www.iozone.org/)

- Hdparm (http://linux.die.net/man/8/hdparm)

RAID

When troubleshooting disk issues, RAID is important to understand. There are a lot of levels of RAID; some of the common ones include the following:

- *RAID 0*: stripping data across disks. There is no redundancy or fault tolerance. The advantage is that performance is increased as a result of multiple reads and writes.

- *RAID 1*: mirroring of data without stripping or parity computation. There is a minimum of two drives; if one fails, you can still access your data

- *RAID 5*: block-level stripping with distributed parity. Parity is distributed among drives. This level requires a minimum of three disks. Loss of a drive results in degraded performance.

- *RAID 6*: block-level stripping with double distributed parity. This strategy allows for two drives to fail.

- *RAID 1+0*: mirroring first and then stripping. This level requires a minimum of four disks.

- *RAID 0+1*: stripping and then mirroring. This level requires a minimum of four drives.

When troubleshooting hardware disk issues, you should know which RAID level is being used, if at all. The reason for this is that some RAID levels run in degraded mode when one or more drives fail, whereas other RAID levels fail completely even if one drive fails. As part of your initial design and implementation, it is always a good idea to keep a spare RAID drive that can be use in case of a RAID drive failure. Most RAID controllers start building a failed drive automatically with a spare drive. During the rebuilding of the RAID volume, performance is usually degraded. The larger the disk size, the longer it takes to rebuild the logical RAID volume.

You can find out more about RAID at

- `https://en.wikipedia.org/wiki/RAID`

- RAID calculator (`https://www.icc-usa.com/raid-calculator/`)

- RAID levels tutorial (`http://www.thegeekstuff.com/2010/08/raid-levels-tutorial/`)

Memory

Memory is managed in blocks known as *pages*, which is generally 4096 bytes; 1MB is equal to 256 pages and 1GB is equal to 256,000 pages. Each page is referenced through a page table entry. The page table entry is in the memory management unit of the CPU.

To manage large memory, CentOS/RedHat increases the page size, which reduces the number of page table entries. The default huge page size is 2MB in RedHat/CentOS 6. For a system with 16GB virtual memory, this translates to 8000 pages. Listing 10-12 shows how to check the current page size and increase it as well. To start using huge pages, set the value of /proc/sys/vm/nr_hugepages to a number based on your memory need. For instance, if your application needs 4GB RAM, you can set the value to be 2000.

■ **Note**   RedHat 6 uses Transparent HugePages, or THP, which does not require you to set the value of huge pages. As such, in Listing 10-12, you can see the value of HugePages being 0. Transparent HugePages is visible in the AnonHugePages setting.

Listing 10-12. Increase Page Size

```
# View Transparent HugePage information
$ cat /proc/meminfo | grep Huge
AnonHugePages:    3162112 kB
HugePages_Total:         0
HugePages_Free:          0
HugePages_Rsvd:          0
HugePages_Surp:          0
Hugepagesize:         2048 kB

# View number of huge pages reserved
$ cat /proc/sys/vm/nr_hugepages
0

# Check if transparent huge pages are used by default
$ cat /sys/kernel/mm/redhat_transparent_hugepage/enabled
[always] madvise never

# echo "2000" >> /proc/sys/vm/nr_hugepages
# cat /proc/sys/vm/nr_hugepages
2000
```

Estimating memory use for any application should be part of application design. The price of memory fluctuates a lot, and buying memory when it is expensive can result in additional costs for an enterprise. The symptoms of memory starvation for an application include the following:

- Slow performance

- Frequent application crash

- Inconsistent performance

- Loss of data

Memory Types

Linux memory can be divided into the following types:

- Physical

- Swap

- Cache

- Buffered

Physical memory consists of the memory modules present on the system. Swap is the portion of the disk that is being used for memory. Cache refers to files loaded in physical memory to speed up disk access. Buffered refers to the raw disk blocks loaded in physical memory. Both the cache and the buffers are released back into the free memory pool for application use as needed. To figure out if your system is running low on memory, the following tools are useful:

- free

- vmstat

- top

- sar

If a system runs out of memory, two things can happen. One is that the kernel panics and the system crashes. The other is that, to prevent kernel panic, Linux activates the out-of-memory (OOM) killer. The OOM killer kills the program causing memory to be exhausted. This strategy prevents the kernel from panicking. Listing 10-13 is an example of using some of these tools to figure out memory issues with a system.

Using the free command, we first check the available memory on a system. This system has 1GB RAM, as shown by the 996 total size. Memory is also confirmed by viewing /proc/meminfo; the MemTotal field shows 1GB RAM. Notice that 18MB is cached and 6MB is in buffers. The "real" free memory is 853MB, which we get by adding the values for free, buffers, and cached (828 + 6 + 18 = 852). This system has no swap memory, so that is showing up as 0.

Listing 10-13. Memory Troubleshooting

```
# free -m
             total       used       free     shared    buffers     cached
Mem:           996        168        828          0          6         18
-/+ buffers/cache:        142        853
Swap:            0          0          0
```

```
# head -5 /proc/meminfo
MemTotal:       1020388 kB
MemFree:         848076 kB
Buffers:           6944 kB
Cached:           19176 kB
SwapCached:           0 kB
```

Let's run a program that consumes a certain amount of memory—say, 300MB.

```
##Consume 300MB of memory
# ./eatmemory 300M
```

When we check the memory after running our 300MB program, we see the used memory has gone up from 168 to 473 (168 + 305). Notice that the cache and buffers stay the same and the -/+ buffers/cache free is reduced to 548 from 853. The difference of 5MB is the program itself running. We can confirm the reduction in free memory by viewing /proc/meminfo, and we see that MemFree is now 535MB instead of 848MB.

```
## Check free memory
# free -m
              total       used       free     shared    buffers     cached
Mem:            996        473        523          0          6         18
-/+ buffers/cache:         447        548
Swap:             0          0          0

# head -10 /proc/meminfo
MemTotal:       1020388 kB
MemFree:         535072 kB
Buffers:           6960 kB
Cached:           19208 kB
SwapCached:           0 kB
```

Let's try to consume more memory than there is on the system by increasing our usage by 900MB. As soon as we try to consume more than what is available, the OOM kicks in and kills our program. When we check free memory after our memory eater has been killed, free is now 845MB. Notice that the disk cache has gone down to 6MB from 18MB. The kernel has given up the disk cache loaded in memory to our program. The same is seen with the buffers; they have gone down to 1MB from 6MB.

```
# ./eatmemory 900M
Eating 943718400 bytes in chunks of 1024...
Killed

# free -m
              total       used       free     shared    buffers     cached
Mem:            996        150        845          0          1          6
-/+ buffers/cache:         142        853
Swap:             0          0          0
```

If we look in /var/log/messages, we see a message about the Linux OOM killer activating and killing the process that was consuming the memory.

```
Sep 28 14:55:15 server kernel: eatmemory invoked oom-killer: gfp_mask=0x280da, order=0, oom_adj=0,
oom_score_adj=0
Sep 28 14:55:15 server kernel: eatmemory cpuset=/ mems_allowed=0
Sep 28 14:55:15 server kernel: Pid: 27950, comm: eatmemory Not tainted 2.6.32-431.5.1.el6.x86_64 #1
Sep 28 14:55:15 server kernel: Call Trace:
Sep 28 14:55:15 server kernel: [<ffffffff810d05a1>] ? cpuset_print_task_mems_allowed+0x91/0xb0
Sep 28 14:55:15 server kernel: [<ffffffff81122950>] ? dump_header+0x90/0x1b0
...[SNIP]...
Sep 28 14:55:15 server kernel: [27830]     89 27830     20340      227     0          0              0
pickup
Sep 28 14:55:15 server kernel: [27950]      0 27950    206967   205992     0          0              0
eatmemory
Sep 28 14:55:15 server kernel: Out of memory: Kill process 27950 (eatmemory) score 779 or sacrifice
child
Sep 28 14:55:15 server kernel: Killed process 27950, UID 0, (eatmemory) total-vm:827868kB, anon-
rss:823932kB, file-rss:36kB
```

If we check vmstat before and after the problem, we can correlate the events as well. Before our memory eater is started, there is 865M free memory. After we start consuming memory, free decreases to 331MB. When we start to consume even more memory, free decreases to 113MB, after which our process is killed and free now returns to 864MB.

```
# vmstat 1
procs -----------memory---------- ---swap-- -----io---- --system-- -----cpu-----
 r  b   swpd   free   buff  cache   si   so    bi    bo   in   cs us sy id wa st
...[SNIP]...
 0  0      0 865280   1824   7184    0    0     0    12  114  217  0  0 97  3  0
 0  0      0 865280   1824   7188    0    0     0     0  110  206  0  0 100  0  0
 0  0      0 857528   3328  11880    0    0  6172    16  309  694  1  1 82 16  0
 0  0      0 857528   3328  11876    0    0     0     0  109  209  0  0 100  0  0
 0  0      0 855984   3508  12476    0    0   780     0  213  516  1  1 94  4  0
 0  0      0 855992   3508  12480    0    0     0     0  111  207  0  0 100  0  0
 0  0      0 855992   3508  12480    0    0     0     0  108  206  0  0 100  0  0
 0  0      0 856016   3508  12480    0    0     0     0  152  278  0  0 100  0  0
 0  0      0 852744   3784  13820    0    0  1612    44  175  330  0  1 91  8  0
...[SNIP]...
 0  0      0 852792   3860  13824    0    0     0     0  126  232  0  0 100  0  0
 0  0      0 852792   3860  13824    0    0     0     0  116  213  0  0 100  0  0

./eatmemory 500M   <--- Start consuming memory; notice that free reduces to 331MB from 852MB.

procs -----------memory---------- ---swap-- -----io---- --system-- -----cpu-----
 r  b   swpd   free   buff  cache   si   so    bi    bo   in   cs us sy id wa st

 0  0      0 331860   3860  13824    0    0    12     0  308  222  3 17 80  0  0
 0  0      0 331860   3860  13836    0    0     0     0  111  210  0  0 100  0  0
 0  0      0 331860   3860  13836    0    0     0     0  108  207  0  0 100  0  0
 0  0      0 331860   3860  13836    0    0     0     4  111  212  0  0 100  0  0
...[SNIP]...
```

```
./eatmemory 900M     <---- Consume even more memory; free now reduces to 113MB from 331MB.
procs -----------memory---------- ---swap-- -----io---- --system-- -----cpu-----
 r  b   swpd   free   buff  cache   si   so    bi    bo   in   cs us sy id wa st
 2  1      0 113420     80    924    0    0  1404    32  503 1079  8 30 63  0  0
```

OOM kicks in at this point and our process is killed, thereby releasing memory. free is back up to 864MB.

```
 0  0      0 864684    432   5164    0    0  4000     0  205  684  0  3 97  0  0
 0  0      0 864684    432   5156    0    0     0     0  111  211  0  0 100  0  0
```

If we observe the system after a few minutes, we notice that buffers and cache have increased. They were at 80MB and 924MB, respectively, but since our process was killed, they have increased to 5112MB and 15,460MB, respectively.

```
## After 10 minutes
# vmstat 1
procs -----------memory---------- ---swap-- -----io---- --system-- -----cpu-----
 r  b   swpd   free   buff  cache   si   so    bi    bo   in   cs us sy id wa st
 0  0      0 850076   5112  15464    0    0     0     1    2    9  0  0 100  0  0
 0  0      0 850068   5120  15460    0    0     0    12  119  216  0  0 98  2  0
```

When the value of panci_on_oom is set to 0 in /proc, the OOM killer activates. This is the default value. If you wish to disable OOM, change the value to 1.

```
# cat /proc/sys/vm/panic_on_oom
0
```

Using sar we can correlate our findings. sar should show output that agrees with vmstat and also with free. One caveat with sar is that, by default, it reports data every ten minutes. This means that if our memory increase and decrease events happen within the ten minutes, we miss them. You can get more granular data from sar using the internal and count options, as in sar <interval> <count>.

```
$ sar -r
09:20:01 AM kbmemfree kbmemused %memused kbbuffers  kbcached  kbcommit   %commit
...[SNIP]...
12:50:01 PM    590372    430016    42.14     99288    172044    157856     15.47
01:00:01 PM    587620    432768    42.41     99304    172068    163948     16.07
01:10:01 PM    563184    457204    44.81     99652    192968    165464     16.22

# At this point we consume 300MB memory; notice kbbuffers goes from 99652 to 5172.
01:20:02 PM    854128    166260    16.29      5172     14820    173072     16.96
01:30:01 PM    854012    166376    16.31      5272     14820    173072     16.96
...[SNIP]...
# Now we run eatmemory with 900MB option, causing kbbuffers to go down even more; same with # kbcached
03:00:01 PM    860088    160300    15.71      2004      8136    181020     17.74
03:10:01 PM    858732    161656    15.84      2400      9180    181020     17.74

# Once the OOM kills the eatmemory process, both kbbuffers and kbcached start to increase
03:20:01 PM    849680    170708    16.73      5076     15312    181020     17.74
```

Tuning Virtual Memory

Virtual memory can be defined as physical memory and swap space. Typically in virtual memory one finds processes, a file system cache, and the kernel. You can control virtual memory through:

- Swappiness
- min_free_kbytes
- dirty_ratio
- dirty_background_ratio
- drop_caches

You can modify kernel parameters using the sysctl utility or by editing the /etc/sysctl.conf file. "Swappiness" is the tendency of the kernel to swap out processes to disk. The value can be set between 0 and 100, with 60 being the default. Increasing the value above 60 causes the kernel to swap aggressively processes that are not active. A lower value causes the kernel to keep inactive processes in memory longer. For instance, if you are using Kernel-based virtual machine (KVM), then it might be better not to swap out inactive virtual machines, because they run as Linux processes on the hypervisor. Therefore, you may chose to reduce the swappiness value from 60 to a lower number.

You cannot disable the Linux page cache (the value seen in the cached column of the free command). However, you can limit the cache value, and some ways of doing this are the following:

- vm.vfs_cache_pressure (default = 100): Controls the tendency of the kernel to reclaim memory. Increasing this value makes the kernel reclaim cache memory frequently and hence reduces the size of the page cache.

- vm.dirty_background_ratio (default = 20): Linux usually writes data out of the page cache using a process called pdflush. This number indicates the percentage of system memory, the number of pages at which pdflush starts writing out dirty data. Decreasing this number causes pdflush to write out the dirty data sooner.

- vm.dirty_ratio (default = 40): Indicates the percentage of number of memory pages at which the processes write out their *own* dirty data. Decreasing this number causes the processes to write out the dirty data sooner rather than later, thereby limiting the size of the page cache.

- vm.dirty_expire_centisecs (default = 3000 , mentioned in milliseconds): Indicates the expire time for dirty pages. Decreasing this number makes them more eligible to be written out by pdflush.

- vm.swappiness (default = 60): Decreasing this number causes the page cache size to be limited.

You can read more about Linux memory at

- https://access.redhat.com/documentation/en-US/Red_Hat_Enterprise_Linux/6/html/Performance_Tuning_Guide/s-memory-tunables.html

- https://access.redhat.com/documentation/en-US/Red_Hat_Enterprise_Linux/6/html/Virtualization_Tuning_and_Optimization_Guide/sect-Virtualization_Tuning_Optimization_Guide-Memory-Huge_Pages.html

- https://access.redhat.com/documentation/en-US/Red_Hat_Enterprise_Linux/5/html/Tuning_and_Optimizing_Red_Hat_Enterprise_Linux_for_Oracle_9i_and_10g_Databases/sect-Oracle_9i_and_10g_Tuning_Guide-Large_Memory_Optimization_Big_Pages_and_Huge_Pages-Configuring_Huge_Pages_in_Red_Hat_Enterprise_Linux_4_or_5.html

- http://www.thomas-krenn.com/en/wiki/Linux_Performance_Measurements_using_vmstat

Domain Name System

One of the most important tools for debugging the domain name system (DNS) is dig. During the setup of a BIND server, and after as well, using dig can help get to the root cause of many issues, and ensures your DNS server is working as expected. The use of dig is generally dig @server name type. If no server is specified, dig looks at the server in /etc/resolv.conf. If no type is specified, dig looks up the A record. Listing 10-14 shows how to use dig to look up DNS records.

Listing 10-14. Using dig command

```
#query the A record of www.example.com
$ dig www.example.org

; <<>> DiG 9.8.2rc1-RedHat-9.8.2-0.23.rc1.el6_5.1 <<>> www.example.org
;; global options: +cmd
;; Got answer:
;; ->>HEADER<<- opcode: QUERY, status: NOERROR, id: 28891
;; flags: qr rd ra; QUERY: 1, ANSWER: 1, AUTHORITY: 0, ADDITIONAL: 0

;; QUESTION SECTION:
;www.example.org.               IN      A

;; ANSWER SECTION:
www.example.org.       21599   IN      A       93.184.216.119

;; Query time: 43 msec
;; SERVER: 8.8.8.8#53(8.8.8.8)
;; WHEN: Tue Aug 26 22:55:38 2014
;; MSG SIZE  rcvd: 49
```

A lot of information useful for troubleshooting is displayed by dig. Let's review some of the information. First, dig gives us the version of dig we are using; in this case, it's v9.8. dig also lists the options we provided, which is +cmd. Although we did not explicitly say +cmd, it's implied. You can specify +nocmd as well on the dig command line and it will not display the options used.

The question section tells you that you are asking for the A record of www.example.org. Similarly, the answer section shows the answer for the question asked.

The query time is also shown—43 msec, in this case—along with the message size received.

You can specify various options for dig in your $HOME/.digrc file. After you set up a DNS server, use the dig command to check for responses from the DNS server.

If you want to get the DNS record without all the debugging information, then you can use the +short option for dig and it returns just the answer, as shown in Listing 10-15.

Listing 10-15. dig options

```
#query the same A record; this time, just return the IP address
$ dig +short www.example.org
93.184.216.119

#find out the start of authority (SOA) for example.org
$ dig +short example.org soa
sns.dns.icann.org. noc.dns.icann.org. 2014080856 7200 3600 1209600 3600
```

```
#query the NS or name server record for example.org
$ dig +short example.org ns
b.iana-servers.net.
a.iana-servers.net.

#see if there is a TXT record for example.org
$ dig +short example.org txt
"v=spf1 -all"
"$Id: example.org 2783 2014-08-07 17:40:21Z mvergara $"

#look up the hostname for the given IP address
$ dig +short -x 74.125.239.51
nuq04s19-in-f19.1e100.net.

#find out the MX record for gmail.com
$ dig +short gmail.com mx
20 alt2.gmail-smtp-in.l.google.com.
30 alt3.gmail-smtp-in.l.google.com.
5 gmail-smtp-in.l.google.com.
10 alt1.gmail-smtp-in.l.google.com.
40 alt4.gmail-smtp-in.l.google.com.
```

nslookup

nslookup was used traditionally to debug DNS; however, dig has become the de facto replacement tool for nslookup. nslookup can also be used in a manner similar to dig, plus it supports interactive querying. Listing 10-16 shows the basic use of nslookup.

Listing 10-16. nslookup Use

```
##
# By default 'nslookup' uses the name server in /etc/resolv.conf
$ nslookup
> server
Default server: 8.8.8.8
Address: 8.8.8.8#53
Default server: 8.8.4.4
Address: 8.8.4.4#53

> www.yahoo.com
Server:         8.8.8.8
Address:        8.8.8.8#53

# The reason this answer is nonauthoritative is because 8.8.4.4 is not the authority for yahoo.com.
Non-authoritative answer:
www.yahoo.com         canonical name = fd-fp3.wg1.b.yahoo.com.
Name:       fd-fp3.wg1.b.yahoo.com
Address: 206.190.36.45
Name:       fd-fp3.wg1.b.yahoo.com
Address: 206.190.36.105
```

```
# To get the 'mx' record, set the type to 'mx'
> set type=mx
> yahoo.com
Server:        8.8.8.8
Address:       8.8.8.8#53

Non-authoritative answer:
yahoo.com        mail exchanger = 1 mta7.am0.yahoodns.net.
yahoo.com        mail exchanger = 1 mta6.am0.yahoodns.net.
yahoo.com        mail exchanger = 1 mta5.am0.yahoodns.net.

> set type=soa
> yahoo.com
Server:        8.8.8.8
Address:       8.8.8.8#53

Non-authoritative answer:
yahoo.com
        origin = ns1.yahoo.com
        mail addr = hostmaster.yahoo-inc.com
        serial = 2014092411
        refresh = 3600
        retry = 300
        expire = 1814400
        minimum = 600
```

BIND Statistics File

BIND can be configured to store statistics about its performance. To enable BIND statistics, enable the options as shown in Listing 10-17 in the named.conf file.

Listing 10-17. BIND Statistics File

```
[ statistics-file path_name; ]
[ zone-statistics yes ; ]
```

To get BIND to dump statistics, use the rndc stats command, which causes BIND to create the statistics file as defined by path_name. Reviewing the statistics file proves very helpful when troubleshooting BIND. If you need to figure out the type of queries your BIND server is receiving, you can find this information in the statistics file. In addition, you can use the statistics information to figure out how to scale the BIND server. BIND statistics can be divided into the following sections:

- Incoming requests: Total incoming requests into the server

- Incoming queries: Requests divided by type, A, NS, SOA, and so on

- Outoging queries: The queries this BIND server made

- Name server statistics

- Zone maintenance statistics

- Resolve statistics

- Cache database resource record sets (DB RRsets)

- Socket I/O Statistics

- Per-zone query statistics

Listing 10-18 shows a brief summary of the BIND statistics file. The statistics are cumulative from the time BIND server was started.

Listing 10-18. BIND Statistics Output

```
+++ Statistics Dump +++ (1412550650)
++ Incoming Requests ++
        2863814921 QUERY
              6239 NOTIFY
++ Incoming Queries ++
        2059811570 A
                12 NS
              9055 SOA
         193324325 PTR
            195930 MX
                21 TXT
         610472679 AAAA
              1275 SRV
                 1 DS
                 1 DNSKEY
                52 AXFR
...[SNIP]...
```

DHCP

Some of the common issues that revolve around troubleshooting DHCP require a basic understanding of the protocol itself. The various messages involved in DHCP are listed in RFC 2131 (`https://www.ietf.org/rfc/rfc2131.txt`). The various options and vendor extensions are defined in RFC 2132 (`https://www.ietf.org/rfc/rfc2132.txt`). Some of the messages are as follows:

- DHCPDISCOVER

- DHCPOFFER

- DHCPREQUEST

- DHCPACK

- DHCPNAK

- DHCPDECLINE

- DHCPRELEASE

- DHCPINFORM

When a client is configured to use DHCP, it sends out a DHCPDISCOVER message. This is a broadcast message to locate available servers. Because it is broadcast, it is restricted to the broadcast domain, unless IP helpers are enabled on routers that forward DHCP broadcast requests to appropriate DHCP servers.

After a server receives a DHCPDISCOVER message, it responds with DHCPOFFER, which includes configuration parameters. The client then requests a DHCP IP using DHCPPREQUEST. The client confirms the parameters that the server sent in the request. The server then sends DHCPACK to the client, confirming the DHCPPREQUEST from the client. The server sends DHCPNAK if the client's lease has expired or if the client has some incorrect parameters in DHCPPREQUEST. The client sends DHCPDECLINE to the server if it rejects DHCPOFFER, which could be because the address is already in use. After the client is ready to give up the DHCP IP address, it sends a DHCPRELEASE message. DHCPINFORM is also a client-to-server message that asks for a local configuration.

When debugging a DHCP issue, if you use tcpdump to view network traffic, some or all of the message will be visible. Listing 10-19 shows how to interpret DHCP traffic.

Using tcpdump, we capture DHCP traffic between the client and the server. The DHCP server is 10.1.1.10, with the MAC address 00:50:56:bd:7d:21. The DHCP client has the MAC address 00:50:56:bd:7f:f6 and gets the IP address 10.1.1.50. The tcpdump options we are using are -v (verbose), -n (don't convert IP to hostname), -e (print link-level header), and -s0 (snarf 0-length bytes of data from each packer, rather than the default 65,535 bytes). We are capturing port 67 and 68 traffic for DHCP.

Initially we see the DHCPDISCOVER message from the client, as is seen in bold type. The destination address of this message is broadcast.

Listing 10-19. DHCP Conversation

```
# tcpdump -vnes0 -i eth0 port 67 or port 68
tcpdump: listening on eth0, link-type EN10MB (Ethernet), capture size 65535 bytes
05:58:12.000470 00:50:56:bd:7f:f6 > Broadcast, ethertype IPv4 (0x0800), length 342: (tos 0x10, ttl
128, id 0, offset 0, flags [none], proto UDP (17), length 328)
0.0.0.0.bootpc > 255.255.255.255.bootps: BOOTP/DHCP, Request from 00:50:56:bd:7f:f6, length 300, xid
0xa033135f, Flags [none]
          Client-Ethernet-Address 00:50:56:bd:7f:f6
          Vendor-rfc1048 Extensions
            Magic Cookie 0x63825363
            DHCP-Message Option 53, length 1: Discover
            Parameter-Request Option 55, length 13:
              Subnet-Mask, BR, Time-Zone, Classless-Static-Route
              Domain-Name, Domain-Name-Server, Hostname, YD
              YS, NTP, MTU, Option 119
              Default-Gateway
```

The server then responds to the client with DHCPOFFER, as seen in bold type.

```
05:58:13.001158 00:50:56:bd:7d:21 > 00:50:56:bd:7f:f6, ethertype IPv4 (0x0800), length 342: (tos
0x10, ttl 128, id 0, offset 0, flags [none], proto UDP (17), length 328)
10.1.1.10.bootps > 10.1.1.50.bootpc: BOOTP/DHCP, Reply, length 300, xid 0xa033135f, Flags [none]
          Your-IP 10.1.1.50
          Client-Ethernet-Address 00:50:56:bd:7f:f6
          Vendor-rfc1048 Extensions
            Magic Cookie 0x63825363
            DHCP-Message Option 53, length 1: Offer
            Server-ID Option 54, length 4: 10.1.1.10
            Lease-Time Option 51, length 4: 600
            Subnet-Mask Option 1, length 4: 255.255.255.0
            BR Option 28, length 4: 172.24.81.255
            Domain-Name Option 15, length 14: "example.com"
            Domain-Name-Server Option 6, length 8: 172.24.0.7,172.24.0.8
            Default-Gateway Option 3, length 4: 172.24.81.3
```

The third step is the client responding with DHCPPREQUEST.

```
05:58:13.001634 00:50:56:bd:7f:f6 > Broadcast, ethertype IPv4 (0x0800), length 342:
(tos 0x10, ttl 128, id 0, offset 0, flags [none], proto UDP (17), length 328)
0.0.0.0.bootpc > 255.255.255.255.bootps: BOOTP/DHCP, Request from 00:50:56:bd:7f:f6, length 300,
xid 0xa033135f, Flags [none]
            Client-Ethernet-Address 00:50:56:bd:7f:f6
            Vendor-rfc1048 Extensions
              Magic Cookie 0x63825363
              DHCP-Message Option 53, length 1: Request
              Server-ID Option 54, length 4: 10.1.1.10
              Requested-IP Option 50, length 4: 10.1.1.50
              Parameter-Request Option 55, length 13:
                Subnet-Mask, BR, Time-Zone, Classless-Static-Route
                Domain-Name, Domain-Name-Server, Hostname, YD
                YS, NTP, MTU, Option 119
                Default-Gateway
```

The fourth step is the client responding with DHCPACK.

```
05:58:13.003958 00:50:56:bd:7d:21 > 00:50:56:bd:7f:f6, ethertype IPv4 (0x0800), length 342:
(tos 0x10, ttl 128, id 0, offset 0, flags [none], proto UDP (17), length 328)
10.1.1.10.bootps > 10.1.1.50.bootpc: BOOTP/DHCP, Reply, length 300, xid 0xa033135f, Flags [none]
            Your-IP 10.1.1.50
            Client-Ethernet-Address 00:50:56:bd:7f:f6
            Vendor-rfc1048 Extensions
              Magic Cookie 0x63825363
              DHCP-Message Option 53, length 1: ACK
              Server-ID Option 54, length 4: 10.1.1.10
              Lease-Time Option 51, length 4: 600
              Subnet-Mask Option 1, length 4: 255.255.255.0
              BR Option 28, length 4: 172.24.81.255
              Domain-Name Option 15, length 14: "example.com"
              Domain-Name-Server Option 6, length 8: 172.24.0.7,172.24.0.8
              Default-Gateway Option 3, length 4: 172.24.81.3
```

Conclusion

In this chapter we covered troubleshooting TCP/IP, CPU, disk, memory, DNS, and DHCP. We looked at a number of tools, specific to the topics, that can be used to debug the various problem you may encounter. Some additional tools that are worth looking into are the following:

- *Valgrind*: For memory analysis (http://valgrind.org/)

- *OProfile*: For application profiling (http://oprofile.sourceforge.net/news/)

- *SystemTap*: For gathering information about running systems
  (https://sourceware.org/systemtap/)

- *Perf*: For statistics on running programs (https://perf.wiki.kernel.org/index.php/Main_Page)

Index

Get the eBook for only $10!

Now you can take the weightless companion with you anywhere, anytime. Your purchase of this book entitles you to 3 electronic versions for only $10.

This Apress title will prove so indispensible that you'll want to carry it with you everywhere, which is why we are offering the eBook in 3 formats for only $10 if you have already purchased the print book.

Convenient and fully searchable, the PDF version enables you to easily find and copy code—or perform examples by quickly toggling between instructions and applications. The MOBI format is ideal for your Kindle, while the ePUB can be utilized on a variety of mobile devices.

Go to www.apress.com/promo/tendollars to purchase your companion eBook.

Apress®
THE EXPERT'S VOICE™